By faith Abraham, when called to go to a place
he would later receive as his inheritance, obeyed and went,
even though he did not know where he was going. . . .
For he was looking forward to the city with foundations,
whose architect and builder is God.

HEBREWS 11:8, 10

OTHER BOOKS BY JAMES MONTGOMERY BOICE:

Witness and Revelation in the Gospel of John
Philippians: An Expositional Commentary
The Sermon on the Mount
How to Live the Christian Life (originally How to Live It Up)
Ordinary Men Called by God (originally How God Can Use Nobodies)
The Last and Future World
The Gospel of John: An Expositional Commentary (5 volumes in one)
"Galatians" in the Expositor's Bible Commentary
Can You Run Away from God?
Our Sovereign God (editor)
Our Savior God: Studies on Man, Christ and the Atonement (editor)
Does Inerrancy Matter?
The Foundation of Biblical Authority (editor)
Making God's Word Plain (editor)
The Epistles of John
Genesis: An Expositional Commentary (3 volumes)
The Parables of Jesus
The Christ of Christmas
The Minor Prophets: An Expositional Commentary (2 volumes)
Standing on the Rock
The Christ of the Open Tomb
Foundations of the Christian Faith (4 volumes in one)
Christ's Call to Discipleship
Transforming Our World: A Call to Action (editor)
Ephesians: An Expositional Commentary
Daniel: An Expositional Commentary
Joshua: We Will Serve the Lord
Nehemiah: Learning to Lead
The King Has Come
Romans (4 volumes)
Mind Renewal in a Mindless Age
Amazing Grace
Psalms (2 of 3 volumes)
Sure I Believe, So What?
Hearing God When You Hurt

TWO CITIES, TWO LOVES

Christian Responsibility in a Crumbling Culture

JAMES MONTGOMERY BOICE

InterVarsity Press
Downers Grove, Illinois

InterVarsity Press® is the book-publishing division of InterVarsity Christian Fellowship®, a student movement active on campus at hundreds of universities, colleges and schools of nursing in the United States of America, and a member movement of the International Fellowship of Evangelical Students. For information about local and regional activities, write Public Relations Dept., InterVarsity Christian Fellowship, 6400 Schroeder Rd., P.O. Box 7895, Madison, WI 53707-7895.

Cover illustration: Roberta Polfus
ISBN 0-8308-1987-8

Printed in the United States of America ∞

Library of Congress Cataloging-in-Publication Data

Boice, James Montgomery, 1938-
   Two cities, two loves: Christian responsibility in a crumbling
culture/James Montgomery Boice.
     p.   cm.
   Includes bibliographical references (p.   ) and indexes.
   ISBN 0-8308-1987-8 (alk. paper)
    1. Christianity and culture—United States. 2. Augustine, Saint,
Bishop of Hippo. De civitate Dei. 3. Kingdom of God. 4. United
States—Civilization—20th century. 5. United States—Church
history—20th century. I. Title.
BR526.B56   1996
261'.0973—dc20   96-8115
                                        CIP

17 16 15 14 13 12 11 10 9 8 7 6 5 4 3 2 1
10 09 08 07 06 05 04 03 02 01 00 99 98 97 96

Preface ————————————————————————————— 7

Part One: The Collapse of a Culture ——————— 11

1 The Barbarians Are Coming ——————————— 13

Part Two: The Biblical Basis for the Two Cities ———— 33

2 The Two Humanities ————————————————— 35

3 Abraham: "He Looked for a City" ———————— 56

4 The Two Cities: Enoch & Nineveh ——————— 72

5 The Two Cities: Babylon & Jerusalem —————— 92

6 Daniel: God's Man in Babylon ————————— 113

Part Three: The Two Cities Today ————————— 135

7 Christianity & Culture ———————————————— 137

8 How We Might Move Forward ————————— 158

9 God & Caesar —————————————————————— 178

10 Nehemiah: Rebuilding the Walls ——————— 200

11 Nehemiah: A Postscript ———————————— 221

Part Four: The Marks of the Church ——————— 229

12 One Nation Under God? ———————————— 231

13 Christ's Prayer for God's City ————————— 243

Notes ————————————————————————————— 265

Subject Index ——————————————————————— 273

Scripture Index ————————————————————— 278

93505

Preface

It has been almost twenty years since I began the series of books on Christian doctrine that InterVarsity Press eventually published as the single volume of theology titled *Foundations of the Christian Faith*. My intention was to write a theology that would have something of the scope of John Calvin's classic *Institutes of the Christian Religion*, though being for our time and dealing with contemporary issues. The book was well received and has continued to be used in many places, particularly in Christian colleges.

I remember thinking, when I was writing that book, that there is another doctrinal classic that needs to be restated for today's world, Saint Augustine's *City of God. The City of God* was the first serious attempt to develop a Christian philosophy of history and was probably the Middle Ages' single most influential volume. The work I am presenting here is my attempt to bring the themes of Augustine's *City of God* up to date. There are several reasons I think this is important.

First, American culture is declining rapidly and, many would say, at an accelerating pace. America was never a "Christian nation." No nation is ever that. Only individuals are Christians. But at one time the country was at least permeated by a Christian ethos so that religion was encouraged, moral values were affirmed, families were intact, authority was respected, schools had wholesome environments, cities were safe, local communities flourished, and people were proud to be Americans. In the eyes of many from abroad America was "a shining city on a hill." They wanted to come here. Today internationals still come, but it is usually only for educational or financial reasons, and it is with fear and trembling. They have a right to be fearful. Some of them get killed here.

Second, evangelicals have not done a very good job recently of relating to our culture. America is very religious by some measures. More people go to church or attend synagogue regularly here than in any other country of the world, about 46 percent on an average weekend. But the influence of this churchgoing on the country's values is almost negligible.

In recent years many Christians have engaged in what has been called the Culture Wars. These are described, on one side, as trying to "take back America" or "reclaim America's soul" and, on the other side, as trying to keep the Religious Right from imposing its values on everyone else. What should be done? Should we intensify the battles, raise money, get out the vote, support Christian lobbying groups in Washington and try to mandate by legislation the kind of country we believe we should have?

What I say in this book is that what Christians need to do above all is to be Christians—that is, to be God's people in the midst of this world's culture. And one thing that will help us to do that is to take a new look at what St. Augustine argued long ago. Augustine distinguished between two entirely different societies: the city of man, which is characterized by self-love, and the City of God, composed of those who love God and want to serve him. The city of man will never be God's city. It has a different origin, progresses along a separate path, and is moving to a radically different end. Yet those who are members of God's city are nevertheless in the world and need to conduct themselves as a renewing force within it.

In this book I explore how we might go about doing that today. This is not a "how-to" book, preparing people to picket abortion clinics, lobby legislators or whatever. It is an attempt to study the problems we face, to think through the options we have, to evaluate these by biblical teaching and to consider what concerned believers might do in our time.

May God help us all to be genuine people of God in the midst of a perishing generation.

Part 1

The Collapse of a Culture

I am raising up the Babylonians,
   that ruthless and impetuous people,
who sweep across the whole earth
   to seize dwelling places not their own.
They are a feared and dreaded people;
   they are a law to themselves
   and promote their own honor.

HABAKKUK 1:6-7

1
The Barbarians
Are Coming

*B*Y THE FIRST DECADE OF THE FIFTH Christian century the Roman Empire had collapsed. Its capital city, great Rome, had been besieged for months by the Visigoth king Aleric, but at last it had been overrun and ruthlessly sacked by his barbarian hordes. The year was A.D. 410.

The city had been besieged by barbarians before. Parts of the empire had already been overrun by foreign armies. But the sack of Rome was politically and psychologically devastating in a way those other defeats were not. Rome had been master of the world. The empire had stood for a thousand years and was the very essence of civilization, at least to all who lived in the west. But suddenly it was gone, swept away by the advancing armies of these wild Germanic tribes. When Rome fell to Aleric, the citizens of the empire could hardly assimilate the scope of this unmitigated tragedy and quite naturally searched about for someone or something to blame.

It was not long before blame fell on the Christians, as it had nearly four hundred years before for less serious troubles—when Nero had been dipping Christians in wax and setting them on fire to illuminate the killing of other Christians in the great arena. The pagans charged that the fall of Rome had resulted from the neglect of the worship of the old gods under whose benevolent protection Rome had grown great. The cause of this neglect, they said, was Christianity.

The Christians were shocked by Rome's fall too. Saint Jerome, the great Latin father of the church and translator of the Vulgate, wrung his hands, crying, "What is to become of the Church now that Rome has fallen?" It was a natural question, since Rome had embraced Christianity under the influence of the emperor Constantine almost one hundred years before and had been the church's benefactor, friend and protector for most of the succeeding decades. Constantine had converted to Christianity after his victory at the Milvian Bridge in 312 B.C.

In God's providence there was a man perfectly suited for the challenges of this great watershed era in world history: St. Augustine of Hippo, a town in North Africa.

Augustine's Early Life
Augustine's first name was Aurelius, though he himself never used it. He was born on November 13, A.D. 354, of mixed pagan and Christian parentage—that is, his mother was a Christian, his father was not—at Tagaste, a small provincial town in North Africa.

His mother's name was Monica, and the passion of her life was that her son might become a Christian. His father wanted him to have a superior liberal education and by this means eventually to become a great and wealthy man. Augustine was educated first in his hometown, then in the renowned but notoriously corrupt city of Carthage. He was trained as a rhetorician, that is, one who made his living by arguing cases of law or giving speeches. He succeeded so well that he moved from Carthage to Rome, and later, in 384, from Rome to Milan, where he was appointed the Government Professor of Rhetoric. This post gave him high standing and brought him into contact with the most influential people in Italy, even members of the court.

In the year 400, fourteen years after his conversion, Augustine published his *Confessions*. This was a book of thirteen relatively short chapters in which he tells of the grace of God in his early life and how God led him to faith in Jesus Christ. On the very first page he wrote something that almost every Christian has heard at one time or another: "Thou hast formed us for thyself, and our hearts are restless till they find rest in thee."[1] He meant that of everyone, of course. But it was especially true of himself and is the major testimony of his life. Augustine had tried everything the world had to offer, but he found it empty.

His Youthful Pleasures

To many people one of the most fascinating parts of the *Confessions* is Augustine's description of his early life. Due to what he says, critics have thought of him as having been something of a libertine or rake. But there are two things wrong with this way of thinking.

First, he was not as depraved as some suppose. By the age of seventeen he had formed a long-lasting relationship with a woman whom he did not marry—his parents did not want him to marry, supposing that marriage at an early age would be an obstacle to his career—and Augustine and this woman were faithful to each other until they were eventually forced apart to make way for a "proper" legal marriage some fourteen years later. Augustine wrote that while they were together he was faithful to her. The *Confessions* contain a tragic passage describing his personal heartbreak when they were forced apart.[2]

The second thing wrong with this thinking is that it makes Augustine worse than we are, and that is just not true. Augustine was no better but also not much worse than anyone else in his time, and the way he lived is all too common today. We too live in an age of so-called sexual liberation, and the pattern of Augustine's early years is duplicated many times over. The only difference is that he confessed his sins while we usually do not.

His Quest for Truth

Augustine did not only have a strong sexual nature. He also had a driving restless mind, and his *Confessions* tell how he journeyed from one popular philosophical system to another to try to discover truth.

He was attracted to the thought of the Manichaeans. The Manichees were dualists. They believed in an eternity of good and evil.

They were also the rationalists of their age. They expressed reverence for Jesus Christ, but their religion was naturalistic, antisupernatural. They were critical of the Bible and had developed a way of looking at life that relieved human beings of responsibility for their failures. This appealed to Augustine. It bolstered his pride, allowed him to speak well of his mother's religion, excused his failings, and freed him to live in any manner he desired.

In time Augustine drifted away from the Manichees and was introduced to the later Platonists. Augustine was deeply affected by their writings. They seemed to have some knowledge of God in the form of an immaterial, eternal, unchangeable mind or *logos*. Yet this system proved unsatisfactory too. Augustine was restless, and he had not yet come to rest in Jesus Christ. In a wonderfully perceptive passage he compares the books of the Platonists with what he later found in Scripture.

> I read, not indeed in the same words, but to the selfsame effect, enforced by many and divers reasons, that, "In the beginning was the Word, and the Word was with God, and the Word was God. The same was in the beginning with God. All things were made by him; and without him was not anything made that was made." . . . But that "he came unto his own, and his own received him not. But as many as received him, to them he gave power to become the sons of God, even to them that believe on his name." That I did not read there.
>
> In like manner, I read there that God the Word was born not of flesh, nor of blood, nor of the will of man, nor of the will of the flesh, but of God. But that "the Word was made flesh, and dwelt among us," I read not there. . . .
>
> That before all times, and above all times, thy only-begotten Son remaineth unchangeably co-eternal with thee . . . is there. But that "in due time Christ died for the ungodly," and that "thou sparedst not thine only Son, but deliveredst him up for us all," is not there.[3]

His Fame

When Augustine arrived in Milan as Government Professor of Rhetoric he was at the apex of his profession. His mother came over from Africa. Wealthy and influential friends sought him out. But, as often happens when we achieve the thing we have been fervently seeking, Augustine discovered that his goal was unsatisfying. This became the most miserable time of his life. He even became sick with a chest or lung infection, and it was doubtful whether he would be able to continue his career in oratory.

His Exposure to Religion

While we are reviewing those elements in his life that Augustine later confessed to have left him unfulfilled and restless, we ought not to forget religion. For Augustine was always somewhat religious, and his religion was never very far from the true evangelical faith of his mother, which was Christianity. Augustine had almost always believed in God, and in these early days he would probably have said that in one way or another he was always striving to know him.

In Milan Augustine came under the influence of Ambrose, the bishop of that city. Ambrose was a man of towering intellect, massive learning and great godliness. Moreover, he was an outstanding preacher. So Augustine went to hear him. At first Augustine was only interested in his homiletical style. But Ambrose was really an expositor of the Bible and thus also an outstanding teacher of Christian doctrine. Augustine began to read the Bible. In spite of himself, he was led deeper into understanding what the gospel of salvation through Jesus Christ was all about, though he had not yet come to trust Christ.

Augustine wrote perceptively of what he was like in those days: "To thee, showing me on every side that what thou saidst was true, I, convicted by the truth, had nothing at all to reply, but the drawling and drowsy words: 'Presently, lo, presently'; 'leave me a little while.' But 'presently, presently,' had no present; and my 'leave me a little while' went on for a long while."[4] "I, miserable young man, supremely miserable even in the very outset of my youth, had entreated chastity of thee, and said, 'Grant me chastity and continency, but not yet.' For I was afraid lest thou shouldest hear me soon, and soon deliver me."[5]

Augustine asked his friend Alypius, "What is wrong with us? . . .
The unlearned start up and 'take' heaven, but we, with our learning,
but wanting heart, see where we wallow in flesh and blood! Because
others have preceded us, are we ashamed to follow, and not rather
ashamed at not following?"[6]

The Scene in the Garden

At last there came the well-known scene in the garden where Augustine was converted. He had been reading the Bible, and he became so distressed at his own lack of spiritual resolution that he
withdrew to a distant part of the garden so he could give vent to his
emotion and so Alypius, who was with him, would not see his tears.
Here is what he says happened:

> I flung myself down, how, I know not, under a certain fig-tree,
> giving free course to my tears. . . . And, not indeed in these words,
> yet to this effect, spake I much unto thee—"But thou, O Lord, how
> long?" "How long, Lord? Wilt thou be angry forever? O, re-
> member not against us former iniquities"; for I felt that I was
> enthralled by them. . . . "Why not now? Why is there not this hour
> an end to my uncleanness?"
>
> I was saying these things and weeping in the most bitter con-
> trition of my heart, when, lo, I heard the voice as of a boy or girl,
> I know not which, coming from a neighboring house, chanting,
> and oft repeating, "Take up and read; take up and read." Imme-
> diately my countenance was changed, and I began most earnestly
> to consider whether it was usual for children in any kind of game
> to sing such words; nor could I remember ever to have heard the
> like. So, restraining the torrent of my tears, I rose up, interpreting
> it no other way than as a command to me from heaven to open
> the book, and to read the first chapter I should light upon. For I
> had heard of Antony, that, accidentally coming in whilst the gospel
> was being read, he received the admonition as if what was read
> were addressed to him: "Go and sell that thou hast, and give to the
> poor, and thou shalt have treasure in heaven; and come and follow
> me." And by such oracle was he forthwith converted unto thee.

So quickly I returned to the place where Alypius was sitting; for there had I put down the volume of the apostles, when I rose thence. I grasped, opened, and in silence read that paragraph on which my eyes first fell,—"Not in rioting and drunkenness, not in chambering and wantonness, not in strife and envying; but put ye on the Lord Jesus Christ, and make not provision for the flesh, to fulfill the lusts thereof." No further would I read, nor did I need; for instantly, as the sentence ended—by a light, as it were, of security infused into my heart—all the gloom of doubt vanished away.[7]

Alypius was converted himself at this time, and both of them went to tell Augustine's mother, Monica. It was not long after this that Monica died, as she and Augustine were on their way back to North Africa, where Augustine eventually became a presbyter and then bishop of Hippo Regius, serving there for more than forty years until his death on August 28, A.D. 430, at the age of seventy-six.

Augustine's Later Life

It is hard to overestimate the importance of Augustine's contribution to Christian theology and the church. Hippo was a second-rate diocese, having no special prominence in itself. Besides, it was overrun by Vandals at the very time Augustine was dying, and the bishopric, school and clergy that Augustine had established and trained were all either widely scattered or destroyed. Nevertheless, Augustine's influence lived on through his writings, perhaps more than any other nonbiblical figure. Adolf Harnack called Augustine the greatest man whom, "between Paul the Apostle and Luther the Reformer, the Christian Church has possessed."[8] Will Durant said of his residence in Hippo, "From this foot of earth he moved the world."[9]

After his conversion Augustine produced polemical works against the Manichaeans, Donatists and Pelagians, interspersed with Bible expositions, theological studies and sermons. He is best known for four works that crown his intellectual achievement: The *Confessions,* written about A.D. 400, *On Christian Doctrine,* written from 397 to 426,

On the Holy Trinity, written from 395 to 420, and above all *The City of God,* written from 413 to 426.

The City of God

Augustine began *The City of God* in A.D. 413, three years after Rome fell to Aleric, and he labored on it for thirteen years. It was the first attempt by any Christian writer to produce what we would call a philosophy of history. Almost instantly it became a Christian classic.

The work itself is in two main parts. The first part (books 1-10) was Augustine's answer to the charge that Rome had been destroyed for forsaking the ancient gods and embracing Christianity. He argued, on the contrary, that the city had been punished for its sins. In its early centuries Rome had been a nation of stoics. It had strong families and honest governors. It had almost created civil law and had given order and peace to the world. But the seeds of decay lay within its debased religions, which encouraged rather than restrained the corrupt sexual nature of human beings. Augustine described the indecency of the Roman stage, which he knew well from his own experience, and he quoted Roman writers such as Sallust and Cicero on the corruption of Roman politics.

As far as the pagan gods were concerned, they had not protected Rome in earlier times—there had been many military and other disasters—nor had they protected other cities or cultures. All they had done was to plunge Rome into increasing vice, for which the gods were notorious.

In the second part of the work (books 11-22) Augustine explained history as the working out of one great universal principle, that of two rival cities or societies. Augustine argued that from the first rebellion of the fallen angels against God "two cities have been formed by two loves: the earthly by the love of self, even to the contempt of God; the heavenly by the love of God, even to the contempt of self."[10] In this work the City of God is the church, composed of God's elect. It is destined to rule the world. The earthly city is the earthly society, having as its representatives the city cultures of Babylon in ancient times and Rome in what was for him immediate past history. The earthly city is destined to pass away.

In this second part of his work Augustine traced the origins of the two cities (books 11-14), their progress (books 15-18) and their ends (books 19-22). It was a masterful way of analyzing history. Durant rightly observed, "With this book paganism as a philosophy ceased to be, and Christianity as a philosophy began. It was the first definitive formulation of the medieval mind."[11]

The central thesis of *The City of God* is one that needs rehearing. It was influential at the time of the Reformation, forming the basis of Martin Luther's and John Calvin's doctrine of the two kingdoms. It needs to be influential again, particularly in our own age in which the line between the sacred and the secular has been so systematically rubbed out. In particular, Christians must discover what it means to be the City of God, to know what it is to be "blameless and pure, children of God without fault in a crooked and depraved generation" (Phil 2:15).

The Barbarians Are Coming

A person might argue that ours is an entirely different age from that in which Saint Augustine wrote and that we need a new approach today, not something that is so old or outmoded. He lived when the culture of the age was collapsing. Ours is not collapsing, we suppose. Our Rome is intact. The barbarians are not knocking at the gates. But is that so? Is it true that the barbarians are not knocking at our gates? Today more than one observer argues that the barbarians are not only coming but are over the drawbridge, across the moat and in the city. They have occupied every one of our contemporary citadels. The signs of the collapse of Western culture are on every hand.

Charles Colson, who served as special counsel to President Richard M. Nixon from 1969 to 1973 and who is now chairman of Prison Fellowship as well as a prolific and popular author, argues this point in a book based on lectures given at an Allies for Faith and Renewal conference held at Wheaton College in 1988. It is called *Against the Night: Living in the New Dark Ages*. In it Colson says,

Today in the West, and particularly in America, the new barbarians are all around us. They are not hairy Goths and Vandals,
swilling fermented brew and ravishing maidens; they are not
Huns and Visigoths storming our borders or scaling our city walls.
No, this time the invaders have come from within. We have bred
them in our families and trained them in our classrooms. They
inhabit our legislatures, our courts, our film studios, and our
churches. Most of them are attractive and pleasant; their ideas are
persuasive and subtle. Yet these men and women threaten our
most cherished institutions and our very character as a people.[12]

Let me share some of Colson's evidence for the presence of these
very cultured "barbarians" in the circles he mentions: our families,
classrooms, government and churches.

Barbarians in the Parlor

Hardly any observer of American society today is not painfully aware
of the collapse of the family. The statistics alone are frightening.
Since 1970 the marriage rate has fallen 30 percent while the divorce
rate has climbed to 50 percent. Each year more than one million
children live through the breakup of their families. Ten million
children now live in one-parent homes. The rate of illegitimate
births has doubled. Over half of today's inner-city children are born
out of wedlock. Even more frightening than mere statistics is the
growth of children from broken families who have no respect for
any adult authority, use vile language, possess no skills, have no wish
to acquire any and who increasingly commit the most horrible of
"adult" crimes: raping, robbing and killing each other as well as
anyone else for no more apparent reason than the pleasure of
watching another person die.

What is wrong? Why are American families self-destructing? "Government policies must bear some of the blame," writes Colson. "Welfare programs subsidize illegitimacy by making it more profitable for
a mother to live alone than with her husband. Liberal divorce laws
make changing spouses a tempting convenience when times get
tough."[13]

But government policies are not the entire problem or even the chief cause of our families' self-destruction, since well-to-do families are also breaking up in increasing numbers and children of privileged suburban homes are becoming increasingly corrupt, crime-prone and disrespectful. What lies at the heart of family breakdown is the same sad philosophy that lies at the heart of the breakdown of American society generally, namely, the cult of self and self-fulfillment to be achieved at the cost of nearly everything else. In other words, the problem is unbridled individualism, which is individualism in the most radical sense ("me alone; no one else matters"), utterly untempered, constrained by not a single moral absolute.

This is the exact opposite of what should be happening in our nation's families. Colson explains:

> Ordained by God as the basic unit of human organization, the family is not only necessary for propagating the race, but is the first school of human instruction. Parents take small self-centered monsters who spent much of their time screaming defiantly and hurling peas on the carpet and teach them to share, to wait their turn, to respect others' property. These lessons translate into respect for others, self-restraint, obedience to law—in short, into the virtues of individual character that are vital to a society's survival.[14]

But when families break down, as is happening nearly everywhere today and at every level of society, these social virtues break down too, and the domestic product becomes the next generation of self-centered, self-seeking, self-serving barbarians.

Surely the barbarians are no longer merely storming at our walls. They are through the front door and in our parlors.

Barbarians in the Classroom

They are also in our classrooms. For years, by any objective measurement, the quality of American education has declined. Test scores have plunged. American students now rank below those of most other developed nations in most subjects. Today's students enter undergraduate and college programs with no goals, exercise no academic or personal disciplines, and scorn education.

Some of this decline might be explained by the deterioration of the American family, which I have just mentioned. But the problem is deeper than this. It concerns the educational establishment itself. In 1987 University of Chicago professor Allan Bloom published a book in which he exposed the demise of education at the university level as a result of the relativism that now dominates virtually all education.[15] Historically the goal of education has been the pursuit of the good, the true and the beautiful. Plato argued that its purpose is to produce good men who will act nobly. But, wrote Bloom, that goal is impossible today, because in a culture dominated by relativism belief in absolutes like the good, the true and the beautiful no longer exists. Relativism and individualism have "extinguished the real motive for education."[16] Since it is useless to pursue these goals education has degenerated into mere pragmatic concerns such as how to operate a computer, keep an accurate ledger or manage an assembly line. No one wants to explore what goals should be pursued or with what moral and not merely expedient means we ought to get there.

Lest someone dismiss this as mere highbrow stuff, the discussion of which is best left to academics like Bloom, we must remind ourselves that among the values being discarded by today's relativism are such things as honesty, respect for other people and even the value of human life. Cheating has become an accepted way of life in most schools. Teachers no longer are respected. As for life itself, well, thousands of students are now using guns and knives to threaten and even kill the classmates and teachers they no longer honor.

In 1992 an ABC *PrimeTime Live* television special, featuring Diane Sawyer, reported that in this country one in five students comes to school with a handgun somewhat regularly, and that there are ten times as many knives in schools as there are guns. What is more, this is as true of the suburbs as it is of the inner city. In Wichita, Kansas, which calls itself mid-America, students must now pass through metal detectors before entering school—and guns and other weapons are still found in buildings. It is common for school districts to install metal detectors and institute other security measures to try to stem the increasing tide of violence.

Colson says we are left with a disturbing paradox.

While higher education is better funded and more accessible than ever before, it has nothing left worth teaching. . . . Each spring these ivy halls graduate a new generation of leaders—doctors, lawyers, politicians, and MBAs—for many of whom personal advancement and "personal truth" are the only guiding principles. Shaped by the forces of individualism, these men and women without ethics go on to mold in their own image the business ethics, legal ethics, and medical ethics of our society. And some of them end up charting the course of our nation on Capitol Hill.[17]

Surely the barbarians are in our classrooms and are moving out from them to infect the entire country.

Barbarians in Power

Americans looked on in wonder and millions rejoiced when the Soviet empire collapsed from within in the last months of the watershed year of 1989. The American way of life seemed to have been vindicated. "God and our country" seemed to have won out over "No God and their country." The Russian barbarians were not going to overthrow the capitalistic Western system after all. True. But neither did we overthrow them. Their "evil empire," as Ronald Reagan called it, collapsed from within, not because of us. It collapsed under its own inherent weaknesses. And is not ours likewise capsizing?

It is pointless here to rehearse the growing avalanche of personal and political corruption that has pushed presidential hopefuls like Gary Hart and Joe Biden out of politics, caused scores of White House aids like Edwin Meese into premature retirement, and relentlessly dogged the footsteps of our most recent presidents: Watergate destroyed Richard Nixon, Irangate tarnished the otherwise exemplary record of Ronald Reagan, Whitewater continued to haunt Bill Clinton. What is most frightening is that our nation hardly seems to care and that millions have simply lost interest in the political process. There is a deep and growing disillusionment with politics, reflected in the steady decline of voter turnout even for presidential elections. In response to the 1988 presidential campaign, which was characterized by vapid television ads and meaningless words about nonissues, nearly half of the eligible electorate did not vote.

In the 1994 midterm elections, to most people's surprise, Republicans managed to reverse Democratic control of both the House of Representatives and the Senate with the promise of fulfilling a "Contract with America," in which the federal budget would be balanced by eliminating wasteful federal spending, and other radical changes in government would take place. But "wasteful government programs" soon began to look like "the other party's programs," and pork-barrel politics continued.

Does no one in Washington have a true guiding sense of right and wrong and the courage to take the right path regardless of the consequences? It is hard to find many.

In the February 13, 1995, issue of *Newsweek* columnist Meg Greenfield wrote an article titled "Right and Wrong in Washington: Why Do Our Officials Need Specialists to Tell the Difference?" She was mocking the so-called ethics committees and ethics offices that are springing up all over Washington as convenient escapes for politicians either unable or unwilling to act morally, and she was asking why they are necessary when most issues of right and wrong should be easy to discern.

> People in Washington don't say "the Devil made me do it" anymore. They say, "I asked the ethics office and they said it didn't fall within the category of impermissible activity." Or, more frequently, when there is a flap about something that has already occurred, they say: "We have directed the ethics office to look into it and report back to us in 60 days." Good old "60 days"—for something that your ordinary, morally sentient person wouldn't need 60 seconds to figure out.[18]

Referring to the congressional page scandal of a few years back, she wrote, "I remember thinking then that if congressmen having sex with underage children who are in their custody as junior employees is not where you draw the line, then there really is no line."[19]

Yet the problem is not just with government officials. True, it is strikingly visible among those with high-profile positions. But the problem is with the character of the electorate itself, with the people who elect such leaders and then keep them in office because of promises to provide what they want even if someone else has to pay for it. A recent poll reported that 74 percent of the American people favor more spending on government programs, but only 30 percent would approve of higher taxes to fund them. In other words, "I want it, but let someone else pay."

Colson knows government from the inside as well as any contemporary critic, and he says, "American politics simply mirrors the loss of character in the American people. If citizens are not willing to put the civic good above their own, they can't expect their leaders to do it for them. In this way, by eroding our sense of societal responsibility, radical individualism paves the way for the death of community."[20]

Surely the barbarians are in the House of Representatives, in the Senate and on Capitol Hill. We have put them there.

Barbarians in the Pews

A final area of national life that Colson sees the new barbarians invading is the church. In a chapter called "Barbarians in the Pews" he notes what pollsters around the country have been noting for years, namely, that interest in religion remains high but that the morality that ought to accompany it is down. Nearly half of all Americans go to church or synagogue regularly, but the differences between the moral behaviors and ways of life of these people and those who show no religious inclinations whatever are nearly unmeasurable. What is the explanation? Colson says,

> The key to the paradox is the fact that those who claim to be Christians are arriving at faith on their own terms—terms that make no demands on behavior. . . . When the not-so-still small voice of self becomes the highest authority, religious belief requires commitment to no authority beyond oneself. Then religious groups become merely communities of autonomous beings

yoked together solely by self-interest or emotion.[21]
Evangelicals will try to view other religious bodies in this category,
but the sad truth is that they perhaps even more than others have
sold out to individualism, relativism, materialism and emotionalism,
all of which are the norm for the majority of evangelical church
services today. Evangelicals may be the most worldly people in America.

We live in bad days for the evangelical church, despite the false
sense of security caused by increasing numbers of church members
and escalating budgets. In the last few years writers such as David
F. Wells *(No Place for Truth: Or Whatever Happened to Evangelical Theology* and *God in the Wasteland: The Reality of Truth in a World of Fading
Dreams)*, Os Guinness *(Dining with the Devil)*, John MacArthur
(Ashamed of the Gospel: When the Church Becomes Like the World and
Reckless Faith: When the Church Loses Its Will to Discern), Michael Scott
Horton *(Power Religion: The Selling Out of the Evangelical Church?)* and
others have pointed out how evangelicals are being swallowed up by
today's secular culture, all because they have abandoned confidence
in the power of God through the Bible to convert sinful, secular
people and to train, establish and strengthen believers in godliness.
They seek to grow worldly programs by worldly methods instead.

To put it another way, evangelicals have abandoned a proper
commitment to revealed truth and have become mere pragmatists.
Instead of proclaiming and teaching God's Word, the Bible, they are
resorting to sermonettes of pop psychology, entertainment-style services and technological approaches to church growth, which is a
formula not for the increase of true religion but for the end of it.
Evangelical churches are growing, but they no longer have anything
distinct to offer. They are popular in many places, but the prophetic,
challenging voice of the Christian preacher and teacher, which has
been the glory and strength of the church in all past ages, has been
lost.

If this is so, then what is called for today is a new generation of
people who are confident that the Bible speaks the truth of God and
who are not afraid to believe what it teaches, build their lives on its

doctrines and proclaim it without compromise to others. What is needed is a generation of Christians who know the Bible well enough and obey it radically enough to be a new people or new society to stand over against the world and its system. To recall Augustine, they must become a people who "love God, even to the contempt of self."

Behold the Hun!

It is time to sum up this chapter by answering in the clearest possible way the question, What is a barbarian? The Greeks, who invented the word, used it to describe anyone who could not speak their language. All such people seemed to be saying was "bar, bar, bar," which is what gave the Greeks the word *barbaros* or barbarian. Dictionaries define *barbarian* as a person who lacks artistic or literary culture, or in adjective form, uncivilized. But what is civilization? Is a barbarian simply a person who has not been exposed to highbrow art or literature?

Let me suggest this definition: A barbarian is a person who lives by power and for pleasure rather than by and for principle. I repeat it again. A barbarian is a person who lives by power and for pleasure rather than by and for principle. If this is right, then we are describing the modern barbarians who live for power and pleasure as well as the older ones who laid siege to and eventually destroyed the Roman Empire.

Think of it in the categories I have been discussing: the home, the school, the government and the church.

If parents live for their own personal fulfillment without a higher concern for the well-being and happiness of their families, if there are no principles to keep them at home doing the right things and living for them even when the going gets tough, are these adults not barbarians? And are they not raising the next generation of barbarians when they fail to teach them that loving God is the first of all human duties and that love of those who are our neighbors, beginning with members of our own families, is next to it?

We call many of our worst schools jungles, since that is what they really are. But is not any school a jungle if it fails to inculcate a love of the good, the true and the beautiful as the goal of learning, so that the educated man or woman might act nobly? If all we are teaching is technical skills so that people can get better jobs, make more money and indulge themselves with pleasures that would have been impossible for nearly everyone as little as a generation ago, is that not barbarism? And are our schools not training centers for barbarism in which old barbarians teach young barbarians to be even more barbarous than those who preceded them?

Politics used to be the arena in which philosophies engaged each other in an effort to find common ground for those actions which most people agreed were right and beneficial to the greatest number. But government is far from that today. The political arena is a place of struggle, all right, but the struggle is not over principle. It is over power. There are no standards, no absolutes for assessing priorities, only a fierce battle for individual "rights" or "felt needs." In the absence of absolutes, every "right" becomes an absolute to be won by power at all costs. Then the will of the majority or of those clever enough to win a majority becomes a new despotism.

If churches are abandoning the teaching of truth for pragmatism, offering entertainment, self-help programs and soporific pep-talks in order to keep people coming and giving with little thought for the ultimate well-being of their souls, is that not a sellout to the pleasure-only principle? And if competition drives leaders to enact only those programs that will bring greater numbers of people to the church and so enhance their personal prestige, is that not a sellout to power religion, as Michael Horton claims it is?[22] We should remind ourselves that barbarians of other ages have also had religion, and theirs was not always very different from our own. Is the church not barbaric when it forgets its unique message and identifies with the aspirations and values of the world culture instead?

We are all a part of this in one way or another. In one of the best-known of all the *Pogo* cartoons, that wise old philosopher opossum Pogo said, "We have met the enemy, and he is us." Where is the

Hun? He is in each of us. We are all barbarians until God removes our proud self-centeredness and enables us to trust and learn from him who alone is good, absolutely true and exquisitely beautiful— Jesus Christ.

Part 2

The Biblical Basis
for the Two Cities

Come, let us build ourselves a city, with a tower
that reaches to the heavens, so that we may
make a name for ourselves and not be scattered
over the face of the whole earth.

GENESIS 11:4

Is not this the great Babylon I have built
as the royal residence, by my mighty power
and for the glory of my majesty?

DANIEL 4:30

I saw the Holy City, the new Jerusalem,
coming down out of heaven from God,
prepared as a bride beautifully dressed for her husband.
And I heard a loud voice from the throne saying,
"Now the dwelling of God is with men,
and he will live with them."

REVELATION 21:2-3

2

The Two Humanities

*T*HE DISTINCTION BETWEEN THE City of God and the city of man is based on the difference between what Francis Schaeffer accurately called "the two humanities,"[1] the origin of which is found in the third, fourth and fifth chapters of the book of Genesis.

According to St. Augustine, who gave us the distinction between "the two cities" in his monumental analysis of history called *The City of God,* this contrast is traceable throughout the Bible. He taught that Scripture unfolds the history of two distinct groups of people, each having a distinct origin, development, characteristics and destiny. These are two cities or societies. The earthly society has as its highest expression the city cultures of Babylon and, in what was for Augustine more modern times, Rome. The other is the church, composed of God's elect. The former is destined to pass away. The latter is blessed by God and is to last forever.

The Two Offsprings
The absolute origin of the two humanities is in the words of God to the serpent following the temptation and fall of Adam and Eve in the Garden of Eden, recorded in Genesis 3. God told the serpent as decree and prophecy,

I will put enmity
between you and the woman,

and between your offspring and hers;
he will crush your head,
and you will strike his heel. (v. 15)

Here are three sets of antagonists: the serpent and the woman, the descendants of the serpent and the descendants of the woman, and Satan himself and the ultimate descendant of the woman, Jesus Christ. These are to be engaged in an age-long conflict, but the point of the prophecy is that the victory of the godly seed will be assured by the ultimate victory of Eve's specific descendant, Jesus Christ.

The Serpent and the Woman

One immediately striking thing about this prophecy is that God presents himself as the author of the strife involved, for that is what the word *enmity* means. Enmity means "ill will on one side or on both; hatred; especially mutual antagonism" (Webster's *New Collegiate Dictionary*).

We might ask how strife can be good or how God can be the author of enmity in any form, but the Bible explains this. It says that Satan is a fallen angel whose first sin consisted in trying to gather the worship of the other creatures about himself rather than about God. His original attempt to seduce the angels had been only partially successful. But now he had appeared on earth to try to do among the new race of human beings what he had failed to do completely earlier. Undoubtedly his temptation of Eve and Adam had in mind two goals: seducing our first parents away from the worship of God and winning their allegiance and worship for himself. He succeeded in the first objective. He did destroy the fellowship of the man and the woman with God. But he did not succeed in his second objective precisely because of what God says here. For in this first announcement of the gospel—theologians call it the *protoevangelium,* which means "first gospel"—God said that he would put enmity between Satan and the woman.

It is significant that these words are spoken to Satan. For the new thing was not Satan's hatred of Eve. Satan had hated Eve from the moment of her creation, even when he was pretending to be her friend and was tempting her to eat of the forbidden tree. The new thing was Eve's (and Adam's and all their true offspring's) hatred of Satan as one aspect of God's gracious preservation of and provision for the race.

This is a great blessing, though we may not think so at times. When we sin we often find that we like sin and would like to continue in it, merely escaping sin's consequences. We would like to destroy ourselves in comfort, like the drug addict who is destroying himself in the dreamlike stupor of his drugs or booze, or the sensualist who is destroying himself by the sin of debauchery. We would like to go to hell happy. But it is one aspect of grace that God does not allow this to happen. God makes sin miserable and sets up an antagonism between ourselves and Satan that modifies the hold of sin on humanity and makes it possible for fallen men and women to hear God's voice, even in their misery.

The Descendants of the Serpent and the Descendants of the Woman
The enmity established by God was not only to be between the woman and Satan, however—that is, an enmity merely on the personal or individual level. It was also to be an enmity between her offspring and his. This could mean between human beings and the demons, but it is unlikely that it does. For one thing, Satan does not really have offspring. He is not engendering little devils. The demons were created once by God, before their fall, and they are not now increasing in number. For another thing, the passage moves in the direction of one specific descendant of the woman, who shall defeat Satan. That is, it is moving from the general to the specific. In view of these factors, the verse probably refers to the godly descendants of the man and woman, influenced by God himself, and the ungodly descendants of the man and woman, influenced by Satan. This distinction is carried forward forcefully in chapters 4 and 5.

If this is the meaning of "your offspring and hers," then it is a message for the godly in every age. It teaches that there is a God-given animosity between the people of God and those who are not

God's people, and that this is for our good. It is to sharpen our minds and wills to serve God. One of Isaac Watts's great hymns ("Am I a Soldier of the Cross?"), written in 1724, asks,

> Are there no foes for me to face?
> Must I not stem the flood?
> Is this vile world a friend of grace,
> To help me on to God?

In the context of Watts's hymn the answer clearly is no. The world is no friend of ours. It is an enemy. Watts wants us to fight against the world for Christ's sake, which we must certainly do. But there is also a sense in which the world *is* a "friend of grace," because its animosity toward us pushes us to a greater measure of dependence on God.

There is also a more specific meaning to this verse. As the book of Genesis unfolds we see God calling out a specific nation, the nation of Israel, through whom he would specifically work, and we see the animosity of Satan (who certainly understood the import of this prophecy) directed particularly against the Jews. His hatred began with attacks on Abraham and the other patriarchs, particularly Joseph, who is a type of the Messiah who was to come, and it extends throughout the entire Bible, even to the book of Revelation. In Revelation we read,

> A great and wondrous sign appeared in heaven: a woman clothed with the sun, with the moon under her feet and a crown of twelve stars on her head. She was pregnant and cried out in pain as she was about to give birth. Then another sign appeared in heaven: an enormous red dragon with seven heads and ten horns and seven crowns on his heads. His tail swept a third of the stars out of the sky and flung them to the earth. The dragon stood in front of the woman who was about to give birth, so that he might devour her child the moment it was born. She gave birth to a son, a male child, who will rule all the nations with an iron scepter. And her child was snatched up to God and to his throne. The woman fled into the desert to a place prepared for her by God, where she might be taken care of for 1,260 days. (12:1-6)

In this passage the dragon is certainly Satan, the woman Israel, and her child the Lord Jesus Christ. Satan's strategy has been to destroy Israel in order to destroy Christ. This is the most basic reason for anti-Semitism. It is also the reason why no Christian should ever have a part in it.

Satan and the Ultimate Descendant of the Woman

The third antagonism in Genesis 3:15 is even more beneficial than the others. The first two give us hope; the third assures us of victory. This prediction of antagonism between Satan and the ultimate descendant of the woman, who is Jesus Christ, was to result in the bruising of Jesus on the cross but also in the crushing of Satan and his power.

If we turn to the Gospel accounts and look behind the visible unfolding of events to the spiritual antagonism behind them, we see the hatred of Satan for Jesus Christ at every turn. Satan moved Herod to kill the babies of Bethlehem two years of age and under in a futile attempt to destroy the infant Jesus (Mt 2:16-18). But God had arranged the escape of the family in advance, having sent the Magi with their valuable gifts of gold, incense and myrrh, which would have paid for the family's flight to Egypt and their maintenance while there. As soon as Jesus began his public ministry the devil was immediately present to tempt him to turn away from the path that had been set down for him by the Father, even promising him the kingdoms of this world if he would only fall down and worship Satan (Mt 4:1-11; Lk 4:1-13). It must have been Satan who stirred up the people of Nazareth to take Jesus to the brow of a hill in order to throw him to his death because of their reaction to his first public sermon (Lk 4:28-30).

Again and again Satan plotted to destroy Jesus Christ. Sometimes he moved people to pick up stones to try to stone him (Jn 8:59; 10:31). He caused the leaders of the people to send soldiers to arrest him (Jn 7:30, 32, 45-46). Always his plots were paralyzed. Jesus described what was happening through the parable of the wicked tenant farmers who beat the servants sent by the owner of the vineyard and eventually plotted to destroy the heir when he was also sent. "They said to each other, 'This is the heir. Come, let's kill him and take his inheritance.' So they took him and threw him out of the vineyard and killed him" (Mt 21:38-39; see vv. 33-41).

On another occasion Satan tried to destroy Jesus by a sudden storm on the Sea of Galilee, but Jesus rebuked the storm, leaving the disciples to ask in awed wonder, "Who is this? Even the wind and the waves obey him!" (Mk 4:41; see vv. 35-41).

Finally Satan saw what he thought was his great opportunity. Judas, one of the Twelve, was disaffected with Jesus, and Satan moved Judas to betray his Master. The leaders of the people sent their temple guards to the garden, Jesus was arrested, and Satan's hatred of Christ, which had been frustrated, now burst forth with vengeance. The Lord was spit upon, mocked, beaten and eventually crucified with great anguish. This was a terrible "bruising," but it was only a bruising, not a defeat. For on the third day after the crucifixion, Jesus rose from the tomb triumphantly with the assurance of forgiveness and life for all who should believe on him.

As for Satan, the victory he believed he had achieved turned out to be only a Pyrrhic victory. He had been instrumental in killing God's Christ. But the death of Christ was God's atonement for sin, which Satan surely had not fully comprehended. Thus it was that even while he was celebrating his apparent victory, the full weight of the atonement, accomplished by the death of Christ, came down on him and his power was broken. His head was crushed, and he discovered that far from being able to contend successfully with the Almighty God, he had actually only been instrumental in advancing the purposes of him who alone is all-wise.[2]

The Two Sons

If Genesis 3:15 were the only text to go on, we might suppose that its second contrast is between the demons, conceived as the seed of the serpent, and humankind in general. But this is not the case, as I indicated earlier. The next two chapters of Genesis make plain that the conflict is between the followers of God, who are believing men and women, and those human beings who do not believe God and who follow Satan and his ways instead.

The Birth of Cain

The first illustration is the conflict between Cain and Abel, the first and second children born to Eve and Adam. Cain was the firstborn, and the meaning of his name is "acquisition." It might be rendered colloquially "Here he is!" The significance of this is that Adam and Eve believed the promise God had given in Genesis 3:15 and were waiting for the Savior God had promised. This was why Adam named his wife Eve—"because she would become the mother of all the living" (Gen 3:20). Eve means "life giver," and this was Adam's way of saying, "I believe God when he says he is going to send a child who will be born of you and who will one day crush the head of our great adversary Satan." And Eve believed too, because the text says that she called her firstborn son Cain (Gen 4:1).

The text is even stronger than that, however. We need to notice two things. First, in the Hebrew text of Genesis 4:1, Eve does not actually say, "With the help of the Lord I have brought forth a man." The words "with the help of" are not in the Hebrew but have been added by the translators to explain in good English what they believe the text means. The actual words are: "the Lord I have brought forth a man." Second, the name of Jehovah ("the Lord") is preceded by the Hebrew particle *'et*, as is the word *man* at the end of the sentence. The particle can mean "with," which is what the translators assume when they add the full expression "*with* the help of." But it usually marks something in the accusative case, which then becomes the object of the sentence. If that is the case here, what Eve actually said was, "I have brought forth a man, even Jehovah."

This is all the more probable because the particle *'et* occurs earlier in the verse before the word *Cain,* which puts the two parts of the sentence in parallel construction. The expanded text would read, "Adam lay with his wife Eve, and she conceived and gave birth to '*eṯ* Cain. [Then, explaining why this was the name chosen] She said, 'I have brought forth [that is the meaning of the word *Cain*] a man, '*eṯ* Jehovah."

The obvious objection to this is that Eve could hardly have thought that she was giving birth to God, at least so early in the history of God's revelation. But the difficulty vanishes when we remember that this *was* early and that God had not yet made himself known to anyone by the name Jehovah. In Exodus 6:3 God told Moses, to whom he did reveal himself as Jehovah, "I appeared to Abraham, to Isaac and to Jacob as God Almighty, but by my name the LORD [Jehovah] I did not make myself known to them." The revelation of the names of God was something that happened over a long period of time, and it may well be that at this stage Jehovah only meant something like "advocate" or "divine deliverer" to Eve and Adam.

Unfortunately, the beautiful baby that Eve held in her arms and beheld with thankful, wondering eyes was not Jesus Christ. Thousands of years would pass before the promise of Genesis 3:15 would be fulfilled. What Eve actually held in her arms was the world's first murderer, the father of the race of human beings that was to "love self, even to the contempt of God." True. But very soon she would hold the father of the godly also! For the next verse says, "Later she gave birth to his brother Abel" (Gen 4:2).

The Offerings of Cain and Abel

The story that follows gives the first clear insights into the nature of the two humanities. Cain and Abel, now fully grown, came to present their offerings to God. The story is brief at this point and omits much that we might like to know. But it suggests that God must have given considerable instruction to Adam and Eve and their descendants as to how they were to approach him in faith by the offering of sacrifices. This is nearly indisputable in light of the emphasis on the approach to God by blood sacrifice that we find in the Bible from beginning to end.

This is not how Cain approached God, however. Cain brought "some of the fruits of the soil" as his offering (4:3) and was rejected.

By contrast, Abel brought a sacrifice of some of "the firstborn of his flock" (v. 4) and was accepted.

This troubles some people who would object strongly, "But why should Cain be rejected? He did the best he could. He brought the best he had." True! But the first great lesson the Bible has to teach about approaching God is that our sinful "good" is not good enough. The best we can do is not sufficient. What we need is a blood sacrifice, the point being that an innocent victim must die in place of the one who has sinned. The sacrifices pointed to the coming of the Redeemer, who is Jesus Christ. So to offer something to God other than a sacrifice is actually to reject Jesus. It is unbelief, which is the first sad, reprehensible characteristic of this ungodly race of people.

I should add that there is a proper place for offering to God the works of our hands. But it is after we have come on the basis of the sacrifice. If Cain had come as God had told him to come, presenting his sacrifice that would have testified to his trust in God's promise to send the Redeemer, and then had offered his first fruits, God would have accepted the offering without question. God accepts what we may offer in the same spirit today, whether it be the fruits of our art or music or intellectual endeavors or whatever. But when Cain refused to come with the blood offering, God was obliged to reject both him and anything else he might offer. The Bible says, "Without the shedding of blood there is no forgiveness" (Heb 9:22).

Yet here is a point in the story that is very significant. Although Cain's offering was rejected, God did not simply walk away from him, as it were, but rather approached him and tried to reason with him about his sacrifice and what he needed to do to be accepted. "Why are you angry? Why is your face downcast? If you do what is right, will you not be accepted? But if you do not do what is right, sin is crouching at your door; it desires to have you, but you must master it" (Gen 4:6-7). So also does God reason with us. " 'Come now, let us reason together,' says the LORD. 'Though your sins are like scarlet, they shall be as white as snow; though they are red as crimson, they shall be like wool' " (Is 1:18).

This reasoning has several important parts.

First, there is an indication that God saw Cain in whatever state he was in. Cain may be downcast and angry and turn away from God. He may withdraw from Abel's society and reject his parents too. He may move to a far country and establish a new city and enter into a new way of life there, but he is unable to get away from God. God sees him regardless, just as God sees you. Ultimately it is God whom we each have to deal with.

Second, Cain need not have been angry. The fault was not outside himself, as if it were something that could not be changed. It could be changed, and the one to change it was Cain. So also with us. We tend to blame others for our troubles. Or our environment. Or our genes. But although these may be factors in our psychological and emotional makeup, the true cause is seldom outside us. It is within.

Third, there is a reminder of the right course of action: "If you do what is right, will you not be accepted?" This is another indication that the way of approach to God by sacrifice had been made clear to these first human beings. If not, how could God call one course "right" as opposed to another? Cain was encouraged to do the "right" thing. In other words, although he had sinned in willful unbelief, refusing to come to God in the way appointed, he still had opportunity to come, if he would humble himself and obey God. Unfortunately, he refused to do that, just as many people today have heard the Word of God and the gospel yet refuse to obey the call.

Fourth, God gave Cain a warning, telling him that sin was crouching at his door and that it wanted to master him. Is that true today? It is for many people. Indeed, it is even worse than that. In many cases, sin has crossed the threshold and has taken up residence within. What can be done in such cases? We cannot drive the demons of sin out. If we try to do that in our own strength, the demon will only come back with seven demons even more terrible than himself and our final state will be worse than our first (see Mt 12:43-45). If we would master sin, we must first be mastered by him who has mastered it. We must belong to Jesus.

The Way of Cain

Cain did not allow himself to be mastered by God, and so he became enslaved to sin and the devil, choosing a path that Jude later called "the way of Cain" (Jude 11). Allowing jealousy and resentment of his brother to build within him, the day came when he found Abel alone in the field and killed him. He must have looked around first to see if anyone was watching, and when he saw no one he did the heinous act. Yet there was one who was watching, one who sees everything. God was watching.

"Where is your brother Abel?" asked God.

"I don't know," Cain answered. "Am I my brother's keeper?"

How evil this reply was. He was his brother's keeper, of course, just as we all have responsibilities for one another. But that was not the worst part of his reply. The worst thing was that he was lying, and he was lying to God. So much had sin mastered him by this point that he believed he could escape the consequences of his sin by lying. Thus far had sin progressed in just one generation! "Am I my brother's keeper?" We hear the voice of modern man in Cain's cruel question.

Cain is mentioned three times in the New Testament: in Hebrews 11:4, which affirms our interpretation of these verses by asserting, "By faith Abel offered God a better sacrifice than Cain did"; in 1 John 3:12, which warns us, "Do not be like Cain, who belonged to the evil one and murdered his brother"; and in Jude 11, which I have already mentioned. Jude expands Cain's actions to what he calls "the way of Cain" in which the wicked walk.

What does this mean? It means that although Cain's case is a sorry one, it is even sorrier than this in that it has become a pattern for many persons who have followed in his wake. If you have rejected God's way of salvation through the death of Jesus Christ for your sin, you are in that way and sin is mastering you. This part of the story warns you of what is happening and calls you to repent of your sin and reject Cain's way. It points you to the way of Abel who, though he was killed, nevertheless has this testimony that "he was . . . a righteous man." The author of Hebrews says, "By faith he still speaks, even though he is dead" (11:4). Let him speak to you, and follow his example.

The Two Genealogies

The remainder of Genesis 4 and all of Genesis 5 show how Cain and Abel gave birth to two radically different societies. Cain is driven away to be a wanderer in the earth, and his descendants are listed: Enoch, whose name Cain gave to the city he was building; Irad, the son of Enoch; Mehujael; and finally Methushael, the father of Lamech. Lamech receives special mention as an illustration of what was happening in the line of those who walked in Cain's way. He had three sons: Jabal, who "was the father of those who live in tents and raise livestock"; Jubal, "the father of all who play the harp and flute"; and Tubal-Cain, "who forged all kinds of tools out of bronze and iron" (Gen 4:20-22). These descriptions speak of a well-developed culture, but it was a cruel culture, as Lamech's boast to his two wives shows.

> Adah and Zillah, listen to me;
>   wives of Lamech, hear my words.
> I have killed a man for wounding me,
>   a young man for injuring me.
> If Cain is avenged seven times,
>   then Lamech seventy-seven times. (vv. 23-24)

This is the story of a man boasting about murder and, since his boasting seems to be in poetry, actually writing a song about it. Francis Schaeffer wrote of this incident, "Here is humanistic culture without God. It is egotism and pride centered in man; this culture has lost the concept not only of God but of man as one who loves his brother."[3]

At this point Genesis introduces the godly family line, which continues through Seth to Noah. The names in this line are Seth, Enosh, Kenan, Mahalelel, Jared, Enoch, Methuselah, Lamech and Noah. Two of these are mentioned in Hebrews 11 as examples of those whose lives were marked by faith: Enoch, who is said to have "pleased God" (Heb 11:5); and Noah, of whom it is written,

"By faith Noah, when warned about things not yet seen, in holy fear built an ark to save his family. By his faith he condemned the world and became heir of the righteousness that comes by faith" (v. 7).

These lines may be traced throughout history, as Saint Augustine does in *The City of God* and I will also begin to do in chapters four and five when I focus on the two cities. The godless line is traceable in the world's cities, states and cultures. The godly line moves forward through Abraham and his descendants, the faithful within Israel, and the church. As far as the cities go, the major contrast is between Babylon, the representative city of the world, and Jerusalem, which is God's city. Here we will need to think not only of historical Jerusalem but of the Jerusalem which is above.

At the very end of Genesis 4, in verses that should really be with those of chapter 5 (4:25-26), the essential characteristics of the godly line are spelled out. We need to look at them closely.

A Proper View of God and His Preeminence
This is seen in Eve's comment at the time of Seth's birth: "God has granted me another child in place of Abel, since Cain killed him." Even on the surface it is plain that Eve (and Adam too) was ascribing the birth of Seth to God, acknowledging that God is the source of life, something no one in Cain's line is said to have done. But this obvious meaning of Eve's words becomes even stronger when contrasted with what she had said earlier when Cain was born. She said, "I have brought forth a man" (Gen 4:1). That was a statement of her faith in God's promise, as I pointed out earlier. It was commendable. But it was nevertheless weak in one sense, which we see as soon as we contrast it with what she says now. It was human-centered. When Cain was born Eve said, "*I* have brought forth a man." But now she changes that to a deeper and nobler confession, saying, "*God* has granted me another child."

Nothing is so characteristic of the diverse natures of the world and Christians as that contrast. The godless culture begins with man— the very essence of what we call secular humanism. The people of

God begin with God, though sometimes even the godly have to learn the hard way, as Eve did.

A Proper View of Man and His Frailty

The second characteristic of Seth's line is its right view of man, particularly its awareness of his frailty. This is not particularly evident in the English translation of these verses, but it emerges in Hebrew because of the meaning of the name of Seth's son Enosh. Seth means "set in place of," because he was given in place of Abel, as Eve said. But Enosh means "frail one" or "mortal." It would seem that Seth, who is a part of the godly line, was so impressed with the frailty of man that he gave his son a name intended to preserve and communicate that truth. Instead of boasting about his strength, as Lamech did, Seth confessed his deep and continuing need of God.

These two doctrines, the doctrine of man and the doctrine of God, go together and are related in a manner that has sometimes been called the seesaw in theology. The basic idea of a seesaw is that when one end is up the other is down. You can never have both ends up or both ends down at the same time. So it is with the doctrines of God and man. If a person exalts man in his or her theology—if man is thought to be strong and good and well able to take care of his own spiritual needs—then God is inevitably lowered in that theological system, for there is no great need of him. In fact, man becomes equal or even superior to God and eventually imagines that he can do without him. On the other hand, if God is up, then man is down and is perceived to be the weak and needy creature Seth saw him to be.

The ungodly object to this conclusion, of course, for they think that lifting God up debases man. But the case is actually the reverse. This is clear in chapter 4. The godless culture of Cain runs on through his godless generations and eventually produces Lamech, the original self-made and self-sufficient man. Lamech does not need God. He can take care of himself. But what is his attitude toward other human beings? Parallel with Lamech's exaltation of himself (at the expense of God) is his lowering of the value of others so that at last he is ready to kill them for so small an offense as wounding him, perhaps (the original permits this) only by words.

We see this devaluing of man everywhere today, and it is a result of the humanistic philosophy that was supposed to exalt him. People with no regard for either God or other human beings are killing people every single hour in our cities, often for nothing, frequently for as little a something as a pair of sneakers or a necklace.

The godly do not have a low view of man, though they have a realistic view and rightly lower him in comparison to the powerful and only holy God. They do not exalt man to an absolute position in the universe. They know his corruption. They speak of his fall. But at the same time they love their fellow human beings as creatures made in the image of God and thus of inestimable worth. Enoch (Gen 5:21-24) became a preacher who tried to warn his generation of the judgment to come. Noah, another in this line, likewise became "a preacher of righteousness" (2 Pet 2:5) who tried to turn back some of his acquaintances before they perished in the flood. The godly care for others so much that they are willing to endure hardship and even suffer personal abuse so that those perishing might hear the gospel and respond by believing on Jesus Christ.

Dependence on God

The final and very important characteristic of the godly line is its dependence on God for salvation and for all other things besides. We have already seen this in Adam, who named his wife Eve because she would become, as he thought, the mother of the Messiah. We have seen it in Eve, in the way she named her firstborn Cain ("here he is"), believing that the Redeemer had arrived. Now we see it at the end of the chapter, where we are told, "At that time men began to call on the name of the LORD" (4:26). The godly knew they were not self-sufficient. So they threw themselves on God, trusting him for their salvation.

The Reformers were very impressed by this text and saw it as an illustration of that utter dependence on God which they had come

to value highly. Martin Luther spoke of Genesis 4:26 as the formation of "a small church . . . in which Adam, as high priest, rules
everything by the Word and sound doctrine."[4] John Calvin saw it as
"a restoration of religion" such as had been effected in his day. He
called it "a miracle, that there was at that time a single family in
which the worship of God arose."[5] He was right. It was a miracle.
And Luther was right too; it was a small church. It was the new
humanity.

The Two Enochs
In the midst of this long genealogy of the godly in Genesis there is
a most interesting man: Enoch. When we discover all there is to
know about him we learn that he is an example and a summary of
all I have been saying in this chapter. Enoch walked with God in an
age when practically no one else did and so became an outstanding
illustration of the nature of the new humanity in every age.

An interesting feature of the biblical references to Enoch is that
more is said about him in the New Testament than in the Old. In
the whole of the Bible only five passages refer to Enoch. Two are
genealogies in which only his name is mentioned (1 Chron 1:3 and
Lk 3:37), so nothing much is learned there. That leaves three key
passages:

Genesis 5:21-23. "When Enoch had lived 65 years, he became the
father of Methuselah. And after he became the father of Methuselah, Enoch walked with God 300 years and had other sons and
daughters. Altogether, Enoch lived 365 years. Enoch walked with
God; then he was no more, because God took him away."

Hebrews 11:5. "By faith Enoch was taken from this life, so that
he did not experience death; he could not be found, because God
had taken him away. For before he was taken, he was commended
as one who pleased God."

Jude 14-15. "Enoch, the seventh from Adam, prophesied about
these men: 'See, the Lord is coming with thousands upon thousands of his holy ones to judge everyone, and to convict all the
ungodly of all the ungodly acts they have done in the ungodly way,

and of all the harsh words ungodly sinners have spoken against him.' "

This makes four Old Testament verses compared to three New Testament verses. But in terms of the number of words, the New Testament (based on the New International Version) has ninety-four words compared to only fifty-one in the Old Testament. The important thing is that the New Testament has important information about Enoch.

The Seventh from Adam

Jude introduces Enoch as "the seventh from Adam." It is a curious phrase, and at first it seems unnecessary. No other Bible character is introduced by such terms. However, it is explained when we turn back to Genesis 4 and 5 and recognize that two Enochs were living at this time. One was the seventh descendant from Adam through the line of Seth. He is mentioned in chapter 5. The other was the third descendant from Adam through the line of Cain. He is mentioned in chapter 4. The Enoch who descended from Adam through the line of Seth was godly. He is our Enoch, the seventh. The one who descended from Adam through the line of Cain was godless. He is the devil's Enoch, the third. So Jude's identification of Enoch as "the seventh from Adam" is a way of distinguishing the two, as if God is saying, "I want you to follow Enoch and be like him. But I don't want you to get the two Enochs confused. I am talking about the Enoch of Genesis 5, not the ungodly Enoch of chapter 4."

This has practical considerations, for it suggests that there is a parallel between those who are God's people and those who are the devil's, and it encourages us to imitate the godly only. I spell it out like this. God has his people, and the devil has his. The devil has his doctors; God has his doctors. The devil has his lawyers; God has his lawyers. The devil has his teachers; God has his teachers. The devil has his convicts and housewives and even preachers, who tell lies. God has his convicts and housewives and preachers, who speak God's truth. Those who are the devil's people live for themselves and by their own rules, "even to the contempt of God." Those who are

God's live for him, "even to the contempt of self," and are a blessing
to others in countless ways. In other words, the existence of the two
Enochs is the very essence of the two humanities.

This is at least part of the answer to the problem of the continuing
existence of evil in the world. For God is using it to demonstrate the
difference between the lives of those who go their own way, sin and
bear the consequences, and those who seek to obey and serve God.
The former are miserable and bring misery in their wake. They
follow the devil, and all the devil can create is misery and confusion.
Even the very word *devil* (*diabolos* in Greek) means "disrupter." God's
people glorify God, and God uses them to bless others. The devil
cannot do that with his children and, in fact, does not even want to.

A Preacher of Righteousness

Jude tells us something else about this important antediluvian: he
was a preacher. And it tells us something about the content of his
preaching. Enoch's message had two essential parts: first, a proclamation of the Lord's coming in judgment and, second, a denunciation of the ungodliness that was all too visible in the degenerate
secular culture of those days. "See, the Lord is coming with thousands upon thousands of his holy ones to judge everyone, and to
convict all the ungodly of all the ungodly acts they have done in the
ungodly way, and of all the harsh words ungodly sinners have spok-
en against him" (vv. 14-15).

When we read those words today we understand that they refer
to the Second Coming of the Lord Jesus Christ in the final judgment.
But when Enoch spoke those words, as the Holy Spirit led him to
do, he must have been looking ahead to the pending destruction of
the race (Noah and his family excepted) by the flood and must have
been warning his contemporaries about it. In fact, we can recall how
the apostle Peter joins the two together, using the first as a warning
of the second. "By these waters also the world of that time was
deluged and destroyed. By the same word the present heavens and
earth are reserved for fire, being kept for the day of judgment and
destruction of ungodly men" (2 Pet 3:6-7). Enoch was warning of the

first judgment, just as Peter did (and we should) warn others of the second.

But isn't the preaching of the gospel to be positive and hopeful? Yes, it is. It was positive to Adam and Eve, who heard it and believed in God's promise of a Redeemer to come. The gospel is a hopeful proclamation of salvation. But it is also negative in the sense that God warns of judgment for those who will not receive Christ. If we are to walk in Enoch's steps, we must be faithful to proclaim the judgment side of the gospel message too.

The second part of Enoch's preaching concerned the ungodliness of his age. He preached that the Lord was coming "to convict all the ungodly of all the ungodly acts they have done in the ungodly way, and of all the harsh words ungodly sinners have spoken against him." This is only part of one sentence from this great man's preaching, but it is significant that in it the word *ungodly* appears four times. In other words, it was the burden of his preaching. What do you suppose is the most used word in preaching today? *Love? Involvement? Self-esteem? Fulfillment?* I do not know, but I am sure it is not *sin* or *judgment* or *ungodliness*.

Enoch lived in the age just before the flood, and it was a very sinful time. There is a brief description of it in Genesis 6:1-7, in which God says that "man's wickedness on the earth" had become very great and that "every inclination of the thoughts of his heart was only evil all the time" (v. 5). We are appalled at the wickedness of that age. But it was not essentially different from our own. We too have sexual promiscuity, materialism, spiritualism and the occult, which are implied in Genesis 6. Moreover, we have rape and murder and drug addiction and prostitution and the killing of the unborn and other evils that are not even mentioned in Genesis in connection with the race before the flood. How can we point our fingers at the antediluvian culture and cry, "Ungodly," when we are so manifestly ungodly ourselves? What would Enoch say if he were here today? Would he not say what he said so many thousands of years ago to the people of his time: "Ungodly . . . ungodly . . . ungodly . . . ungodly"? And would he not be right? Ungodliness is the single most characteristic feature of our own decadent civilization.

Enoch Walked with God

From what we are told about Enoch in Jude, we turn back to the
original mention of Enoch in Scripture, the text in Genesis. This
passage does not mention his preaching at all, but in its short fifty-
one words, much as Jude 14 and 15 repeat the word *ungodly* four
times, Genesis 5:21-24 repeats the words "Enoch walked with God"
twice. The full text says, "When Enoch had lived 65 years, he became
the father of Methuselah. And after he became the father of Methuselah, Enoch walked with God 300 years and had other sons and
daughters. Altogether, Enoch lived 365 years. Enoch walked with
God; then he was no more, because God took him away."

What does it mean to walk with God? It means a number of things.
It means to believe in God, to obey God, to stay close to God, to seek
the way in which God would have us live and the things he would
have us do. It has to do with godliness. If Enoch walked with God,
clearly it was because he was not fighting against God or resisting
him but was delighting to walk as God directed him.

Moreover, the text tells us that he was doing this for a long time.
The first use of these words is in connection with the birth of
Enoch's son Methuselah, when Enoch was 65 years old. The second
time is of the end of his life when he was 365 years old. So Enoch
walked with God for 300 years. That is no casual stroll. It was the
walk of a lifetime. Moreover, it was a walk and not a sprint or a run.
Nearly anyone can sprint for a short time or distance, but no one
can sprint for long. For the long haul you need to walk, and that is
what Enoch did. That is what we need today too. We need people
who will walk with God year in and year out. Not flashes-in-the-pan.
Not shooting stars who attract for an instant by their sudden flashing
brilliance but soon burn out. We need steady, faithful people who
know God and are coming to know him better day by day.

Enoch Pleased God

I turn finally to the third of the three texts that tell us about Enoch:

Hebrews 11:5, which says that "Enoch . . . pleased God." This is the obvious culmination of the account of Enoch's life, for having walked with God and having thereby come to recognize sin as sin and to have turned his back on it, Enoch inevitably pleased God in what he did. What could be a better testimony for any human life? What could be a better achievement than to have it said that you or I pleased God?

If we please God, however, we will not be in a position to please most other men and women, because the new humanity is abhorred by the old humanity and vice versa. By the time Enoch died, by the sheer mathematics of birth and reproduction, given their long recorded lifetimes, there were probably several million of Adam's descendants on earth. These were Enoch's relatives, mostly cousins. It was these whom Enoch called "ungodly." Do you think that would have made Enoch popular? Hardly! We can be certain that he was not popular with his many ungodly cousins. But although Enoch may not have pleased his cousins, he had this testimony—that he pleased God. And that is what counted!

May it also be true of us. If possible, we want to please people too, like Jesus of whom it was said that in his youth he "grew in wisdom and stature, and in favor with God and men" (Lk 2:52). But it is not always possible. Sometimes a determined choice is necessary. And when that is the case, may it never be said of us that we chose to please other people rather than God, but that we pleased God regardless of the consequences. When we stand before our maker in heaven may we hear him say to us, as he did to the faithful servants in the Lord's parable, "Well done, good and faithful servant! You have been faithful with a few things; I will put you in charge of many things. Come and share your master's happiness!" (Mt 25:21, 23).

3

Abraham: "He Looked for a City"

*I*T IS ALMOST IMPOSSIBLE TO THINK about the two humanities, as I have done in the last chapter, studying Genesis 3—5, without moving on to Abraham, who is the greatest example of the new humanity in the first half of Genesis. He may be the greatest single example of the new humanity in all of the Bible.

What most characterizes those who are members of God's city is that they live by faith in God with their eyes on what is invisible rather than what can be seen, and this is the way Abraham is presented to us—in Genesis and elsewhere. The treatment of Abraham in Hebrews 11 is a good example. There he is brought forward a hero of faith, one who "looked for a city with foundations," that is, God's city, rather than an earthly city with earthly foundations that will pass away. Hebrews 11:8-10 says,

> By faith Abraham, when called to go to a place he would later receive as his inheritance, obeyed and went, even though he did not know where he was going. By faith he made his home in the promised land like a stranger in a foreign country; he lived in tents, as did Isaac and Jacob, who were heirs with him of the same promise. For he was looking forward to the city with foundations, whose architect and builder is God.

The Obedience of Faith

What that means practically is spelled out for us in a series of faith steps, marked by a fourfold repetition of the words "by faith" in Hebrews 11:8, 9, 11 and 17. We need to look at each of these in turn. The first of these steps was Abraham's calling by God and his response to that call while he was in Ur of the Chaldeans. This is recounted in Genesis 12:1-9 and is referred to in Hebrews 11: "By faith Abraham, when he was called to go to a place he would later receive as his inheritance, obeyed and went, even though he did not know where he was going" (v. 8).

There are two important things about this initial step in Abraham's pilgrimage. First, it was initiated by God entirely. Abraham did not seek God of himself any more than we do. In fact, Abraham was a worshiper of false gods and at the start had no appreciation of the true God at all (cf. Josh 24:2). He was in the category of those who have repressed the truth lest the knowledge of the true God spring up to force a change of allegiance in their lives and a reordering of their lifestyles.

Nothing could be clearer than this from the verses in Genesis 12 that describe God's call (vv. 1-3, 7). They contain seven great "I will's."

1. "I will show you [a land]."
2. "I will make you into a great nation."
3. "I will bless you."
4. "I will make your name great."
5. "I will bless those who bless you."
6. "I will curse [those who curse you]."

And later, after Abraham had reached Canaan,

7. "I will give [you] this land."

In no case does Abraham do anything to merit the appearance of God to him. Nor does he contribute anything to the promises God utters. It is a matter of election pure and simple, as in our own salvation.

"But surely Abraham did something?" someone queries. That is true, of course, and it is the second important thing about Abraham's

initial step of faith: Abraham obeyed God (Heb 11:8). But notice, this
came after God's commands and was provoked by it. God told Abraham, "Leave your country, your people and your father's household
and go to the land I will show you" (Gen 12:1). So Abraham did. The
text says, "So Abram left, as the LORD had told him" (v. 4).

We would think about the Christian life more accurately than we
do if we would learn to think of our own responses to God in this
way. And our presentation of the gospel would be more accurate too.
The way we usually present the gospel suggests that we think of
becoming a Christian as a work of ours—"deciding for Jesus" or
"letting Jesus into our hearts." But that makes it all human-centered.
It would be better if we thought of faith simply as obedience to what
God tells us to do.

To Be a Pilgrim

The second stage of Abraham's walk of faith concerns his early years
in the Promised Land. In one sense, Abraham had arrived. He was
now where God had sent him. But at the same time, Abraham knew
that he was only a pilgrim in this earthly land, since his true goal
and inheritance from God were in heaven. Hebrews makes this
plain by saying, "By faith he made his home in the promised land
like a stranger in a foreign country; he lived in tents, as did Isaac
and Jacob, who were heirs with him of the same promise" (11:9). He
did this in spite of many difficulties (Gen 12:10—14:16).

We have a hymn in English that uses the pilgrim image, but in a
way that suggests a wrong idea. It goes:

A pilgrim was I, and a wand'ring,

In the cold night of sin I did roam,

When Jesus the kind shepherd found me,

And now I am on my way home.

That is a pretty rhyme, of course, and it is true for the most part. But
its use of the word *pilgrim* suggests that this is what we were before
Jesus found us and that now we are no longer pilgrims. Actually a
pilgrim is what we have become. To be a pilgrim, two things must
have happened to us.

We Must Have Left Home

Abraham did that. God told him to leave his "country . . . [his] people and . . . [his] father's household" (Gen 12:1). Similarly, we are called to leave our past to follow Jesus. This is why Jesus told us to "deny" ourselves, "take up [our] cross daily and follow [him]" (Lk 9:23). It is why he said, "If anyone comes to me and does not hate his father and mother, his wife and children, his brothers and sisters—yes, even his own life—he cannot be my disciple" (Lk 14:26). Jesus was not teaching us literally to hate members of our family, of course. He was teaching that lesser loyalties must be subordinated to our loyalty to him. We must turn from anything that would keep us from true discipleship.

We Must Follow Jesus

A person who has merely left home is not a pilgrim. He is a drifter. To be a pilgrim, a person must have his or her eyes on a goal toward which he or she is moving.

This does not mean that a Christian cannot have warm human friendships. In fact, Christian friendships will be greater and deeper than those of non-Christians, if only because people will have become more valuable than things to the Christian. And speaking of things, living the pilgrim life does not mean that Christians cannot also have a reasonable share of earthly riches. Abraham, though a pilgrim, became a rich man. He had flocks and herds and servants. Yet he was a pilgrim still. Why? Donald Grey Barnhouse answers:

[Because he left] his native land and [began] to walk with God, everything he owned was now held in the reality of its true and eternal value. Nothing was held for any intrinsic worth. Henceforth all that was touched or possessed was looked upon as a gift from God—of value if it enhanced the glory of God and brought the Lord nearer to the heart, and of no value at all if it caused the light of God to grow dim and the memory of the glory to fade.[1]

You may complain that you have too many things to worry about to be a disciple of Jesus—your studies, a job, a mortgage or other impediments—or that you are too old to take a rigorous following of

Jesus Christ seriously. But think of Abraham. He had many possessions even when he started out from Haran (Gen 12:5). Moreover,
he was already seventy-five years old (v. 4). If you are a follower of
Jesus Christ, doesn't God want you to be a true pilgrim, regardless
of your circumstances?

God of the Impossible

The next stage of Abraham's life is a great one. Hebrews 11:11-12
refers to it, as do other passages, such as Romans 4:18-22. The verses
in Hebrews say, "By faith Abraham, even though he was past age—
and Sarah herself was barren—was enabled to become a father
because he considered him faithful who had made the promise. And
so from this one man, and he as good as dead, came descendants
as numerous as the stars in the sky and as countless as the sand on
the seashore."

The promise of numerous descendants that Hebrews refers to is
in Genesis 15:5. It was a solemn promise. Yet although Abraham was
seventy-five years old when he started out for Canaan, eleven more
years passed in which he and his wife Sarah remained childless. It
became a great problem for them—an embarrassment, of course,
but more than that. It was a spiritual problem since the promise of
a deliverer from sin was wrapped up in the promise of this son.
Abraham and Sarah's hope was set on this promise, as it should have
been. Yet for all these long years no son was born to them.

In its original form Abraham's name was Abram, which meant
"father of a people." That was appropriate in view of God's promise
that he and Sarah would have many children. But they had no
children for years. Whose fault was it? Was it Abraham's fault? Was
he impotent, unable to engender children? Or was the problem
Sarah's? Was she unable to bear a child?

Sarah must have been a proud woman who wanted to settle once
and for all whether the problem lay in her inability to bear children
or in her husband's infertility. So Sarah gave her handmaid Hagar
to Abraham to see if he could father a child by her, and although
Abraham should have refused, trusting God to provide the promised

heir in his own time, he listened to Sarah and so had Ishmael by Hagar. How proud Abraham was of Ishmael, since he was fathered in his old age. Thus when God came to renew the promise of the heir again later, Abraham pleaded with God to select Ishmael, saying, "If only Ishmael might live under your blessing!" (Gen 17:18).

Still Ishmael was only one child for a man whose name meant "father of many." The jokes at the patriarch's expense must have been as painful to him as they were many.

God appeared to Abraham again when he was ninety-nine years old to say that the promise had not been forgotten and that the couple would have a child by the same time the next year. When Ishmael had been conceived, the act of intercourse was by Abraham's own physical strength. That is one reason why he was so proud of Ishmael. But Abraham was past the age of engendering a child now, and Sarah was past the age of childbearing. If there was to be a child at this stage, a miracle was required. Yet this is precisely what Abraham was enabled to trust God for. It is why Hebrews speaks of Abraham being "as good as dead" (Heb 11:12) and why Paul writes in Romans,

> Against all hope, Abraham in hope believed and so became the father of many nations, just as it had been said to him, "So shall your offspring be." Without weakening in his faith, he faced the fact that his body was as good as dead—since he was about a hundred years old—and that Sarah's womb was also dead. Yet he did not waver through unbelief regarding the promise of God, but was strengthened in his faith and gave glory to God, being fully persuaded that God had power to do what he had promised. (Rom 4:18-21)

When God appeared to Abraham to announce the birth of this son he also announced a change in Abram's name, from Abram to Abraham. A change in name was important then as now, perhaps even more important. There must have been a moment when Abram would have announced this change to the hundreds of people who were part of his encampment at Haran. What interest there would have been when Abram intimated that he was going to change his name!

"Have you heard? Abram is going to change his name!"

"I'm not surprised."

"I wonder what he's going to change it to."

"He's been Abram, 'father of a people,' for many years. That must have been difficult to live with. Perhaps he's going to change it to Abechad, 'father of one.' That's all he is, after all."

Then Abraham made his announcement: "God appeared to me last night and told me that I am to change my name from Abram to Abraham." It is hard to capture the full effect of this change by a bare translation of the two names. Abram means "father of a people" literally. Abraham means "father of a nation (or nations)." But the effect was to heighten the contrast greatly, changing it from what we might call "father of many" to "father of a vast, vast multitude."

I suppose the laughter broke out behind the scenes at that point and was only barely suppressed by those who were closest to Abraham. For what could be more ridiculous than such a change of name? Foolish! Laughable! Preposterous! Yet it was not foolish to Abraham, because he was looking at things from the perspective of God's promise and was willing to act publicly on his convictions regarding God's power, truth and faithfulness. The next year Isaac, the son of the promise, was born to him, when Abraham was one hundred years old and Sarah was ninety.

Abraham had been living by his faith in God all along. But his faith rises to a great height at this point, and several qualities of this faith are worth thinking about carefully.

Abraham's Faith Was in God's Promise

That is clear from Paul's handling of the incident in Romans 4:18, where he quotes one expression of God's promise to Abraham recorded in Genesis 15:5. It is also a theme throughout the latter half of Romans 4, in which the word *promise* appears four times (in vv. 13, 14, 16, 20) and the verb *promised* once (in v. 21). God made a multifaceted promise to Abraham, involving personal blessing, a land to be given to him and his posterity, blessing on his descendants and a Redeemer to come. Therefore, the first and most important thing about Abraham's faith is that it was faith in this promise.

When we first look at this, the fact that Abraham believed God may seem obvious. Because it seems obvious it may also seem unimportant. But it is neither obvious nor unimportant.

It is not *obvious* because most of our natural thinking about faith moves in different categories entirely. What do we think of chiefly when we think of faith? We think in subjective categories. We identify faith with our feelings about something, which really means that we are human-centered in this area rather than being God-centered.

Occasionally, when I want to see what others have said about a certain subject, I look in various books of quotations in my library, and when I did that in reference to "faith," I found that the quotations made this point dramatically. Here are some that appear in *Roget's International Thesaurus*. The Roman poet Ovid (43 B.C.—A.D. 18) said, "We are slow to believe what hurts when believed." The epic poet Virgil (70-19 B.C.) wrote, "They can because they think they can." The Roman playwright Terence (185-159 B.C.) said, "As many opinions as men." The French writer Montaigne (1533-1592) declared, "Nothing is so firmly believed as that we least know." George Santayana (1863-1952), the Spanish-born American philosopher, spoke of "the brute necessity of believing something so long as life lasts." And then there were popular sayings like: "Believe that you have it, and you have it" and "I believe because it is impossible."[2]

These sayings all have at their root the belief that faith is grounded in man and is a subjective quality. This is the way the world thinks. But in the Bible faith is grounded in God and is something that springs from his encounter with the individual.

Again, the fact that biblical faith is faith in God's promise is not *unimportant,* because it is along these identical lines that we must believe God today if we, like Abraham, are to be saved. We are not saved because we have a strong subjective faith. That is to focus the matter on us, and besides, our faith is not strong. It is weak and vacillating. We are saved because of the promises of God made

known to us in the pages of the Bible. In other words, Christian faith
is a Bible-based faith. Or, to put it in still other words, we are saved
not because of our faith but because of God's word. Faith is merely
our receiving God's promises and believing them on the basis of
God's character.

Abraham's Faith Was Based on the Word of God Only

That is, it was based on what D. Martyn Lloyd-Jones has called "the
bare Word of God and on nothing else whatsoever."[3] In Genesis 15
God promised Abraham numerous offspring (as numerous as the
stars in heaven) at a time when he was old and had no children. To
be sure, the situation was not as hopeless as it was later to become.
Abraham was then about eighty-five years old, but he was still able
to engender a child, as he proved by fathering a child by Sarah's
handmaid Hagar. Fourteen years later, at the time of the conception
of Isaac, Abraham was not able even to father a child. Still, at the
time of his life described in Genesis 15, Abraham had lived most of
a century without having any children. It seemed that he and Sarah
would die childless. Yet here was God promising not only that they
would have an heir but that they would eventually have children
beyond any human possibility of counting.

Where could Abraham find external support to assist him in
believing this "wild" promise? There was no external support. From
the point of view of human experience the situation was desperate.
He had no prior examples of fecundity in old age that he could rest
on. So if Abraham believed God, as he did, it was only because it was
God who had made the promise.

It is the same when we trust God in the matter of salvation today.
God says that he has given his Son in death for us so that "whoever
believes in him shall not perish but have eternal life" (Jn 3:16). What
else in life can sustain you in believing a promise like that except
the bare Word of God? Apart from God's Word, we do not know
anything about eternal life, let alone how to obtain it. The invisible
world is hidden from us. No human being can tell us anything. If
we find salvation, it is by believing God's Word pure and simple.

Is that too hard to do? In some ways it is. But why should we not believe God? Human beings can deceive us and often do. God's Word is his bond, and he never breaks it. Therefore, although we do not have *external* support for believing God, we do not need it. In fact, it would be an insult to the character of God to maintain that we believe God only because of the word or experience of some human being.

Lloyd-Jones writes, "There is always this naked element in faith. It does not ask for proofs, it does not seek them; in a sense it does not need them. Faith is content with the bare Word of God, because he is God."[4]

Abraham's Faith Was in God Despite Contrary Appearances

As Paul points out in the closing verses of Romans 4, it was not a case of Abraham's merely believing God in the absence of all external supports; he believed God when the external evidences were actually and sharply to the contrary. This is the meaning of the sentence "against all hope, Abraham in hope believed" (v. 18). It means that Abraham was willing to believe God despite the circumstances. Here Paul's thought is moving beyond the situation described in Genesis 15 to the entirely impossible conditions of Genesis 17. By this time Abraham was ninety-nine years old and there was no longer any hope that the aged couple could have their own child. That is why the text says, "Without weakening in his faith, he [Abraham] faced the fact that his body was as good as dead—since he was about a hundred years old—and . . . Sarah's womb was also dead" (v. 19). When the chips were down, Abraham believed God rather than his own inadequate observations or understanding.

I do not often cite the testimony of the Swiss theologian Karl Barth in my studies. But Barth had an enviable sense of the greatness of God and, by contrast, the utter weakness and hopelessness of all things human, and at this point in his highly esteemed Romans commentary he quotes with evident approval some strong words about faith by Martin Luther. Luther was aware that faith must rest on God in spite of circumstances.

What could be more irrational and laughable, ridiculous and impossible, than God's words to Abraham? . . . Moreover, all the articles of our Christian belief are, when considered rationally, just as impossible and mendacious and preposterous. Faith, however, is completely abreast of the situation. It grips reason by the throat and strangles the beast. It effects what the whole world and all that is in it is impotent to do. But how can faith do this? By holding on to God's word and by accounting it right and true, however stupid and impossible it may appear. By this means did Abraham imprison his reason. . . . And in the same fashion do all other believers who have entered the dark recesses of faith throttle reason, saying: "Listen, Reason, thou blind and stupid fool that understandest not of the things of God. Cease thy tricks and chattering; hold thy tongue and be still! Venture no more to criticize the Word of God. Sit thee down; listen to his words; and believe in him." So do the faithful . . . achieve what the whole world is incompetent to achieve. And thereby they do our Lord God supreme and notable service.[5]

No one should understand this as meaning that faith is an irrational thing, though Barth sometimes wrote as if it were. Nothing is more rational than to believe God even in the face of evidence to the contrary. When God says something, it is irrational to trust our own opinions. Nevertheless the point is that faith stands always with God and his Word, even when doing so appears foolish from a human perspective. And it often does, simply because the world's way of thinking is so contrary to everything spiritual.

Abraham's Faith Was Fully Confident

The fourth characteristic of Abraham's faith is assurance. Paul says this in a number of ways in Romans: "without weakening in his faith" (4:19); "he did not waver through unbelief" and "was strengthened in his faith" (v. 20). The chief statement is in verse 21: "being fully persuaded that God had power to do what he had promised." Some of the other versions of this verse are worth noting. The Revised Standard Version says that Abraham was "fully convinced."

The New English Bible speaks of a "firm conviction." Phillips says that Abraham was "absolutely convinced." The New American Standard Bible speaks of him being "fully assured." True faith should always have this assurance.

But how does faith achieve this in a world where flesh is weak and circumstances are usually more powerful than we are? There is only one answer. Faith has assurance because it is directed neither to ourselves nor to circumstances but to God. We are weak, and faith grounded in ourselves will always be weak and will weaken further, waver and slip away. Faith that is grounded in the character of God will go from strength to strength, since God is faithful. This was characteristic of the faith of all the heroes mentioned in Hebrews 11. By faith they were able to move mountains.

Abraham's Faith Was Active

Finally, we dare not omit and need to remind ourselves of one more characteristic of Abraham's faith. It is that faith acts. Faith believes God, but it also acts decisively. In fact, I define true biblical faith as "believing God and acting upon it." How do we know that Abraham believed God? We know because of what he did. He believed God enough to leave Ur for Canaan, to remain in the Promised Land even when the going got rough, to engender Isaac when he was ninety-nine years old and, above all, to announce his change of name to those who lived with him—even before Isaac's conception.

I admit that this is a very high example of faith. That is why the New Testament refers to Abraham's faith so often. But this is the kind of faith we should all have—if we are Christians. The God we serve is the God of Abraham, and God is developing faith like this in those who know him. God brings life out of death, love out of hate, peace out of turmoil, joy out of misery and praise out of cursing.

Faith in Search of Understanding

Hebrews 11 ends its overview of Abraham's faith with a fourth incident, Abraham's willingness to sacrifice Isaac on Mount Moriah. We need to end this study with that story too. The text says,

> By faith Abraham, when God tested him, offered Isaac as a sacrifice. He who had received the promises was about to sacrifice his one and only son, even though God had said to him, "It is through Isaac that your offspring will be reckoned." Abraham reasoned that God could raise the dead, and figuratively speaking, he did receive Isaac back from death. (vv. 17-19)

Abraham had come to love Isaac greatly over the years. So the call to sacrifice him was at least a test of Abraham's devotion to God. Had Isaac grown too dear to Abraham? Had he begun to take the place of God in his affections? The Chinese evangelist Watchman Nee thought so and wrote that "Isaac represents many gifts of God's grace. Before God gives them our hands are empty. Afterwards they are full." As a result, when God reaches out his hand to take ours in fellowship, we have no hand to give him and the things that have filled our hands must go. "Isaac can be done without," Nee wrote, "but God is eternal."[6]

Isaac may have begun to take the place of God in Abraham's thinking, though we cannot be sure of that since the Bible does not teach it. But one thing the Bible does teach is that the testing of Abraham was spiritual and that it involved Abraham's perception of who God is and whether or not he would continue to trust him as the only truthful God.

The problem was not merely that Abraham loved Isaac. What was even more important was that God had promised that the blessing of salvation was to come through Abraham's descendants. God told Abraham that Isaac was to have a family, and that from that family there would come one who would be the world's Savior. Now God said that Isaac was to be sacrificed, and for the first time in all of Abraham's experience with God he was confronted by a conflict between God's command and God's promise. Earlier, Abraham had been tested as to whether he would believe that God could do what seemed impossible, but that was not as hard a test as this one. This test involved a conflict within God's words themselves. God had *promised* a Savior through Isaac. But God had now also *commanded* Abraham to kill him.

How could this contradiction be explained?

There were only two ways. Abraham could have reasoned that God was erratic, wavering from one plan to another because he did not know his own mind. This had not been his experience of God. The long wait for the son had taught him better than that. Or Abraham could have concluded that, although he, being finite and sinful, was unable to work out a resolution of the difficulty, God could nevertheless be trusted to have a resolution and would certainly disclose it to Abraham in due time. This was the harder of the two solutions to accept, but Abraham's experience of God led in this direction.

Abraham did not understand the solution. But the power of the story comes from the fact that Abraham did come to understand it somewhat. In other words, it was a case of what Anselm of Canterbury described centuries later by the words "faith in search of understanding."

It must have gone something like this. Abraham must have reasoned: "God is no liar. He told me beyond any question that I should have a son, and I have had one, though in my old age. Isaac stands beside me now. He is a proof of God's faithfulness. But God has also said that Isaac will have children through whom the Messiah will come. Isaac is not married. He has no children. If I put him to death, the promises of God cannot be fulfilled. Here is a contradiction. But there are no contradictions in God. This is a foundational truth. What must I conclude then? Since I am commanded to sacrifice Isaac and since, at the same time, God cannot be unfaithful to himself, the only solution I can imagine is that God is going to do a miracle and bring Isaac back from the dead. There will have to be a resurrection."

But Abraham, there has never been a resurrection.

"That doesn't matter," Abraham replies. "A resurrection is compatible with the nature of God. God is the author of life. It would be a small matter for him to bring life back into a dead body. But the one thing God cannot do is lie. God must tell the truth. He must keep his promises. So I expect a resurrection."

This is not just speculation, since the Genesis story actually teaches that Abraham expected a resurrection, though subtly. When Abraham got to the base of the mountain with Isaac, he told his servants who were accompanying them, "Stay here with the donkey while I and the boy go over there. We will worship and then *we* [plural] will come back to you" (Gen 22:5). In other words, although Abraham intended to sacrifice his son in obedience to God, he also expected God to raise Isaac from the dead so that he and the boy could return home together.

This is truly great faith. It is faith in search of understanding.

Obedience from First to Last

There is one more thing. At the very end of the account, after Abraham has proceeded to the point of binding Isaac and raising his knife and God has intervened to stay his hand and provide a ram as a substitute, the angel speaks to praise Abraham. But what Abraham is praised for—notice this, it is of great importance—is not his perception in figuring out God's plan or even the magnitude of what we might call his "blind faith," but *obedience.* The story ends on this note. It tells us that at the very end the angel spoke to Abraham for God again, saying, "Your descendants will take possession of the cities of their enemies, and through your offspring all nations on earth will be blessed, *because you have obeyed me*" (Gen 22:17-18).

That is where it began too—with Abraham's obedience in leaving his own land and setting out for Canaan. Faith begins with obedience. Faith ends with obedience. It is a matter of obedience from the very first to the very last, until we appear before God and see him face to face. If you are in Abraham's line, if like him you are looking for the city with foundations, you must obey God in everything.[7]

How to Grow Your Faith

A number of years ago the Philadelphia Conference on Reformed Theology held a spring meeting on the theme "How to Grow Your Faith." It was on what theologians call the means of grace, and it dealt with such subjects as prayer, worship, Bible study, fellowship and the sacraments. In the course of the weekend it was said again and again that the most important, indeed, the foundational means of growing faith is Bible study.

Why is that? It is because of the very matter we are studying. True biblical faith is not something you and I are able to work up ourselves, as if we could merely decide to be men and women of faith in the same way we might decide to take up aerobics or pursue a degree in higher education. Faith is only as strong as its object, and it is created in us by God and built up by God through our coming to know him. The only way we can come to know God is by studying God's revelation of himself in Scripture—and then applying it to our own circumstances.

Here is the way Lloyd-Jones puts it toward the end of his commentary on Romans 3 and 4.

> If you want to have strong faith, read your Bible; go through it from beginning to end. Concentrate on the revelation that God has given of himself and of his character. Keep your eye especially also on prophecy, and then watch his promises being fulfilled. That is the way to develop strong faith—be grounded in all this. Then read the historical portions of the Bible, and the stories of the great heroes. That is why the author of the Epistle to the Hebrews gives that gallery of portraits of these great saints in the eleventh chapter. He says, Look at these men, who were men like yourselves. What was their secret? It was that they knew God, they gave glory to God and relied utterly upon him and his word. Turn that over in your mind, keep on speaking to yourself about it; mediate upon it. . . . Then, finally, you apply all that in practice to particular cases as they arise in your own life and experience. "He staggered not, but gave glory to God." That is the secret of faith. It is our ignorance of God that constitutes our main trouble.[8]

Ours is not an age of great faith, and the reason we are weak in faith is that we do not know the Bible's God. Or if we do, we do not put what we do know into practice.

4

The Two Cities:
Enoch & Nineveh

*I*N THE LAST CHAPTER OUR ATTENTION was focused on the two humanities, which means that it was focused on individuals as the basic unit of the two cities, the City of God and the city of man. But individuals do not exist in isolation. They form societies or civilizations. Therefore our next responsibility is to look at these two societies as they grew out of the actions of those who created them. They are pictured in the Bible as actual cities. So the task of this chapter is to begin to study them.

Cain's City: Enoch

Our starting point once again is Genesis 4. In the midst of the account of the ungodly race of Cain, his son Enoch and Enoch's subsequent descendants Irad, Mehujael, Methushael and Lamech, there is mention of Cain building a city and a description of its corresponding civilization. The text says, "Cain was then building a city, and he named it after his son Enoch." So far as we know, this was the first of the world's cities and it was called Enoch, the name of the very man we learned in chapter two not to imitate. We are to imitate the Enoch who was the seventh from Adam instead.

Four characteristics of Enoch's city are worth noting.

A Loss of Roots and a Restlessness

To understand this first characteristic we have to go back to God's words of judgment on Cain for the murder of his brother Abel: "You will be a restless wanderer on the earth" (Gen 4:12). This becomes somewhat of a theme for what follows, for Cain immediately picks it up, complaining, "I will be a restless wanderer on the earth, and whoever finds me will kill me" (v. 14). It is even present in the name that is given to the land to which Cain goes: Nod, which means "wandering" (v. 16). The point is that Cain remained a wanderer at heart even when he attempted to settle down. Having rejected God, who is the only true home for anyone, Cain had severed his roots and was condemned to be homeless.

Adam and Eve had suffered something similar, for when they sinned they were cut off from Eden. Sin always produces separations, from God and from other people. But the result was different in the case of our first parents. Adam and Eve remained close to God through the provision of the sacrifices. Cain had rejected both God and the sacrifices as a means of approaching God and was therefore rootless. His restlessness was an early illustration of what Saint Augustine had in mind when he wrote in his *Confessions,* "Thou hast formed us for thyself, and our hearts are restless until they find rest in thee."[1]

In Jacques Ellul's *The Meaning of the City* this well-known French author wrote about Cain,

> He is to be a wanderer and a vagabond. As such he can find no rest. He is therefore condemned to a perpetual searching for God's presence, the God with whom he wanted nothing to do and in whom he does not believe, and his very condition keeps him from ever finding him. Whatever he does, he cannot succeed, and that is the hopelessness of it all.[2]

This rootlessness is a basic ingredient of all secular cultures and especially of our own. If there was ever a day in which civilization was attempting to form itself without God, it is the day in which we live. But never has restlessness been more evident. Simone Weil, a brilliant French writer who lived in London during the occupation of France by Germany during World War II and who died there in 1943, wrote a book entitled *The Need for Roots,* in which she analyzed the uprootedness of her day. She described it in terms of what she saw in the cities, in the countryside and in relation to nationhood. She concluded that the only cure for uprootedness is a rediscovery of the human being as God's creature and of God himself as the source of those basic elements without which a proper civilization cannot function: order, liberty, obedience, responsibility, equality, the right to express one's opinion, security, private property, truth and others.[3] She was exactly right. Our only true roots are in God. If we will not have God, we are condemned to be vagabonds.

This is why our civilization engages in so much frantic activity—to disguise our lack of roots and consequently our loss of a sense of destiny. Years ago the noted English agnostic Thomas Huxley was in Dublin, Ireland, for a speaking engagement, and when it was over he left his hotel in a hurry to catch a train. He jumped into one of the city's famous horse-drawn taxis and, thinking the doorman at the hotel had told the driver where he was going, simply shouted to the driver to drive fast. The taxi set off at a breakneck pace, but after a few minutes Huxley realized that it was headed away from the station. "Do you know where you're going?" he shouted to the driver.

"No, your honor," the driver answered, "but I'm driving fast."

So is our civilization and with similar confusion. For many of our contemporaries the situation is as Franklin Delano Roosevelt described it in his first inaugural address: "We don't know where we are going, but we are on our way."

Closeness Without Community

The second characteristic of this first world civilization (and the many others that have followed it) was closeness without community. We see this in Genesis 4:17 in the first two acts of Cain following his judgment by God. First, Cain "lay with his wife" so that she became pregnant and gave birth to Enoch. Second, he "was . . . building a city." These go together psychologically as well as textually. For having been driven from the company of family and from the area of Eden, Cain tries to surround himself with other people through procreation and the consolidation of these people into the first metropolis.

Some might wonder where the people to populate Cain's city might have come from, but we can be sure there were many. One writer has estimated that if during the several hundred years that Adam lived only half of the children that would normally be born grew up (and they probably all grew up) and if only half of those who grew up got married (and they probably all got married) and if only half who got married had children (and they probably all had children), even at that half, half, half rate Adam would probably have lived to see more than a million of his descendants. Thus many more people were living at this time than the text specifically mentions, certainly enough to fill Enoch and many other cities.

As I read this chapter I sense that this must have been an unpleasant city to live in. If we are to take as an indication the only example of Cain's descendants who is pictured at length, Lamech, it must have been a culture of hard, arrogant and cruel self-seekers. In other words, rootless people are no less rootless for having gathered together in groups. Nor are they less hard for being together. The loneliest people I know are in the city. The saddest stories I know concern city people. This is one reason why the greatest task facing the Christian church today is winning the city person to Christ.

Some Christians are opposed to the city for reasons based on the very points I am making. They regard the city as godless. They think of urban cultures as being man's invention and therefore alien to God, who placed the first man and woman in a garden, not a city. That is true, but it is not the whole story. The city is godless. But the problem with the "godless city" is not the city but the "godless," and people living in the country without Christ are godless too. Again, the problem of "civilization without God" is not civilization itself but rather its godless characteristics. And so far as the garden goes, while it is true that the Bible begins with a garden, it is also true that it ends with a city, the new Jerusalem. Our task is not to abandon earthly kingdoms but to build God's kingdom in the midst of the godless ones and in so doing look forward and show the way "to the city with foundations, whose architect and builder is God" (Heb 11:10).

Cult of Physical Beauty

The third characteristic of this first civilization was its worship of beauty, reflected for us in the names of Lamech's wives. Lamech was the first bigamist in history, and if the names of his wives are a guide (and they should be since these names are always significant), Lamech chose them for their physical attractions rather than their moral stature or spiritual commitments. Adah, the name of the first, means "pleasure, ornament or beauty." Zillah, the second, means "shade," probably referring to a luxuriant covering of hair. Lamech's daughter's name, Naamah, means "loveliness." This points to a culture committed to physical pleasure, charm and beauty rather than to those inner qualities that Peter rightly describes as "the unfading beauty of a gentle and quiet spirit, which is of great worth in God's sight" (1 Pet 3:4).

Few things so aptly describe our own culture as a glorification and pursuit of beauty. Many protest against it, women particularly, who object to such blatant forms of marketing beauty as the Miss America Pageant or the sale of nearly every product by sexually explicit advertising. They resent having women reduced to such a gross commercial level. But the marketing goes on. Why? Not because it has not been seen to be destructive of better values, but because the better values that would drive out the lesser ones are missing. Women (and also men) perceive themselves to be exploited and rightly protest the exploitation. But they will continue to be exploited in the worst way and will even willingly submit to that exploitation until they discover that they are creatures made in the image of God, not of the latest rock star or movie idol. They need to learn that they are of value not because of their outward beauty, which they may or may not have, but because they are capable of communion with God and possess eternal souls.

And what about religion? Did this early civilization have religion? It may have, judging from the names of two of Cain's descendants,

Mehujael and Methushael, which contain the simple name for God, *el*. But this concession would have been only an early expression of what Paul later calls "a form of godliness" by those who deny its power (2 Tim 3:5). It would be the kind of religion Cain chose by his aesthetically human-pleasing but God-displeasing offering.

We have exactly this today in the beautiful words, music and liturgies of spiritually dead and even God-denying churches. It is not that religious words, music or liturgies are necessarily bad. David was a poet, and the psalms had liturgical uses in the temple worship of the Jews. But these things are displeasing to God if they are offered as a substitute for simple faith in the promise of God's forgiveness of sin through the shed blood of Jesus Christ.

This point is also true of the various professions, suggested here by the occupations of Lamech's children: Jabal, who raised livestock; Jubal, an inventor of music and musical instruments; and Tubal-Cain, who worked in bronze and iron. Remember that Abel was also a herdsman, as was Jabal. Abraham, Isaac and Jacob, as well as David, tended sheep. Later in Israel's history God's Spirit came on certain craftsmen to enable them to create the works of art used in the tabernacle and temple (Ex 31:1-11). David was a musician. Obviously it is legitimate to participate in the arts and enjoy the most beautiful things, if you can afford them, provided your enjoyment is in line with your obedience to God and results in thankfulness to God for such beauty. But God help the person or culture that puts beauty first and worships and serves the creature rather than the Creator. It was this reversal that characterized Cain's civilization.

Pride in Power and Blind Passion

The last striking characteristic of this early civilization was arrogance, culminating in a blatant defense of murder. The boast is expressed in poetry, the first recorded poetry of the human race. It is the song of Lamech, which I mentioned in the previous chapter.

> Adah and Zillah, listen to me;
>> wives of Lamech, hear my words.
> I have killed a man for wounding me,

a young man for injuring me.
If Cain is avenged seven times,
    then Lamech seventy-seven times. (vv. 23-24)

Here Lamech was boasting of his violence in killing a man who had merely wounded him, saying that he was better able to take care of himself by murdering other people than God was able to take care of Cain—because God is nowhere to be seen, while Lamech is present to be both seen and feared.

Our culture does not say this in such explicit language, but it says it nonetheless. When we banish God from public life, even from our courtrooms, so that it is no longer even legal to hang the Ten Commandments where they can be seen by witnesses or juries, what we are saying is that we do not need God to enact or maintain justice. We think we can do it by ourselves. We cannot, of course, and we are not doing it. In many areas of our national life justice has become a joke, crimes are committed without the least bit of remorse on the part of the perpetrator, and violence in the most extreme forms is increasing at geometric rates.

What is to happen to a society like ours? We should be helped by remembering Enoch's city and by recalling that Genesis 4:24 is the last recorded mention of Cain's ruthless civilization. In the silence between verse 24 and verse 25 (which begins to trace the generations of the godly line from Adam through Seth) we can hear the rising waters of the flood. Cain's generation was wicked, and its wickedness brought the just recompense of its reward.

Nimrod's City: Nineveh

The next place cities are mentioned in Genesis is in a short paragraph that appears in the middle of the table of the genealogy of nations in chapter 10. They are associated with Nimrod, who is said to have been "a mighty warrior" and "a mighty hunter."

The important part of this paragraph reads: "The first centers of his kingdom were Babylon, Erech, Akkad and Calneh, in Shinar. From that land he went to Assyria, where he built Nineveh, Rehoboth Ir, Calah and Resen, which is between Nineveh and Calah; that is the great city" (vv. 10-12). Most of these cities are barely mentioned again, if at all. But two stand out: Nineveh and Babylon, each of which has an important place in Bible history. We will look at Nineveh in this chapter and Babylon in the next. (We will study Babylon side by side with Jerusalem, God's city, for which it is an important contrast and foil.)

Genesis 10:10-12 contains the first use of the word *kingdom* in the Bible. Later we will read of the kingdom of God. But here the word is used of the first great rival kingdom of Nimrod. This must have been a matter of some importance to Moses, for a related parenthesis occurs in the first nine verses of chapter 11, in the story of the tower of Babel.

What is so significant about Nimrod? The fact that he founded cities and built a kingdom is important; it carries the account of the construction of the world's culture just a bit further. But more can be said of Nimrod.

Nimrod is the first person in history to have become a "mighty" man; these verses call attention to this by using the adjective three times in describing him: "Nimrod . . . grew to be a *mighty* warrior on the earth. He was a *mighty* hunter before the LORD; that is why it is said, 'Like Nimrod, a *mighty* hunter before the LORD' " (vv. 8-9). An adjective like this can be used to indicate what is either good or bad, of course. We recall that God himself is called mighty. But a little thought will show that "mighty" is used in a bad sense here. The empires of Nineveh and Babylon were an affront to both God and man, an affront to God in that they sought to do without him (Gen 11:1-9) and an affront to man in that they sought to rule over other people tyrannously.

Martin Luther was therefore precisely on target when he suggested that this is the way the word *hunter* should be interpreted. This is not talking about Nimrod's ability to hunt wild game, Luther said. Nimrod was not a hunter of animals. He was a hunter of men, a warrior. It was through his ability to kill and rule ruthlessly that the first kingdom of the Euphrates valley city-states was consolidated. Building on Luther, another commentator renders this paragraph:

Cush begat Nimrod; he began to be a mighty despot in the land. He was an arrogant tyrant, defiant before the face of the Lord; wherefore it is said, Even as Nimrod, the mighty despot, haughty before the face of the Lord. And the homeland of his empire was Babel, then Erech, and Accad, and Calneh, in the land of Shinar. From this base he invaded the kingdom of Asshur, and built Nineveh, and Rehoboth-Ir, and Calah, and Resin between Nineveh and Calah. These make up one great city.[4]

Great? Yes, a great city. But it was great not as Jerusalem was to become great (as God's city), but great in its defiance of God. It was the secular city. It was *of* man, *by* man and *for* man's glory.

The Growth of Nimrod's City

In secular sources Nineveh is first mentioned in the Code of Hammurabi (c. 2200 B.C.). Hammurabi calls himself the king who made the name of the goddess Ishtar famous in the temple of Ishtar in Nineveh (4.60-62). Still, for centuries after this little is heard about the city. We have the name of a Ninevite king from about 1900 B.C. and other scattered references. But not until the middle 800s (when Israel first came into contact with the expanding empire of Assyria) are there significant historical records.

Shalmaneser III, who reigned from 858 to 824 B.C., made Nineveh the base for his campaign to subjugate the northern Jewish kingdom. He relates that he met "Ahab the Israelite" with two thousand chariots and ten thousand soldiers. In the account of his fourth campaign (824 B.C.), he declares that "at that time I received tribute . . . of Jehu, son of Omri." This scene is represented on the famous Black Obelisk in the British Museum. On it Jehu is seen on his knees before the king of Assyria, and the inscription reads: "Tribute of Jehu, son of Omri. Silver, gold, a golden bowl, a golden beaker, golden goblets, pitchers of gold, lead, staves for the hand of the king, javelins, I received from him."[5] Significantly, this first great humbling of the Jews was effected by an Assyrian king setting out from Nineveh.

Tiglath-pileser III (745-727 B.C.) invaded Judah and received tribute from Azariah. In 733-732 B.C. he invaded Israel, deposed Pekah, placed Hoshea over the nation as an Assyrian vassal, received tribute and deported many of the people.

The final blow against Israel came in 722 B.C. when Tiglath-pileser's son Shalmaneser V returned and besieged Samaria. He died early in this campaign and was succeeded by Sargon II (721-705 B.C.), the founder of a new dynasty. Samaria fell to Sargon, and the history of the northern Jewish kingdom ended. The conqueror recorded: "At the beginning of my rule, in my first year of reign . . . I carried away 27,290 people of Samaria. I selected 50 chariots for my royal equipment. I settled there people of the lands I had conquered. I placed my official over them as governor. I imposed tribute tax upon them, as upon the Assyrians."[6]

In 701 B.C. occurred the well-known invasion of Judah by Sennacherib (705-681 B.C.), Sargon's son (2 Kings 18—19; Is 36—37). Sennacherib's account is as follows:

As for Hezekiah, the Jew, who did not submit to my yoke, 46 of his strong, walled cities, as well as the small cities in their neighborhood, which were without number—by leveling with battering rams and by bringing up siege engines, by attacking and storming on foot, by mines, tunnels and breaches—I besieged and took 200,150 people, great and small, male and female, horses, mules, asses, camels, cattle and sheep without number, I brought away from them and counted as spoil. Himself, like a caged bird, I shut up in Jerusalem, his royal city. . . . As for Hezekiah, the terrifying splendor of my majesty overcame him, and the Urbi (Arabs) and his mercenary troops which he had brought in to strengthen Jerusalem, his royal city, deserted him.[7]

The Bible tells this story differently. It acknowledges the force of Sennacherib's invasion. But it tells how Sennacherib's field commander stood before the walls of Jerusalem and boasted that Assyria's gods were stronger than the God of Judah. He demanded the surrender of the city. After this the emperor sent Hezekiah a letter, saying, "Do not let the god you depend on deceive you when he says, 'Jerusalem will not be handed over to the king of Assyria.'

Surely you have heard what the kings of Assyria have done to all the countries, destroying them completely. And will you be delivered? Did the gods of the nations that were destroyed by my forefathers deliver them?" (2 Kings 19:10-12). Hezekiah spread this letter before the Lord in the temple and prayed for deliverance. Isaiah sent a message saying that God would deliver the people, and that night "the angel of the Lord went out and put to death a hundred and eighty-five thousand men in the Assyrian camp" (v. 35). This so weakened Sennacherib's army that he returned to Nineveh without achieving Jerusalem's capitulation.

The Assyrian monarch may have been checked by God in 701 B.C., but these were still great days for Nineveh. Sennacherib more than doubled the city's size, making it the world's largest city for that time. The inner city was surrounded by a wall eight miles in circumference. It was one hundred feet high and so wide that three chariots could race around it abreast. It had twelve hundred towers and fourteen gates. Beyond this was a much longer, outer wall. There was an inner city, an outer city, and what we would call extensive suburbs beyond that. In Jonah this wide expanse is termed a "three days" journey (Jonah 3:3).

Sennacherib's palace was called "The Palace With No Rival." It was of cedar, cypress and alabaster. Lions of bronze and bulls of white marble guarded it. Its great hall measured forty by one hundred and fifty feet. Sennacherib's armory, where he kept his chariots, armor, horses, weapons and other equipment, covered forty-six acres and took six years to build.

What a magnificent city this was! Yes, but what a wicked city! And with what cruelty and violence was it constructed! And here is the really important thing: the violence of Nineveh was not overlooked by God. An entire book of the Bible, Nahum, one of the minor prophets, is written to expose the city's evils, condemn it and promise judgment.

In chapter 3 of his prophecy Nahum cites Nineveh's crimes—violence, deception, plunder and witchcraft—and tells of the judgment that was to come. The first of the crimes, violence, gets the most attention since it was the characteristic vice of Nineveh: "Woe to the city of blood . . . never without victims! The crack of whips, the clatter of wheels, galloping horses and jolting chariots! Charging cavalry, flashing swords and glittering spears! Many casualties, piles of dead, bodies without number, people stumbling over the corpses" (vv. 1-3).

When Nahum calls Nineveh a "city of blood," his words are a massive understatement. In all the ancient world no single city had matched the Assyrian capital for its calculated cruelty. Indeed, none had boasted about it as the rulers of Assyria had done. On a monument commemorating the first eighteen years of his reign, Ashurnasirpal II (885-860 B.C.) declared:

Great number of them in the land of Kirhi I slew . . . 260 of their fighting men I cut down with the sword. I cut off their heads, and I formed them into pillars. . . . Bubo, son of Buba, I flayed in the city of Arbela, and I spread his skin upon the city wall.

I flayed all the chief men [in the city of Suru] who had revolted, and I covered the pillar with their skins; some I walled up within the pillar, some I impaled upon the pillar on stakes, and others I bound to stakes round about the pillar; many within the border of my own land I flayed, and I spread their skins upon the walls; and I cut off the limbs of the officers, of the royal officers who had rebelled. Ahiababa I took to Nineveh, I flayed him, I spread his skin upon the wall of Nineveh.

600 of their [the people of the city of Hulai] warriors I put to the sword; 3,000 captives I burned with fire; I did not leave a single one among them alive to serve as a hostage. . . . Their corpses I formed into pillars; their young men and maidens I burned in the fire.

3,000 of their [the people of the city of Tela] warriors I put to the sword. . . . Many captives from among them I burned with fire. From some I cut off their hands and their fingers, and from others I cut off their noses, their ears, and their fingers, of many I put out the eyes. I made one pillar of the living, and another of heads, and I bound their heads to posts [tree trunks] round about the city.[8]

The utter fiendishness of impaling defeated soldiers on stakes, skinning commanders alive, cutting off limbs, noses and ears, putting out eyes, heaping up skulls in the city squares, and burning vast numbers alive was without parallel in the ancient world, though it has been matched in frightening measure by the atrocities of our more "civilized" times. We dare not be self-righteous.

In his exhaustive study of Nahum, Walter A. Maier writes,

To Nineveh came the distant chieftains who kissed the royal feet, rebel leaders paraded in fetters, distant and deceitful kings tied with dog chains and made to live in kennels. To Nineveh were sent gifts of far-off tribute, heads of vanquished enemies, crown princes as hostages, beautiful princesses as concubines. In Nineveh rulers who experienced rare mercy carried brick and mortar for building operations. There recalcitrant captives were flayed, obstinate opponents crushed to death by their own sons. The Nineveh against which the prophet thunders divine denunciation had become the concentrated center of evil, the capital of crushing tyranny, the epitome of cruelest torture. Before the beginning of the seventh century and Sennacherib's reign, other cities had been royal residences: Calah, Ashur, Dur Sharrukin; but Sennacherib made Nineveh the source of unmeasured woe for Judah, as for other, far greater nations.[9]

This great city had existed almost from the beginning of time. Under Sennacherib it rose to unparalleled strength and splendor. But it was to end. Within ninety years of Sennacherib's encampment before Jerusalem's walls, Nineveh, the largest city in the world, was overthrown—never to be inhabited again.

The Avenging God

Historians give varied reasons for Nineveh's fall—internal corruption, the rise of Babylon, external and otherwise unpredictable factors. But however these may have contributed, the true answer is given by Nahum in his prophecy. The avenging wrath of God destroyed it.

Many people do not like to think of God as a God of wrath. They prefer to think of him as a God of saccharine love and sentimental indulgence. What a weakening this is of the biblical concept of the only true God! It is true that God is a God of love and mercy—a holy love and an utterly undeserved and sovereign mercy. But it is also true that God is a God of wrath against sin. Peter describes him as being "patient . . . not wanting anyone to perish" (2 Pet 3:9), but even this welcome description is set in the context of God's sure, though postponed judgment: "The day of the Lord will come like a thief. The heavens will disappear with a roar; the elements will be destroyed by fire, and the earth and everything in it will be laid bare" (v. 10).

This is the point at which Nahum begins his prophecy, a prophecy directed almost entirely against the wickedness of Nineveh. Nahum means "comfort," but there is no comfort for Nineveh in what Nahum says. For Nineveh, God is to be a God of vengeance. The city is to fall.

Vengeance Is God's
Nahum develops the thought of God's vengeance in 1:1-6. First, he puts an emphasis on vengeance itself. The word is repeated three times in verse 2: "The LORD is a jealous and *avenging* God; the Lord takes *vengeance* and is filled with wrath. The LORD takes *vengeance* on his foes and maintains his wrath against his enemies." Vengeance is retaliatory punishment for wrong done. The Ninevites had committed great wrongs. Now they were to be repaid for those wrongs by the one who had solemnly declared, "It is mine to avenge; I will repay. In due time their foot will slip; their day of disaster is near and their doom rushes upon them" (Deut 32:35; cf. Rom 12:19).

Wickedness and Guilt
The second point is the Ninevites' guilt. When we think of God taking vengeance we instinctively react against it, as if vengeance is unjust and uncalled for. But our reaction only shows how insensitive we are to sin both in ourselves and in others. God's wrath is not capricious, but he will take vengeance, which is why we read that

although God is "slow to anger, . . . [he] will not leave the guilty unpunished" (1:3). Not in Nineveh! Not anywhere!

Judgment Is Certain

The third point of Nahum's opening verses is the certainty of God's judgment. This theme occurs throughout the prophecy, but it is developed in particularly powerful language here. Nahum looks at nature, noting that God dries up seas and makes the rivers run dry. There are times when even Bashan, Carmel and Lebanon (proverbial sites of lush vegetation) wither (v. 4). Mountains quake before God; hills melt away; the earth trembles (v. 5). If this is true of nature, what mere mortal can stand against God's fierce indignation? Who can endure when "his wrath is poured out like fire [and] the rocks are shattered before him" (v. 6)?

God and God's People

According to Nahum's prophecy, God had three reasons to destroy Nineveh. Two have already been suggested: first, God is a jealous God, who will have no other gods before him (cf. Ex 20:3-6), and second, he is an avenging God, who will always do right (cf. Gen 18:25). The prophet gives another reason in the second half of chapter 1 (vv. 7-15). It is God's goodness to his people. They have been abused by Nineveh. Now God is going to rise up and make an end to the oppressor.

This passage was especially meaningful to Martin Luther, who found it a source of comfort in his own difficulties during the Reformation period. He called verse 7 ("The LORD is good, a refuge in times of trouble") "an outstanding statement, overflowing with consolation." He wrote,

> We must relate and apply it not merely to that trial of Judah but to absolutely every day of our trials and adversities, so that we may learn to flee for refuge in any trial at all to this sweetness of the Lord as if to a holy anchorage. Many psalms are filled with statements of this sort. Thus Psalm 9:9 has "a stronghold in times of trouble." The Lord is a sweet stronghold at the very time when

we are greatly afflicted, when we hunger, when we suffer adversity, when our consciences trouble us, as he says elsewhere in the psalm (Ps. 50:15): "Call upon me in the day of trouble; I will deliver you." He commands us to flee to him for refuge, to call upon him. Yet such is the weakness of the human heart that even if it is ordered to seek out and escape to this sweetness, it fears and loses faith in temptation. In this way, clearly the Lord comforts in tribulation. That is, even when temptation presses us hard, yet he will not allow us to succumb. Paul says the same thing in every detail (1 Cor. 10:13): "God is faithful, and he will not let us be tempted . . . but with the temptation will also provide the way of escape."[10]

Not only is the Lord going to punish Nineveh, according to Nahum; he is going to destroy it completely. Nahum announces this as a comfort to Judah at least seven times in chapter 1.

1. "With an overwhelming flood he will make an end of Nineveh; he will pursue his foes into darkness" (v. 8). This was a literal flood, as the historical accounts indicate and I will note in a moment.

2. "Whatever they plot against the LORD he will bring to an end; trouble will not come a second time" (v. 9). Trouble will not come a second time because there will be no need for it. God will have finished his work with the first attack.

3. "They will be consumed like dry stubble" (v. 10). This too was fulfilled. Stubble is consumed by fire. Following the flood that broke through a section of the walls, the city was burnt.

4. "Although they have allies and are numerous, they will be cut off and pass away" (v. 12). One hundred and eighty-five thousand had been destroyed outside the walls of Jerusalem. Thousands more would perish in the collapse of Assyria's capital.

5. "You will have no descendants to bear your name" (v. 14). The Ninevites were lost to history. And not only that: even their city was lost until it was rediscovered by archaeologists about the middle of the nineteenth century.

6. "I will prepare your grave, for you are vile" (v. 14). In this verse *vile* actually means "light." It is the word used of Babylon in Daniel

5:27: *"Tekel*—You have been weighed on the scales and found wanting."

7. "No more will the wicked invade you; they will be completely destroyed" (v. 15). The invasion of Judah by Sennacherib was the last by Assyria, for Assyria was utterly destroyed. The next threat to Judah would come from Babylon.

All of this is precisely what happened, as I have indicated. The Assyrian empire had experienced rebellions for some time, as would be expected of so oppressive a state. Many of these were repulsed by the armies of Nineveh supported by her allies. But in the year 612 B.C. the city's doom arrived. Combined armies of Babylonians and Scythians marched up the left bank of the Tigris River and surrounded the city. This happened in early spring at the time of the annual rainfalls. Since the rains were especially hard that year, the Tigris flooded and washed away a portion of the city's walls, leaving a breach for the hostile armies to enter.

The Greek historian Diodorus Siculus (c. 20 B.C.) says that the river not only broke down the walls of the city but also inundated part of it. At this point, the king, Sardannapalus, remembering an oracle to the effect that Nineveh would only fall when the river itself declared war against it, believed that the oracle was fulfilled and abandoned any hope of saving himself. He built a gigantic funeral pyre in the royal precincts, heaped up large quantities of gold and costly clothes, shut his concubines and eunuchs in a chamber he had made in the midst of the pyre, and then burned himself, his family, his concubines and eunuchs, and the palace. Whatever had not been burned in the conflagration was destroyed by the entering armies. There was a terrible slaughter. Diodorus said, "So great was the multitude of the slain that the flowing stream, mingled with their blood, changed its color for a considerable distance."[11]

There was unparalleled looting. For centuries the wealth of the ancient world had been pouring into Nineveh as a result of the Assyrian conquests. Now it poured out. Diodorus says, using a phrase that he did not employ in any other description of a city's fall, "They plundered the spoil of the city, *a quantity beyond counting."*[12]

What would the plunder of a city like this be like? Nahum tells us: "Nineveh is like a pool, and its water is draining away. 'Stop! Stop!' they cry, but no one turns back. Plunder the silver! Plunder the gold! The supply is endless, the wealth from all its treasures! She is pillaged, plundered, stripped! Hearts melt, knees give way, bodies tremble, every face grows pale" (2:8-10). It is an impressive confirmation of this prophecy that nothing of all this gold and silver has been discovered in the ruins of Nineveh by archaeologists. Nineveh was indeed stripped bare.

The points of agreement between Nahum's prophecy and the details of Nineveh's fall are so precise that some commentators have supposed Nahum's prophecy to be a *vaticinium ex eventu* (a "prediction" made after the event). But Nahum did not write after Nineveh's fall. He wrote at the height of her power, shortly after the invasion of Judah by Sennacherib. That a Judean author, writing at a time when the invincible armies of Assyria were running unchecked across Asia, plundering all in their path, should have predicted the sudden destruction of the Assyrian capital and do so in such minute detail is surely another evidence of the divine origin and nature of the Word of God.

An Astonishing Account

I close this chapter with two thoughts. First, Nahum's prophecy against Nineveh was intended to be a source of comfort to God's people and can be a similar source of comfort today. We too are surrounded by evil. But we can know that evil does not go unjudged. Though delayed, God's vindications of his own and his condemnation of the wicked are both certain. Luther saw this in his day and wrote,

> These consolations ought also to fill us all with courage in any need, so that we may have confidence and trust absolutely that the Lord will not allow foes of God's Word to prevail against us. . . . He will be near us in every need, physical or spiritual. Indeed, our God is still the same one who redeemed Judah, who said that a hair on our head would not fall without his will.[13]

My second thought is this. It is an encouragement for those who may yet be members of the secular city rather than of the city of God. Earlier in the collection of minor prophets, another book is also concerned with Nineveh. It too preaches a message of judgment on this city for its violence. It is the book of Jonah. Jonah was sent to Nineveh with the message "Forty more days and Nineveh will be overturned" (Jonah 3:4). But Nineveh was not destroyed, not on that occasion. And the reason was that the inhabitants of the city repented as a result of Jonah's preaching. The text says,

When the news reached the king of Nineveh, he rose from his throne, took off his royal robes, covered himself with sackcloth and sat down in the dust. Then he issued a proclamation in Nineveh:

"By the decree of the king and his nobles:

Do not let any man or beast, herd or flock, taste anything; do not let them eat or drink. But let man and beast be covered with sackcloth. Let everyone call urgently on God. Let them give up their evil ways and their violence. Who knows? God may yet relent and with compassion turn from his fierce anger so that we will not perish."

The text continues: "When God saw what they did and how they turned from their evil ways, he had compassion and did not bring upon them the destruction he had threatened" (Jonah 3:6-10).

If you are not yet a believer in the Lord Jesus Christ, you are in a position similar to Nineveh on the earlier occasion. Judgment hangs over you because God is a God of justice, and justice will be done. But this is still the day of God's grace. Judgment, though real and imminent, has not yet come. There is still time to turn from your sin and embrace him who said, "Come to me, all you who are weary and burdened, and I will give you rest" (Mt 11:28). But let it be a firm and permanent decision. And remember that although Nineveh appeared to turn from her sin for a time, she was not really changed and eventually fell back into that pattern of cruelty and repine for which God eventually wiped her from the surface of the earth.

There is a wide and treacherous gulf between the city of man and the City of God. It is the difference between death and life, God's judgment and everlasting grace. But it is a gulf that can be crossed quickly, in a moment, by true faith in Jesus Christ.

5

The Two Cities:
Babylon & Jerusalem

*T*HE DESTRUCTION OF THE NORTHERN kingdom of Israel by Assyria, which had its capital at Nineveh, was a foretaste of the destruction of the earthly city of Jerusalem by the armies of Babylon under Nebuchadnezzar. But there is more in this second contrast than in the first. For in both the Old and New Testaments both Babylon and Jerusalem take on more than life-size dimensions and become symbols of two entirely different relationships to God and ways of life.

Babylon stands for earthly relationships and an earthly way of life. Jerusalem stands for spiritual realities, and God is its life. This was true of the earthly Jerusalem only at its best and in part. But it becomes so in full measure when the new Jerusalem rises on the ruins of the old. Or rather descends from heaven, for that is the way John describes it in Revelation:

> I saw the Holy City, the new Jerusalem, coming down out of heaven from God, prepared as a bride beautifully dressed for her husband. And I heard a loud voice from the throne saying, "Now the dwelling of God is with men, and he will live with them. They will be his people, and God himself will be with them and be their God. He will wipe every tear from their eyes. There will be no more death or mourning or crying or pain, for the old order of things has passed away." (21:2-4)

This vision of the City of God in Revelation 21 is a utopia. But it is not like the utopias envisioned by human beings. Most human utopias either present what the writer would like to see happen (examples would be Plato's *Republic* and Henry David Thoreau's *Walden*) or warn against what may happen if evil is unchecked (for instance, Aldous Huxley's *Brave New World* or George Orwell's *1984*). The biblical utopia has already happened in part, but it is to happen fully and perfectly when Jesus Christ returns.

Nimrod's Second Great City: Babylon

Chapters 10 and 11 of Genesis are composed of genealogies of the world's nations designed to link the account of Noah and the flood, which fills chapters 6 through 9, with the story of Abraham and his descendants, which fills the remainder of the book. But at two points there are parentheses dealing with the founding of Babylon, the capital of the first world empire, by the tyrant Nimrod. The first parenthesis is Genesis 10:8-12. The second is Genesis 11:1-9.

These two accounts go together. The first tells of Nimrod's exploits. In this passage we learn that Babylon was the initial city of Nimrod's city-building empire. The second account does not speak of Nimrod, but it tells about the attempt to build Babylon, focusing on "a tower that reaches to the heavens" (v. 4). Moreover, as we study both passages we see that the founding of Babylon and the building of the tower of Babel in chapter 11 are an elaboration of the salient features of the earlier narrative. The first is an emphasis on Nimrod—what he was like, what he did, what his goals were. The second is a treatment of the same theme from the perspective of the people who worked with Nimrod. In both cases the people were trying to build a civilization without God.

United We Stand

The account of the building of Babylon begins by saying that the world had one common language, as would be expected from humankind's common descent from Noah. Some of these people moved eastward to settle on the plain of Shinar, which was a fulfillment of God's command to Noah and his sons to "increase in number and fill the earth" (Gen 9:1), itself a restatement of the command originally given to Adam and Eve before the Fall (Gen 1:28). Yet as we read on in this story we find that the goal of this particular settlement was not to obey God's command but to defy it. This is because the explicit goal of building Babylon was to resist any further scattering of the world's peoples and instead to create a metropolis where the achievements of a united and integrated people could be centralized.

The Bible reports this desire as an invitation to "come" together to work on the great project. It is the first important "come" in the story. The people "said to each other, *'Come,* let's make bricks and bake them thoroughly.' . . . Then they said, *'Come,* let us build ourselves a city, with a tower that reaches to the heavens, so that we may make a name for ourselves and not be scattered over the face of the whole earth' " (Gen 11:3-4).

This invitation involved three things: a vision for the city, a desire for a name or reputation and a plan for a new religion. So far as a vision for the city goes, we have already looked at what was involved when we were studying Cain's city and Nimrod's Nineveh. The important point is that it was not God's city, as Jerusalem was meant to be. It was man's city, and it was constructed for human glory. So far as the desire for a name or reputation goes, the desire was for a reputation apart from God. It was for achievement without God, independence from God, and it was to be earned by human power alone. It was to be man's reputation and not his Maker's.

A New Religion

The strikingly new thing in this description is the desire of the builders to create a new religion, one, as might be expected, from which the true God would be excluded. This is what the famous "tower of Babel" is about. We know from archaeological ruins in this area of the world that among the notable characteristics of its ancient cities were ziggurats or step-pyramid temples, which in one sense or another must be lineal descendants of this "tower." A few of the earliest Egyptian pyramids have this form, which must have been borrowed from Babylon. But aside from these nothing quite like these "towers" is to be found anywhere else in the ancient near-Eastern world.

Most commentators have sensed that the original tower, like its later copies, must have been constructed for religious purposes, though they do not agree on exactly what form this religion would have taken. Martin Luther wrote that the words "reaches to the heavens" should not be applied to the height alone but should be seen as denoting "that this was to be a place of worship."[1] Robert S. Candlish said, "The building of the tower 'unto heaven' had undoubtedly a religious meaning."[2] Henry M. Morris writes that in his desire to build a great empire, Nimrod realized that the people needed a religious motivation strong enough to overcome their knowledge that God had commanded them to scatter abroad on the earth. The tower satisfied that need and was therefore "dedicated to heaven and its angelic host."[3]

From the broadest biblical perspective there can be little doubt that this tower must have had a religious meaning, for the Bible traces the source of all false religions to Babylon, and this is the only element in the description of early Babylon that can suggest it. Besides, Romans 1:23 says that when people reject knowledge of the true God they inevitably turn to false gods, making them like "mortal man and birds and animals and reptiles." The citizens of Babylon had rejected God. Therefore, we should expect the creation of a false religion as part of their dubious cultural achievements.

Historical evidence shows that this was the case. Morris notes that "the essential identity of the various gods and goddesses of Rome, Greece, India, Egypt and other nations with the original pantheon of the Babylonians is well established." In fact, "Nimrod himself was apparently later deified as the chief god (Merodach or Marduk) of Babylon."[4]

The description of the tower also serves as evidence. Most translations speak of a tower that should "reach" to heaven, but it is hard

to think that these ancient people could have been foolish enough
to suppose that they could do this literally. Or even if they did, it is
hard to think of them being foolish enough to build their tower on
the plain of Shinar, that is, almost at sea level, when they could
equally well have built it on top of a nearby mountain and thus have
begun with at least a few thousand feet head start. Actually, this is
probably not what was involved at all. The word *reach* does not occur
in the Hebrew text. Instead the text speaks of the top of the tower
only as "in," "on," "with" or "by" the heavens. This could mean that
the top was dedicated to the heavens as a place of worship. Or it
could mean that it had a representation of the heavens, a zodiac,
on it.

I think the latter is the real interpretation, because astrology is
based on the zodiac, and by all accounts astrology originated in
Babylon. It came from the Chaldeans, which is another name for the
citizens of Babylon. From there it passed to Egypt where it mingled
with the native animism and polytheism of the Nile. The pyramids
were constructed with mathematical relationships to the stars. Even
the Sphinx has astrological significance.

By the time the Jews left Egypt for Canaan, astrology had infected
the population there. Thus some of the strictest warnings in the
Bible against astrology date from this period (see Lev 19:31 and Deut
18). Still later, astrology entered the religious life of Rome.

The most interesting thing about these biblical denunciations
of astrology is that astrology is identified with demonism or Satanism in the sense that Satan and his hosts were actually worshiped
in the guise of the zodiac signs or planets. This is the reason for the
Bible's particularly stern denunciation of these practices. Are we to
think that Satan was entirely absent from this attempt to build a
civilization without God? Was he absent from the formation of the
first nonbiblical religion? Probably not. And if he was present,
then the religion of the tower of Babel was a satanic attempt to direct the worship of the human race away from God to himself and
those former angels who, having rebelled against God, were now
demons. From such beginnings there must have emerged the entire

complex of human religion, including pantheism, polytheism and demonism.

The Response of God
The time when the Lord Jesus Christ was to crush the head of Satan was still far off, but in the meantime God was going to crush this first attempt to worship Satan. He was not going to flood the earth, as he had in the time of Noah. He was going to do it in an entirely unlooked-for manner. Instead of destruction, God performed a miracle in the minds and vocal cords of the builders, confusing their language so that now, instead of speaking and working together, their words brought confusion and an inevitable scattering of these people over the surface of the earth. The text says, "So the LORD scattered them from there over all the earth, and they stopped building the city. That is why it was called Babel—because there the LORD confused the language of the whole world. From there the LORD scattered them over the face of the whole earth" (Gen 11:8-9).

That is a very good description of human civilization from that early time to this. It is culturally confused, one race or group of people struggling against or competing with another. And it is scattered, lest the human race be able to unite its forces in its fight against God.

Jerusalem
Scattered? Yes. But now God begins to gather together a new people for himself, starting with Abraham, whose story begins in the next chapter (Gen 12), and ending with the planting of this new elect people in the great and holy city of Jerusalem. God said to Abraham, "Leave your country, your people and your father's household and go to the land I will show you.

"I will make you into a great nation
     and I will bless you;
I will make your name great,
     and you will be a blessing.

I will bless those who bless you,
   and whoever curses you I will curse;
and all peoples on earth
   will be blessed through you." (Gen 12:1-3)

This is a first expression of many promises that were given to the leaders of this new people, but already several important characteristics of God's plan are evident. First, the promise is that God will revive or reconstitute a new people, the new humanity that has already been disclosed in the earlier chapters of Genesis. Second, this new people are to become a nation, a nation set apart from the other "gentile" nations of the world. Third, this new people was to become a blessing to the others. This became true in the sense that God used Israel to give divine law and true religion to the world. But it was preeminently true in that it was through the historical people of Israel that Christ the Savior came. Fourth, this is to be God's doing, not man's. Note the five "I will's" in the passage. This is the exact opposite of the plan of the builders of Babylon, who said, "Come, let us build ourselves a city, with a tower that reaches to the heavens, so that we may make a name for ourselves and not be scattered over the face of the whole earth" (Gen 11:4).

In time Jerusalem became the capital city of this new people, the Jews. In the Bible Jerusalem is first mentioned as the city of which Melchizedek was king (Gen 14:18). The site had been inhabited from about 3500 B.C. onward, judging from the pottery remains that have been found there. But it became a Jewish city and achieved biblical prominence only under the great King David.

David made Jerusalem his political capital, first by wresting it from the Jebusites by conquest and then by constructing his palace there (2 Sam 5:6-12). He made it the Jews' religious capital by bringing the ark of the covenant to Jerusalem, a story that is told at great length in 2 Samuel 6 and 1 Chronicles 15 and 16. Later Solomon built the temple, which David had wanted to build, and the ark was placed in the Most Holy Place. The people were to present themselves before the Lord at the temple three times a year. Psalms that were written to praise Jerusalem form a collection known as the "Psalms of Zion"

(Ps 46, 48, 76, 84, 87). Other psalms were known as "Psalms of Ascent" because pilgrims would sing them as they made their way upward to the elevated mountain city (Ps 120—134). We catch something of the emotional and spiritual importance of Jerusalem from these psalms. For example,

> How lovely is your dwelling place,
>   O LORD Almighty!
> My soul yearns, even faints,
>   for the courts of the Lord;
> my heart and my flesh cry out
>   for the living God.
>
> Even the sparrow has found a home,
>   and the swallow a nest for herself,
>   where she may have her young—
> a place near your altar,
>   O LORD Almighty, my King and my God.
> Blessed are those who dwell in your house;
>   they are ever praising you. . . .
>
> Better is one day in your courts
>   than a thousand elsewhere;
> I would rather be a doorkeeper in the house of my God
>   than dwell in the tents of the wicked. (Ps 84:1-4, 10)

In these psalms Jerusalem becomes almost synonymous with the divine presence, a truly holy city. But alas, it was still just an earthly city, and the people themselves were far from holy. Which is why, in the end, the city was overthrown and the people deported to Babylon.

Nebuchadnezzar's City: Great Babylon

We have already looked at Babylon once, as the city founded by Nimrod but then broken up and its people scattered by God because of their attempt to build the tower of Babel. The people of this world do not give up easily, however, and sometime along the way the old site was refounded and became a great metropolis once again. In fact, under Nebuchadnezzar and his immediate predecessors Babylon became the dominant world city of the age and eventually the conqueror of Judah and its capital.

Nebuchadnezzar attacked Jerusalem three times. The first invasion was in 605 B.C., a little more than a hundred years after the northern kingdom had fallen to the Assyrians. The second invasion occurred in 597 B.C., when Jehoiakim, the Jewish king, was compelled to surrender Jerusalem and go into captivity with many of the Jewish leaders, including the royal family, the commanders of the army, and even some of the priests like Ezekiel. The third invasion, in 586 B.C., is the one we think of most often since it was then that Jerusalem was destroyed. Jeremiah was in Jerusalem at the time of this final destruction of the city.

It is helpful at this point to think of the early chapters of Daniel, for Daniel was one of a number of the youth of Judah who were carried off to Babylon to be trained for service in the ever-expanding Babylonian empire. Daniel lived in Babylon a long time, through the reigns of four successive kings: Nebuchadnezzar, Belshazzar, Darius and Cyrus. And he produced the book of Old Testament history and prophecy that bears his name. This is a critical book for our study, because it deals with the sovereignty of God over this world's kingdoms and develops what we would today call a Christian philosophy of history.

The theme of Daniel is established in the very first verses of the book where we are told that after Nebuchadnezzar had conquered Jerusalem, he carried articles from the temple of God in Jerusalem "to the temple of his god in Babylonia and put [them] in the treasure house of his god" (Dan 1:2). It was a way of saying that, in his opinion, the god of Babylon was stronger than the God of Israel. And so it seemed! Nebuchadnezzar had conquered Jerusalem. He was victorious. What he did not understand was that God had only used him as an instrument for judging his own persistently disobedient people, as he had said he would do.

But Nebuchadnezzar was not really interested in proving that his *god* was stronger than the Jews' God; he was not really a religious man. Nebuchadnezzar's god was only a projection of himself, an alter ego, and the real struggle of the book is therefore between Nebuchadnezzar himself and Jehovah. In other words, it is exactly the struggle that Paul depicts in Romans as being between sinful humanity and God. Nebuchadnezzar did not want to acknowledge God, which is precisely what Paul says we do not want to do. He wanted to run his own life, achieve what he wanted to achieve and then claim the glory for himself for those achievements.

The climax of his rebellion comes in chapter 4 when Nebuchadnezzar looked over Babylon from the roof of his palace and took the glory of God for himself, saying, "Is not this the great Babylon I have built as the royal residence, by my mighty power and for the glory of my majesty?" (Dan 4:30). This is the cry of the secular humanist. It describes life as *of* man, *by* man and *for* man's glory.

Insanity

We read that as soon as Nebuchadnezzar made his boast, God spoke from heaven to pronounce a judgment on this powerful but arrogant emperor. Sometimes we think of God dispensing judgments somewhat arbitrarily, as if he were merely going down a list of punishments to see what punishment he had left for some special sinner. "Let's see now," he might muse. "Nebuchadnezzar? What will it be? Not leprosy, not kidney stones, not paralysis, not goiter. Ah, here it is: *insanity*. That's what I'll use with Nebuchadnezzar." We may think that is what happened when we read, "This is what is decreed for you, King Nebuchadnezzar: Your royal authority has been taken from you. You will be driven away from people and will live with the wild animals; you will eat grass like cattle. Seven times will pass by for you until you acknowledge that the Most High is sovereign over the kingdoms of men and gives them to anyone he wishes" (Dan 4:31-32).[5]

But this is not the way it happened. God is not arbitrary. He does not operate by going down a list of options. Everything God does is significant. So when God caused Nebuchadnezzar to be lowered from the pinnacle of human pride and glory to the baseness of insanity, it was God's way of saying that this is what happens to all who suppress the truth about God and take the glory of God for themselves. The path is not uphill. It is downhill, and it ends in that moral insanity by which we declare what is good to be evil, and what is evil to be good. From God's perspective this is one chief characteristic of the world's godless cultures. They are out of their minds, as we say. They are insane.

Bestial Behavior

Nebuchadnezzar's case is one not only of insanity but also of bestial behavior. We see this in the words decreeing that Nebuchadnezzar would "live with the wild animals [and] eat grass like cattle." Indeed, later on it is even worse. We are told that "he was driven away from people and ate grass like cattle. His body was drenched with the dew of heaven until his hair grew like the feathers of an eagle and his nails like the claws of a bird" (v. 33). A horrible picture! But it is merely a dramatic Old Testament way of saying what Paul is saying in Romans, namely, that if we will not have God, we will not become like God (that is, "like God, knowing good and evil," Gen 3:5), but we will become like and actually live like animals.

At this point I always think of these verses in Psalm 8:

When I consider your heavens,
    the work of your fingers,
the moon and the stars,
    which you have set in place,
what is man that you are mindful of him,
    the son of man that you care for him?
You made him a little lower than the heavenly beings
    and crowned him with glory and honor.

You made him ruler over the works of your hands;

you put everything under his feet:
all flocks and herds,
   and the beasts of the field. (vv. 3-7)

These verses fix humanity at a very interesting place in the created order: lower than the angels but higher than the animals—somewhere between.[6] This is what Thomas Aquinas saw when he described man as a mediating being. He is like the angels in that he has a soul. But he is like the beasts in that he has a body. The angels have souls but not bodies, while the animals have bodies but not souls.

Here is the point. Although humans are mediating beings, created to be somewhere between the angels and the animals, in Psalm 8 we are nevertheless described as being somewhat lower than the angels rather than somewhat higher than the beasts. In other words, although we are between the angels and beasts, we are destined to look not downward to the beasts but upward to the angels and beyond the heavenly beings to God, becoming increasingly like him. But if we will not look up, if we will not look to God and thus become increasingly like God, we will inevitably look down and become like the animals. Like Nebuchadnezzar, we will become beastlike.

Over the years of my ministry in America in the last quarter or so of this twentieth century I have noticed something very interesting about our culture. I have noticed a number of articles (and sometimes books) that tend to justify or at least explain bestial human behavior on the ground that we are, after all, just animals. We have perversions, but . . . well, the animals have perversions too.

Sometime ago an article appeared in a scientific journal about a certain kind of duck. Two scientists had been observing a family of these ducks, and they were reporting something that they called "gang rape" in this duck family. I am sure they did not want to excuse this crime among humans by the inevitable comparison they were making. But I think their point was that gang rape among humans is at least understandable given our animal ancestry. These scientists had an evolutionary, naturalistic background, and I think they were saying, "After all, gang rape is not all that surprising when you consider that even the ducks do it."

A story of a similar nature appeared in the September 6, 1982, issue of *Newsweek* magazine. It was accompanied by a picture of a mature baboon that was supposed to be holding a dead infant baboon, and over this was the headline "Biologists Say Infanticide Is as Normal as the Sex Drive—and That Most Animals, Including Man, Practice It." The title says everything. It identifies man as an animal, and it justifies his behavior on the basis of this identification. The logic goes like this: Man is an animal, animals kill their offspring, therefore it is all right (or at least understandable) that human beings kill their offspring. But, of course, the argument is fallacious. Most animals do not kill their offspring. They protect their young and care for them. And even if, in a few rare instances, some animals do kill their young, this is still nothing to compare to the crimes regarding the young of which human beings are capable. In this country alone, to give just one example, we kill over one and a half million babies each year by abortion—in most instances, simply for the convenience of the mother.

Even more recently *Discovery* magazine ran an article on the sexual life of a relatively rare apelike family known as bonobos. Bonobos enjoy free sex, practicing open heterosexual exchange of partners as well as male-male and female-female couplings. There was no doubting the facts, because the article was illustrated with very graphic pictures of these couplings. The headline read: "What's Love Got to Do with It?" The point was that bonobos get along very peaceably with this arrangement, and the application to us was clearly: "Why don't we try it? We might find that free sex will lessen tensions and reduce war among human beings." Of course, the long history of the human race shows this to be fallacious.

Worse Than the Animals

But not only do we behave like animals in our cultural rush to free ourselves from God. In our rebellion we end up doing things even the animals would not do. Teaching about human depravity and

trying to make a point, John Gerstner, professor emeritus of Pitts-
burgh Theological Seminary, compared men and women to rats. A
question and answer period followed his address, and someone who
had been offended by the comparison asked Gerstner to apologize.
Gerstner did. "I do apologize," he said. "I apologize profusely. The
comparison was terribly unfair . . . to the rats." He then went on to
show that what a rat does, it does by the gifts of God that make it
ratlike. It does not sin. But we, when we behave like rats, behave
worse than we should and even worse than rats. We are worse than
"beasts" in our behavior.

Do ducks commit rape? I do not know if they do or not. Perhaps
so. But if rape occurs in the animal world, it is uncommon. I do not
know if baboons kill their young. They may. But they do not systematically murder them for their own convenience, as we do our young.
As far as free sex goes, well, the bonobos may do it innocently and
without sin. But when we do it, we sin and pay the due penalties for
our perversions (Rom 1:27).

How Low Can You Go?

Everything I have said to this point illustrates the downhill passage
of the human race when it turns away from God. Paul writes about
this explicitly in Romans 1:18-32, and the last verse of this section
describes the nadir of our fall: "Although they know God's righteous
decree that those who do such things deserve death, they not only
continue to do these very things but also approve of those who
practice them." I call this the lowest point on the downward sliding
scale. But is it really the lowest point? Is it the bottom? Or is there
a bottom? Is there a point beyond which sin will not go?

I have asked this question from time to time in terms of our
declining Western culture—not so much in an absolute sense but in
terms of the moral sensibilities of our nation. I have asked if there
is a point at which people will pull back from our increasingly rapid
decline and say, "This is where we stop; this is terrible; this is a point
beyond which we will not go." Is there such a point in our culture?

If there is, it is certainly not adultery. We have plenty of that.

It is not prostitution. Prostitution is actually legal in some places.

It is not pornography. Where is the point beyond which our culture does not want to go?

I have noticed that in recent years there has been an attempt to define this point at the place perversions impinge on children. The argument goes, "It is not possible to forbid anything to adults so long as they want to do something or consent with each other to do it. But we must not allow these things to affect children. Pornography? Yes, but not child pornography. Prostitution? Yes, but not child prostitution." That sounds good, of course. It gives us the feeling that we are both tolerant—God forbid that we should be intolerant—and moral. But it is sheer hypocrisy.

I remember noticing, when I was first beginning to think along these lines, that at the very time articles were appearing that protested against child pornography and child prostitution, a movie appeared starring Brooke Shields, who was only twelve years old at the time. She played the part of a child prostitute in a brothel in New Orleans at the turn of the century. It was called *Pretty Baby*. It suggested that the child "matured" through her experience.

When we are sliding downhill we delude ourselves into thinking that we are only going to dip into sin a little bit, or at least that there are points beyond which we will never go or lines that we will never cross. But this is sheer fantasy. When we start down that downhill path, there are no points beyond which we will go and no lines that we will not choose to cross—if we live long enough. And even if we die, hell is still continuing along this dismal, downhill path forever.

God's Image Restored

I do not want to leave Nebuchadnezzar and the study of Nebuchadnezzar's Babylon at the edge of this bottomless pit, however. It is true that our rejection of God has left us looking to the beasts and becoming increasingly like them—indeed, even worse than the beasts—and that left to ourselves there can be no end to this grim descent into depravity. But the gospel says that God has not left us to ourselves. In Christ, he has acted to restore what we are intent on destroying. I see it in five steps.

1. We were made in God's image.

2. We rejected God in Adam and therefore lost that image.

3. Having lost God's image and having ceased to become increasingly like him, we became like beasts and, as I have been pointing out in this study, even worse than beasts.

4. Christ became like us, taking a human form on himself.

5. He died for us and thus made it possible for us to be renewed after his image.

I think even Nebuchadnezzar got it. For at the end of the story in Daniel 4, after Nebuchadnezzar had been judged by insanity for seven years, the king came to his right mind and praised the true God as God Most High. Nebuchadnezzar confessed,

His dominion is an eternal dominion;
  his kingdom endures from generation to generation.
All the peoples of the earth
  are regarded as nothing.
He does as he pleases
  with the powers of heaven
  and the peoples of the earth.
No one can hold back his hand
  or say to him: "What have you done?"

He added, "Now I, Nebuchadnezzar, praise and exalt and glorify the King of heaven, because everything he does is right and all his ways are just. And those who walk in pride he is able to humble" (Dan 4:34-35, 37). He is not only able to humble them; he does humble them, as the king found out.

The Fall of Mystery Babylon

We now move to the end of the story, to the book of Revelation and a powerful climax to all that earthly Babylon and earthly Jerusalem stand for throughout the Bible. We have studied the origin of these two cities and have seen something of their progress throughout history. Now we are to see their ends, and in the case of Babylon, its fall.

Chapter 18 heralds the fall of "Mystery Babylon." Babylon had been a sister city to Nineveh and had become a symbol of secular man united in opposition to God, just as Nineveh had become a symbol of man united in opposition to other men and women. By the time Revelation was written, earthly Babylon had long since fallen. So the Babylon mentioned in Revelation is termed "Mystery Babylon" (17:5), which is a way of identifying it as a city representative of all cities of all ages of human history that wickedly opposed God. Chapter 18 begins with an angel coming from heaven to announce in a mighty voice, "Fallen! Fallen is Babylon the Great!" (18:2). The announcement of Babylon's fall by this and another angel fills eight verses.

It is a striking feature of this chapter that Babylon's fall is marked by three mournful dirges, each beginning with the words "Woe! Woe!" First, the kings of the earth express their grief. They are terrified and stand a great distance away crying:

Woe! Woe, O great city,

O Babylon, city of power!

In one hour your doom has come! (v. 10)

Then the merchants, who have lost the best market for their wares, join in:

Woe! Woe! O great city,

dressed in fine linen, purple and scarlet,

and glittering with gold, precious stones and pearls!

In one hour such great wealth has been brought to ruin!

(vv. 16-17)

At last the sea captains, sailors and all who earn their living from the sea express their grief. They throw dust on their heads, exclaiming, "Was there ever a city like this great city?"

Woe! Woe, O great city,

where all who had ships on the sea

became rich through her wealth!

In one hour she has been brought to ruin! (vv. 18-19)

The grief is so poignant that an angel adds his words, observing that "the music of harpists and musicians, flute players and trumpeters, will never be heard in you again" (v. 22).

Then something tremendous happens. These sounds die away, and the scene shifts to heaven where, in chapter 19, the people of God are singing God's praises. Their words are not words of woe. The word that comes to their lips is "Hallelujah!" ("Praise God"). A multitude cries out:

Hallelujah!
Salvation and glory and power belong to our God,
    for true and just are his judgments.
He has condemned the great prostitute
    who corrupted the earth by her adulteries.
He has avenged on her the blood of his servants. . . .

Hallelujah!
The smoke from her goes up for ever and ever. (vv. 1-3)

At this the twenty-four elders exclaim, "Amen, Hallelujah!" (v. 4).

Again the multitude, like the roar of rushing waters and like loud peals of thunder, cries out loudly, shouting:

Hallelujah!
    For our Lord God Almighty reigns.
Let us rejoice and be glad
    and give him glory! (vv. 6-7)

In these two important chapters what is mourned on earth is applauded in heaven. On earth the fall of Babylon is judged an unmitigated tragedy, a tragedy for all who were in her and for all who profited by her. In heaven her fall is a cause for the deepest rejoicing before God.

The New Jerusalem

Then the scene shifts again. First we see Jesus, who appears as a rider on a great white horse. He bears the name KING OF KINGS AND LORD OF LORDS, and he comes to execute judgment on Satan and on the dead and living among mortals. John writes, "The dead were judged according to what they had done as recorded in the books. The sea gave up the dead that were in it, and death and Hades gave up the dead that were in them, and each person was judged according to what he had done. . . . If anyone's name was not found written in the book of life, he was thrown into the lake of fire" (Rev 20:12-13, 15).

At last the Holy City, new Jerusalem, descends from heaven. It is no mere copy of the old earthly Jerusalem that had been destroyed by earthly Babylon for its sins. It is a glorious new city described in what we would call surrealistic terms.

> It shone with the glory of God, and its brilliance was like that of a very precious jewel, like a jasper, clear as crystal. It had a great, high wall with twelve gates, and with twelve angels at the gates. On the gates were written the names of the twelve tribes of Israel. There were three gates on the east, three on the north, three on the south and three on the west. The wall of the city had twelve foundations, and on them were the names of the twelve apostles of the Lamb. (21:11-14)

John describes the city as a perfect cube, about 12,000 stadia or 1,400 miles long on each of three dimensions. John looked for the city's temple, but he did not see one. It was because

> the Lord God Almighty and the Lamb are its temple. The city does not need the sun or the moon to shine on it, for the glory of God gives it light, and the Lamb is its lamp. The nations will walk by its light, and the kings of the earth will bring their splendor into it. On no day will its gates ever be shut, for there will be no night there. The glory and honor of the nations will be brought into it. Nothing impure will ever enter it, nor will anyone who does what is shameful or deceitful, but only those whose names are written in the Lamb's book of life. (21:22-27)

A river of life is in the city, flowing down from the throne of God. It causes trees to bear fruit, and their leaves are for "the healing of the nations" (22:2). The description ends by glancing to God's servants, who will see God's face and bear his name on their foreheads. They will dwell in perpetual light and reign with him "for ever and ever" (v. 5).

It is hard to know what to do with these symbols. They bear ties to reality, for heaven is a real place, not merely an idea. Yet they are also clearly symbols, all with a rich biblical history, pointing to the glories, joys and eternal security of those who are truly God's people.

Perhaps the best way to think about heaven is like coming home. I said at one point that the Bible begins in a garden and ends in a city. But while that is true, it is probably a superficial way to think of it. The important thing about Eden is that it was home to Eve and Adam. When they were driven from the Garden they were driven from home, just as Cain was later driven from his home to become a wanderer on the earth. Cain tried to make a new home for himself by constructing an earthly city. Adam and Eve did not. But God began to make a home for them. He gave them a family, first of all. The family of those who love God and worship him together becomes a taste of heaven. At last God gave them a nation and a church.

Alas, neither the family, the nation nor the church is the whole of what God intends for us. But one day we will have it, when we enter that new heavenly home which Jesus has gone to make ready for us (Jn 14:1-3). That is our destiny, and it is a great destiny indeed. John Newton wrote,

Savior, if of Zion's city
I, through grace, a member am,
Let the world deride or pity,
I will glory in thy name:
Fading is the worldling's pleasure,
All his boasted pomp and show;
Solid joys and lasting treasure
None but Zion's children know.

I close this chapter with a story. When our children were small and we could take them out of school each winter, after the pressures of the Christmas and New Year's services in Philadelphia were behind us, my wife and I would take a short four-day vacation to the Pocono Mountains in eastern Pennsylvania. We would stay at a beautiful lodge called Skytop, and we looked forward to this very much each year as the vacation approached. It was about a three-hour drive, and we usually arrived at dusk. We would park, open the door and be greeted by doormen who, in some cases, had been there for twenty or more years. It was their practice to take our suitcases and say, "Welcome home!"

Skytop was not our home, of course. The greeting was only a clever device on the part of the lodge to make its guests feel welcome. But one day we are going to glory, where those words will be spoken to us literally by Jesus, who has gone ahead to make home ready for us. "Welcome home!" he will say. And we really will be home. Forever.

6
Daniel: God's Man in Babylon

*I*T IS ALMOST IMPOSSIBLE TO THINK of Babylon as it was under the rule of Nebuchadnezzar or, even more, of what it means for a godly person to live and labor in a secular environment like Babylon today without thinking of Daniel, whose life under four Babylonian kings and whose prophecy of the history of the world's nations and the coming of the Messiah is recorded in the book that bears his name.[1] Consider these facts.

First, Daniel was a godly man sent to live in ungodly Babylon at a time when God's blessing on the Jewish nation seemed to have been withdrawn or at least postponed. This means that his position was much like that of believers trying to live in a secular environment today.

Second, the Babylon of Daniel's day was a type of all kingdoms that do not acknowledge God or that think they can dispense with him. This is an apt description of most of the world in our time, including so-called Christian America.

Third, Daniel and his three friends, Hananiah, Mishael and Azariah, were under tremendous pressure to conform. That is, their religion was tolerated, even respected, as long as it did not intrude into public life or "rock the ship" of state. That is our situation also. We can practice our religion so long as it is not in the schools, at work, or in any public place. We have to keep it "on the reservation."

The fourth point is that the world seemed to be winning. Nebuchadnezzar (and after him Belshazzar and others) reigned. Nebuchadnezzar in particular believed himself to be above having to answer to anybody.

Nevertheless, in spite of these things, God showed Daniel that it is he, God, who is in control of history and that his purposes are being accomplished, even in the overthrow and captivity of his people. Moreover, in the end God will establish a kingdom that will endure forever. The destiny of the people of God is wrapped up in that eternal kingdom.

I do not know of any message that is so valuable for Christians living in our own secular and materialistic times as is this message. Indeed, in Daniel we have a stirring and helpful example of a man who not only lived through such times and survived them, but actually triumphed in them and excelled in public life to the glory of God. Daniel did not compromise. He did not bow to this world's idols. He was hated and plotted against. But he triumphed because he knew God and trusted him to do with his life whatever was best.

We need people like that today—people who are aware of the dangers of trying to serve God in this world, but who trust God in spite of the danger and who will not compromise. They are the ones who really triumph, regardless of appearances, and in the last analysis they are the only ones who make a difference.

A Secular Environment

In order to understand Daniel we must realize that the Babylon to which he and his three friends were taken was a secular, worldly place, and that their initial experiences there were intended to blot out of their minds the remembrance of the true God of Israel and their homeland.

We see this in several ways. For one thing, Nebuchadnezzar ordered Ashpenaz, chief of his court officials, to choose young men who would be easily molded by their new environment. Again, he attempted to lure them with the delicacies of food and drink that the great city of Babylon could provide.

Chiefly, we notice Nebuchadnezzar's intentions in the changing of the young men's names. The Hebrew names of these men were Daniel, Hananiah, Mishael and Azariah. They were changed to Belteshazzar, Shadrach, Meshach and Abednego. It should be immediately evident to anyone with even a limited knowledge of Hebrew that the Jewish names contain a name of God and have spiritual meanings. Daniel and Mishael contain the syllable *el,* which means "God" and is the basis of the frequently appearing (plural) name *Elohim.* Daniel means "God is my judge." Mishael means "Who is like God?" The other two names, Hananiah and Azariah, both contain a shortened form of the name Jehovah. Hananiah means "Jehovah is gracious." Azariah means "Jehovah is my helper." The very names of these men were reminders of their heritage and a challenge to them to remain faithful to the Lord. But now, deported into a strange pagan land, their names were changed, and the names they were given each contain references to the false gods of the ancient Babylonians, Aku and Nego. It was a way of saying that those who had been servants of the Jewish God were now servants and worshipers of the gods of the pagan civilization.

Yet the change accomplished nothing. Nebuchadnezzar changed the men's names, but he could not change their hearts. They remained faithful to the true God of Israel, as the story shows.

It is exactly the same today. One thing the world seems always to try to do—it has happened in the past, and it is happening in our own time—is to take Christian words and rework them to convey the world's ideas. An alternative is to substitute words drawn from a non-Christian vocabulary. Sometimes Christians even go along with this. Thus, a word like *sin* is either dropped out of common speech entirely, or it is replaced by concepts like "sickness," "dysfunctional," "environmentally deprived" or "alternate lifestyle." Sometimes it is just trivialized, as in, "It would be a sin to eat that whole dessert, but I'm going to try." Worse even than this, the names God and Jesus Christ are used for swearing.

This is a significant attack on Christian ideas. But if the truth of what is behind these words remains strong in the minds and hearts of those who really know God, then the vitality of the faith will remain regardless of the words' corruptions.

The most important verse in the first chapter of Daniel is verse 8, which says, "But Daniel resolved not to defile himself with the royal food and wine."

Daniel was a young man at this time. We know from the development of the story that he lived for a very long time after this— through the rule of four emperors. He was probably in his eighties when he died. So at this point he was probably between fifteen and seventeen. At this young age he was taken away from his own country and culture, plunged into the strange but exciting life of the great world capital, and lured to loyalty by the best of all possible educations and by provision of the very food served to Nebuchadnezzar. Yet Daniel refused to partake of this food. Does this seem a small thing? Can we think of Daniel's decision as the mere immaturity of youth? Would we have gone along with Nebuchadnezzar's decree? Would we have said, "Why should we have to live by Jewish dietary laws when we are now in Babylon? Let's eat and drink what they give us, and enjoy it. After all, it's just a small thing."

It was a small thing. Yet that is just the point. For it is in the small matters that great victories are won. This is where decisions to live a holy life are made—not in the big things (though they come in time if the little things are neglected), but in the small details of life. If Daniel had said, "I want to live for God in big ways, but I am not going to make a fool of myself in this small matter of eating and drinking the king's food," he would never have amounted to anything. Because he started out for God in small things, God used him greatly.

Nebuchadnezzar Dreamed a Dream
At the end of Daniel 1 we are told that God gave Daniel three things. Because of his decision not to defile himself with the food and culture of the Babylonians, God granted Daniel *wisdom* beyond the wisdom of the Babylonians, *influence* beyond that of any in the kingdom and *health,* which resulted in a long life. However, when we

move from the end of the first chapter to the beginning of the second chapter, we find that each of these is at once either disregarded or threatened.

Nebuchadnezzar's Dream

At the end of his period of training Daniel was presumably graduated into the company of wise men and statesmen referred to by Nebuchadnezzar as "the magicians, enchanters, sorcerers and astrologers" (2:2). Daniel was still only about eighteen or nineteen years of age, and undoubtedly many of those wise men were far greater and far more influential than he was. In that company Daniel would have been just a beginner. Indeed, when the king had his dream, which is the central episode of chapter 2, and an inquiry about it was made to these men, Daniel did not seem to have been consulted and, in fact, did not even know what was happening until the order was given to execute the wise men. So Daniel had no power or influence. And so far as health and long life are concerned, we find that when the wise men were unable to tell the king what his dream was and the king threatened to kill them all, Daniel, who was not even consulted and whose influence did not amount to anything at the time, was nevertheless also on the verge of extermination.

Nevertheless, although his gifts were disregarded and although he was now under sentence of death by Nebuchadnezzar, Daniel *was* wise, and the crisis became the occasion through which God brought him to the forefront of leadership.

That is the important thing: God brought Daniel to the fore! For here as elsewhere in the story we see the overriding sovereignty of God in this young man's affairs. In fact, the sovereignty of God is the connection between these chapters. In chapter 1 God gave Daniel wisdom, influence and health or long life. Now, in spite of the threat to Daniel's life, God fulfills what he has promised. He does it by being sovereign over the details of history, which is the book's theme. If God does not control our lives—from the actions of kings and others in positions of power to the most minute circumstances—

then everything in life is uncertain. We are the toys of circumstance, and whatever happens will happen regardless. *Que será, será!* But if God is sovereign, as the Bible declares him to be, and if he is our God—if the promises he makes and the actions he takes are certain of fulfillment—then we can be confident of the future and know that we will be able to live our lives in a way that will please God.

The Crisis

Nebuchadnezzar was not the first monarch in history to have troublesome dreams. Nor was he the last. Statesmen are often troubled by the past and have forebodings about the future. But the king's dream was not like the dreams that other rulers have. His dream had been given to him by God, and he must have sensed that it was an important revelation. The trouble was, he was unable to remember it.

The king had people around him who were supposed to be able to deal with such things, however. So he called the magicians, enchanters, sorcerers and astrologers together and announced, "I have had a dream that troubles me and I want to know what it means" (v. 3).

The astrologers said, "O king, live forever! Tell your servants the dream, and we will interpret it" (v. 4).

Nebuchadnezzar ignored their request and repeated what he had said at first, but with the addition of a threat if they did not tell him the dream and its interpretation. "This is what I have firmly decided: If you do not tell me what my dream was and interpret it, I will have you cut into pieces and your houses turned into piles of rubble. But if you tell me the dream and explain it, you will receive from me gifts and rewards and great honor. So tell me the dream and interpret it for me" (vv. 5-6).

At this point we may probably detect a rising note of dismay in the wise men's voices. "Let the king tell his servants the dream, and we will interpret it" (v. 7).

This was going nowhere quickly. Each side kept insisting on its own position. The astrologers said, "There is not a man on earth who can do what the king asks! No king, however great and mighty, has ever asked such a thing of any magician or enchanter or astrologer. What the king asks is too difficult. No one can reveal it to the king except the gods, and they do not live among men" (vv. 10-11). True. But there is a God who does reveal himself to people, one who would later say through his prophet Amos, "Surely the Sovereign LORD does nothing without revealing his plan to his servants the prophets" (Amos 3:7). In this case, God revealed to Daniel what the king had dreamed and what he himself was about to do in history. So the stage was set for the first great revelation to Nebuchadnezzar of the sovereignty, wisdom and power of the one true God.

The Meaning of Nebuchadnezzar's Dream

As Daniel explained it, the king had dreamed about a great statue— "enormous, dazzling [and] awesome in appearance" (2:31). It was made of different kinds of metal. The head of the statue was of gold. The chest and arms were of silver. The middle portions were of bronze. The legs were of iron, and the feet were of iron mixed with baked clay. While the king was watching, a rock that was not "cut out . . . by human hands" struck the statue on its feet, and the whole thing toppled over and broke in pieces. The pieces were swept away by the wind like chaff at threshing time, and the rock that struck the statue grew into a huge mountain that filled the whole earth. After he reminded the king what the dream was, Daniel explained it, showing what was to come.

According to Daniel's interpretation, the gold head stood for the emperor himself. Daniel said, "You, O king, are the king of kings. The God of heaven has given you dominion and power and might and glory; in your hands he has placed mankind and the beasts of the field and the birds of the air. Wherever they live, he has made you ruler over them all. You are that head of gold" (vv. 37-38).

This brief description of the importance of Babylon in world history is surprisingly accurate, and it is significant that this is the point at which the vision starts. One reason is that Nebuchadnezzar was then living and Babylon was the world empire of the time. Another is that in the Bible Babylon is also the prototype of all world empires, as I have shown in an earlier chapter. The Bible introduces Babylon in the early chapters of Genesis as the center of Nimrod's empire (Gen 10:8-12), the place where men first banded together against God, who scattered them by the confusion of their language (Gen 11:1-9). Babylon had risen to heights of previously unmatched splendor under Nebuchadnezzar. It was there, for example, that the famous "hanging gardens," one of the wonders of the ancient world, were located.

The second part of the statue was the silver part, representing a kingdom that would follow but would be inferior to that of Nebuchadnezzar. In the unfolding of history this became the kingdom of the Medes and Persians, brought to its zenith of power by King Darius, who is introduced at the end of Daniel 5.

The third part was made of brass. It represented the kingdom of the Greeks established by Alexander the Great.

The fourth part of the statue, the part made of iron and the feet made of iron mixed with baked clay, represented the Roman Empire. This kingdom was still hundreds of years in the future, but Daniel predicted it accurately. "There will be a fourth kingdom, strong as iron—for iron breaks and smashes everything—and as iron breaks things to pieces, so it will crush and break all the others. Just as you saw that the feet and toes were partly of baked clay and partly of iron, so this will be a divided kingdom" (2:40-41).

According to this vision, each of the coming world kingdoms was to be inferior to the one before it in terms of its glory, while also being stronger in military might. The golden head represented Babylon, the most glorious of the world's kingdoms. The kingdom of the Medes and Persians, which followed it, was less glorious, just as silver is less glorious than gold. But it is also stronger, which is why it was able to subdue Babylon. Greece had less glory than the Medes and Persians, though it was stronger than they were. Finally, the Roman Empire, though less glorious still, nevertheless was more powerful than any kingdom on earth. Yet strikingly, the description of Rome does not end with strength, but with a divided empire whose strength, represented by the iron, was mixed with clay.

This is the opposite of the humanistic view of world progress. In its purest form the doctrine of progress insists that progress must always occur on all fronts. This is not true, of course. There are declines as well as gains. So modified expressions of the "progress" philosophy argue that losses in one area (glory or magnificence, for example) are more than compensated for by gains in other areas (strength or power, to preserve the example). But even this is an illusion, according to this chapter. When we walk with God, as Daniel and his friends were doing, we go from strength to strength and from victory to victory. This produces genuine progress, both personal and social. But apart from God even our imagined advances are declines. Is the United States not morally and spiritually weaker today, though physically stronger, than it was a generation ago? Is not the same thing true for most other technically advanced societies?

The Stone Not Made with Human Hands

The climax of the king's dream was the rock that struck the statue and destroyed it and then grew to be a great mountain that filled the whole earth. Daniel interpreted this part of the dream, saying, "In the time of those kings, the God of heaven will set up a kingdom that will never be destroyed, nor will it be left to another people. It will crush those kingdoms and bring them to an end, but it will itself endure forever" (2:44). It is obvious from the vision itself and from the way the stone image is used throughout the Bible that the rock is Jesus Christ and his kingdom.

So the vision comes down to this. The kingdoms of this world may well be powerful and sometimes even glorious, from our point of view. But even their strength is given to them by God, and just as God sets up kingdoms, so does he bring them down and dispose of them. He was to do that with King Nebuchadnezzar. He has done it with all the prior kingdoms of this world, and he will do it with those of our own time too.

Our duty is to recognize that "the kingdom of the world has become the kingdom of our Lord and of his Christ" (Rev 11:15) and bow down to him and thank him for the salvation he brings.

Faith in the Furnace

But the story continues. In the next chapter of Daniel Nebuchadnezzar takes it into his head to build a great statue, which he sets up on the plain of Dura. Made of gold, it was ninety feet high and nine feet wide—twice as high as most houses. So even if it was only covered with gold, it would still have taken a prodigious amount of this most precious metal. The fact that it was made entirely of gold is the point of chief importance.

The significance of the gold is because of Nebuchadnezzar's vision. As Daniel had interpreted the dream, the head represented the glorious kingdom of Babylon, the silver a less glorious but stronger kingdom that would follow Nebuchadnezzar's, the brass a still less glorious but stronger kingdom, and the iron the strongest but basest kingdom of all. At the end of this history, a rock, representing Christ, would strike the world's kingdoms, destroy them, and then grow to fill the whole earth. As we read this today, none of it seems very threatening. Kingdoms do succeed other kingdoms, after all, and Christians at least do look forward to Christ's kingdom.

This is not the way Nebuchadnezzar must have seen it. After Daniel had revealed the dream and its meaning, Nebuchadnezzar had praised Daniel's God, saying, "Surely your God is the God of gods and the Lord of kings and a revealer of mysteries, for you were able to reveal this mystery" (2:47). But when he started thinking about it, Nebuchadnezzar was not pleased. He must have said to himself, "Why should just the head of the statue be of gold? The gold empire represents the kingdom of Babylon, my kingdom. Why should my kingdom be succeeded by other kingdoms? Why shouldn't this great Babylon that I have built last forever?" So the king built a statue that represented his will for the future. It was all of gold, and everyone was required to bow down to it on pain of death. Those who refused were to be thrown into a blazing furnace. In this way the king was defying God, saying in effect, "I will not allow the God of Daniel to set my kingdom aside."

Daniel does not appear at this point in the story. We do not know why and can only guess that because he was still young at this point he was probably serving at some other place in the empire. Whatever the cause, he was absent and the storm broke on Shadrach, Meshach and Abednego, his three friends.

These three men were among those required to bow down before the great golden statue. To their great credit we do not read that they hesitated even for a minute or asked for time to think the issues through. Even the great Martin Luther asked for an evening to pray and think when he was required to recant his writings. But Shadrach, Meshach and Abednego seem to have refused categorically and at once, and the king was furious when he heard about it. He hauled them in and demanded their immediate compliance. They responded in what is probably my favorite passage in the entire book. "O Nebuchadnezzar, we do not need to defend ourselves before you in this matter. If we are thrown into the blazing furnace, the God we serve is able to save us from it, and he will rescue us from your hand, O king. But even if he does not, we want you to know, O king, that we will not serve your gods or worship the image of gold you have set up" (3:16-18).

How could these three men find the strength to resist this all-powerful human monarch in such a bold way? Three things gave them the ability to stand firm in this great test of their commitment, and they are equally necessary if the people of God are to stand for what is right and make a difference in our similarly secular culture today.

First, they knew that God was sovereign. Nothing is clearer in their response to Nebuchadnezzar than this. "The God we serve *is able* to save us," and if he chooses to do so, "*he will* rescue us from your hand, O king." This was no airy speculation. This was faith in the furnace. It was a firm conviction of the sovereignty of God in the midst of all things seemingly contrary to it. These men were convinced that God is sovereign, and therefore it was not foolish but wise for them to entrust their lives to him in this matter.

Second, they knew the Scriptures. This is the reason they refused to bow down. God had forbidden it. But knowing the Scriptures is also important for us, for the reason that moral issues seldom come to us in black-and-white terms. The world makes moral issues as ambiguous as possible because, when that is the case, it seems to free us to do whatever we want to do—at least to do what we judge best in the circumstances. If we are to do the right thing in such circumstances, we must know the Word of God because only the Word of God will cut through such ambiguity. Shadrach, Meshach and Abednego triumphed because their minds were filled with Scripture and because they kept coming back to Scripture as the only fully trustworthy and inerrant authority in all matters.

Third, they were willing to die for their convictions. This is important too because, although it is possible to believe in a sovereign God and to know from the Bible what the sovereign God requires, we can still fail to do the right thing if we are unwilling to pay the price of obedience. It is true that not many of us are likely to be faced with a sharp choice between compromise or execution. But the issue is the same regardless of the penalty. Many fail to do the morally right thing because they will not pay the price of a loss of popularity or loneliness or ridicule or persecution or economic hardship. Only those who are willing to pay such prices make a difference.

I think of Joseph Tson, the Romanian pastor who was called before the communist authorities to answer for his religious convictions and preaching. He expected to be killed. So he set his affairs in order, and when he appeared before the interrogating officer he said, "I have to tell you first that I am ready to die. I have put my affairs in order. Your supreme weapon is killing. My supreme weapon is dying, because when you kill me people all over Romania will read my books and believe on the God I preach—even more than they do now."

The interrogator replied, "Who said anything about killing?" and eventually let him go. Although Joseph Tson was exiled to America for quite a few years, today he is back in Romania. The communist regime has fallen, and Christians like Tson are trying to rebuild the country along Christian lines.

In Daniel a similar thing happened. Shadrach, Meshach and Abednego were thrown into the furnace. But God protected them from the heat of the fire, even sending his Son, the Lord Jesus Christ, to stand with them in the furnace—as I suppose the fourth person who looked "like a son of the gods" (3:25) to have been. And they were delivered.

We need Christians who will stand for the right today. So let us refuse to compromise. Let us stand with unbowed heads and rigid backbones before the golden statues of our godless, materialistic culture. Let us declare that there is a God to be served and a race to be won. Let us shout that we are determined to receive the approval of God, a prize that is far greater than this world's tinsel toys. Let us be bold servants of him before whom every knee will one day bow.

Belshazzar Gave a Party

"Belshazzar gave a party, and he invited all his friends." I do not often remember exact sentences of sermons I have heard preached, but I do remember that one. It was the way Billy Graham began a sermon on Daniel thirty or more years ago. What a party it was! The king assembled one thousand of his nobles, plus many wives and concubines. Wine flowed. The palace roared with laughter. At the height of the party Belshazzar called for the gold and silver goblets that his predecessor King Nebuchadnezzar had taken from the great temple at Jerusalem years before when he had sacked the city. Belshazzar, his nobles, his wives and his concubines drank from the goblets and praised the gods of Babylon—gods of gold and silver, of bronze, iron, wood and stone.

Suddenly a disembodied hand appeared and began to write on the wall. The king and his nobles believed in dark omens, and this was the most unusual and terrifying omen that they had ever seen. We are told that the king's "face turned pale and he was so frightened that his knees knocked together and his legs gave way" (5:6).

Belshazzar called for the enchanters and diviners to read the writing and explain what it meant, but they were baffled. At last Daniel was summoned. By the time of this story Daniel was a much older man. He read the writing. It was a judgment.

O king, the Most High God gave your father Nebuchadnezzar sovereignty and greatness and glory and splendor. . . . But when his heart became arrogant and hardened with pride, he was deposed from his royal throne and stripped of his glory. He was driven away from people and given the mind of an animal; he lived with the wild donkeys and ate grass like cattle; and his body was drenched with the dew of heaven, until he acknowledged that the Most High God is sovereign over the kingdoms of men and sets over them anyone he wishes. But you his son, O Belshazzar, have not humbled yourself, though you knew all this. (vv. 18, 20-22)

Then Daniel read the inscription, MENE, MENE, TEKEL, PARSIN, and explained it. *Mene* meant "God has numbered the days of your reign and brought it to an end." *Tekel* meant "You have been weighed on the scales and found wanting." *Peres* meant "Your kingdom is divided and given to the Medes and Persians" (vv. 26-28). And so it happened. That night Darius the Mede attacked Babylon and overthrew it, killing Belshazzar. He did it by damming up the river that flowed through the city and then entering through the space provided when the water dropped and the river's portals into the city were exposed. The conquest was an example of God's judgments in human history and a warning about the pride that affects us all.

A Busy Man's Devotional Life

The last incident in the life of Daniel is recounted in chapter 6; chapter 7 begins a quite different section of the book, chiefly an insight into the details of future history that God gave this important Old Testament prophet. Chapter 6, however, is about Daniel's prayer life, and it contains a verse that I wish could be spoken of every believer in the Lord Jesus Christ, though I confess that it probably cannot be. Daniel had been promoted to a position of prominence, and those about him were jealous. They wanted to find something for which to accuse him and pull him down. They could not. Finally they confessed, "We will never find any basis for charges against this man Daniel unless it has something to do with the law of his God" (6:5).

Wouldn't it be wonderful if that could be said of every Christian today, especially of us? I am afraid that it cannot usually be said of us, because there are many things of which we can rightly be accused. At times we can be accused of wrong actions. The world says, "That Christian is doing something that is not right. His (or her) actions are against what all people everywhere believe." If this is the case with us, we need to confess the sin and have it cleansed and forgiven by Jesus Christ. At other times we can be accused of laziness. Daniel's jealous peers tried to fault him for negligence (v. 4), but they could not prove that he had been neglectful of anything. Sometimes people accuse Christians of pride. They say, "Those Christians are no better than we are. In fact, they are much worse. They sin and are lazy, and then, to top it off, they are proud of being like that." This may be an unjust accusation in most instances, but Christians sometimes have been terribly prideful.

Are we? If so, perhaps it will yet be said of us—even if it cannot properly be said of us at this moment—"We will never find any basis for a charge against these people unless it has something to do with the law of their God."

But to the story. The account in which this comment is made is the best-known incident in Daniel and one of the best-known stories in the Old Testament. It involves Daniel's being thrown into a den of lions during the reign of King Darius, who succeeded Belshazzar as the ruler of Babylon.

Daniel must have been over eighty years old at this time, and his enemies had observed him for many years. Since there was nothing in his performance about which they could honestly or successfully accuse him, they resorted to a stratagem. They approached Darius with the flattering suggestion that a law be passed according to which no one would be allowed to make a request or pray to any god or man for the next thirty days, except to Darius himself. They suggested further that if anyone should disobey this law, he should be thrown into a den of hungry lions. It was proposed that this be done in the most binding way, according to the laws of the Medes and Persians, which could not be annulled.

Darius was trapped by this evil plot. He did not want to condemn his valuable administrator Daniel, but he was caught by the deception.

God or Caesar?

What did it mean for Darius to issue a law forbidding anyone to make a request of any god or man except himself for a period of thirty days? The answer is obvious. It meant that Darius was putting himself in the place of God—unwittingly perhaps, but nevertheless doing so. He was saying, "I am the one to whom people should look for all things. I am sovereign." This is what Belshazzar had done in the desecration of the temple vessels and what Nebuchadnezzar had done before him when he boasted that he alone was responsible for Babylon's great glory. It was the ultimate blasphemy, a sin that God will not tolerate.

But this is the besetting sin of every secular culture—the sin of putting oneself in God's place. Expressions of this sin abound in Babylon. But think also of the kingdom of Rome, whose coming Daniel prophesied. Rome was extremely arrogant, and the ultimate arrogance was the cult of the Caesars. Citizens of the empire were required to burn a pinch of incense to the reigning Caesar and utter the words *Kyrios Kaisar,* meaning "Caesar is Lord." This is what the early Christians refused to do and for which they were themselves thrown to the wild lions or crucified. It was not that Christians were forbidden to worship God. They were free to worship any god they chose so long as they also acknowledged Caesar. Rome was tolerant. But when Christians denied to Caesar the allegiance that they knew belonged to the true God only, they were executed.

Is it any different today? We think that we are in a more enlightened age, and we are in some respects. In most places in the world a person is not killed for an exclusive worship of Jesus Christ, though it continues to happen more often than we like to admit. But there are different kinds of executions, and the attacks on Christians even in enlightened countries are often no less vicious than the attack on Daniel.

Here is a recent example. In early 1981, after Ronald Reagan's election as president of the United States, the distinguished pediatric surgeon C. Everett Koop was appointed deputy assistant secretary of Health and Human Services, which put him in line to become surgeon general of the United States. Koop was then surgeon-in-chief of Children's Hospital in Philadelphia, where the entire surgical center is named in his honor. He was a pioneer in pediatric surgery and an inventor of many pediatric surgical techniques. He founded and was at that time editor of the *Journal of Pediatric Surgery*. He had been awarded the French Legion of Honor.

But Koop had opposed abortion on the grounds that the fetus is made in the image of God and that to abort it is to commit murder. Indeed, he was nominated to be surgeon general because of this conviction. Because his opposition to abortion was unpopular at that time, the media especially, but also many political opponents, embarked on a scurrilous campaign in which his medical accomplishments were ignored and he was repeatedly portrayed as merely a close-minded fundamentalist. The *Washington Post* described him as "a fundamentalist Christian with a Lincolnesque beard . . . the narrator of a controversial anti-abortion film, *Whatever Happened to the Human Race?*" (March 6, 1981). The *Boston Globe* dismissed him as a "clinician . . . with tunnel vision." One journalist called him "Dr. Kook."[2]

These and other attacks delayed Koop's appointment as surgeon general for nearly a year, although in the end he was appointed. The battle over Koop was a case of our society wanting to play God in the matter of the life of the unborn, and of its fierce hostility to anyone, however distinguished, who dares to stand against it in obedience to God. If we practice our religion on the reservation and do not attempt to bring it out into the real world, the world will tolerate us. But if we determine to take a stand on any important issue on the grounds of genuine religious principle, the fury of our secular society will break all bounds.

To Pray or Not to Pray

Daniel was an experienced courtier, so he knew at once what the king's decree meant and where it came from. For thirty days Daniel would need to abandon his customary practice of praying thrice daily before his open window in the direction of Jerusalem, or else be thrown into the den of lions. *Thirty days!* "Well," we say, "that's not too bad. It isn't as if he had to bow down to an idol as his friends Shadrach, Meshach and Abednego had been required to do. All he had to do was stop praying openly for one month." Indeed, he could even be subtle. He could close his window so his prayers would not be seen or, better yet, pray in bed at night. He could let his devotions slide for a month. After all, many so-called Christians today probably allow a month or more to slide by without any significant devotions.

We may think like that. Doubtless many do. But not Daniel. Instead we read that "when Daniel learned that the decree had been published he went home to his upstairs room where the windows opened toward Jerusalem. Three times a day he got down on his knees and prayed, giving thanks to his God, just as he had done before" (6:10).

I like those last words: "just as he had done before." They indicate that this was a lifetime devotional pattern with Daniel. The outside world may have been changing, but God had not changed and Daniel was not going to allow his relationship to God to change either, regardless of the shifting circumstances.

There are two important things to notice at this point.

First, Daniel was the smallest of all possible minorities, a minority of one. Yet although he was only one man among many hostile enemies, he was the one man who knew the true state of affairs in this struggle. Darius did not know what was going on. He had not even been able to see through the strategy of his administrators and satraps, and of course he perceived nothing of the spiritual struggle. The conspirators did not understand the situation. They did not know Daniel's God. They were not taking God into account at all. This is why they thought that it would be an easy matter to get Daniel executed.

And what about Shadrach, Meshach and Abednego? At this time Daniel probably did not even have the support of his three friends, for they are not mentioned as they were in the incident involving Nebuchadnezzar's dream (see 2:17-18). Either they had been moved to other parts of the empire or they had died, which is likely since Daniel himself was now elderly. Here was one man standing alone in the midst of an utterly pagan culture. All were against him. Any who knew his convictions would have laughed at them. Yet in all this vast empire Daniel was the only person who actually had it together. He knew that God was all-powerful. He knew that God could deliver him, if he chose to do so. Above all, he knew that obeying and serving this one true God had to be the supreme goal in his life.

Second, what Daniel did he did openly. Some people maintain their belief in God privately and confess him if asked, but they do not want to go public. They do not want to offend anyone. They do not want to be seen to be religious. So they back off. They retreat. They privatize their convictions. Daniel did not do that, and in this he showed his true greatness. Instead of hiding his convictions, he knelt before his window in the sight of all Babylon and prayed as he had always done. We need more Daniels. We need more people who are willing to bring their awareness of God and his laws off the reservation, who are willing to open their windows and honor him before a watching world.

Safe with the Lions

For most of us, the end of the story is the least interesting part since we know it already. But it is nevertheless dramatic and has its own lessons. Darius did not want to see his friend and faithful administrator killed. So he tried to discover a way to escape the force of his unchangeable edict. It was to no avail. The law had to be enforced, and at last the king had Daniel thrown to the lions, calling out, "May your God, whom you serve continually, rescue you!" (6:16).

A detail from an earlier moment in the story is of special interest now. We are told that when the conspirators burst in on Daniel while he was praying, they found him "asking God for help" (v. 11). This means that Daniel was not oblivious to his danger, even though his outward calm might have suggested that he was not taking the threat of execution seriously. Actually, Daniel was very much aware of his danger. He knew that he stood to lose his life. He was asking God to help him. And of course, that is exactly what God did. God stopped the lions' mouths so they could not attack Daniel, and while Daniel was with them he was kept from harm, not only from the lions but from his enemies too. They could not get to him. He was in the safest place in all Babylon, and that night, I am sure, Daniel slept marvelously.

It was the king who could not sleep. Darius thrashed about, and very early in the morning he rushed to the lions' den to see what had become of his most influential administrator. "Daniel, servant of the living God, has your God, whom you serve continually, been able to rescue you from the lions?" he called (v. 20).

I do not know what kind of an answer Darius was expecting, perhaps a growl from the lions. But when the answer came back it was not the lions who were making noise. God had shut their mouths. It was Daniel who was speaking, and his voice was heard clearly: "O king, live forever! My God sent his angel, and he shut the mouths of the lions. They have not hurt me, because I was found innocent in his sight. Nor have I ever done any wrong before you, O king" (vv. 21-22). Then the king had Daniel drawn from the den. He had the conspirators and their families thrown into it, and he issued a decree concerning God with which the story ends:

> For he is the living God
>   and he endures forever;
> his kingdom will not be destroyed,
>   his dominion will never end.
> He rescues and he saves;
>   he performs signs and wonders
>   in the heavens and on the earth.

He has rescued Daniel

from the power of the lions. (vv. 26-27)

It was not a very profound decree, but it was profound for the king and it was certainly true enough. It is true today. God is God, and he had indeed rescued Daniel. In the same way, in our time, God rescues his servants from evils that threaten them whenever they determine to live for him and serve him in spite of dangerous circumstances.

In all honesty, however, we must say that God does not always rescue his servants in this fashion. Hebrews 11:33 speaks of those who by faith "shut the mouths of lions," a clear reference to Daniel. But immediately after that the book also speaks of others who were

> tortured and refused to be released, so that they might gain a better resurrection. Some faced jeers and flogging, while still others were chained and put in prison. They were stoned; they were sawed in two; they were put to death by the sword. They went about in sheepskins and goatskins, destitute, persecuted and mistreated—the world was not worthy of them. They wandered in deserts and mountains, and in caves and holes in the ground. (11:35-38)

God calls some to win by living out long lives for him, sometimes in very pagan places. Others are called to win by dying. But whether in life or death, God rules, and we are called to serve him faithfully, fearlessly and to the very best of our ability. Will we? The world does not know this, but it needs scores of people who know God and who will live for him and his righteousness even when the entire culture turns ferociously against them.

Part 3

The Two Cities Today

If my people, who are called by my name,
will humble themselves and pray and seek my face
and turn from their wicked ways, then will I hear from heaven
and will forgive their sin and will heal their land.

2 CHRONICLES 7:14

Give to Caesar what is Caesar's, and to God what is God's.

MATTHEW 22:21

The weapons we fight with are not the weapons of the
world. On the contrary, they have divine power to demolish
strongholds. We demolish arguments and every pretension
that sets itself up against the knowledge of God, and we take
captive every thought to make it obedient to Christ.

2 CORINTHIANS 10:4-5

7

Christianity
& Culture

*A*S SOON AS WE TALK ABOUT TWO "CITIES" rather than individuals
formed into what has been called "the two humanities," we have
begun to talk about society and the cultures that are its product. And
the question arises, What should the relationship of Christianity to
culture be? Or, to put it in other terms, How should Christians relate
to the world in which they live? This is a complex question because,
on the one hand, Christians are part of that culture, even if they do
not realize that they are or do not like it, and on the other hand,
they are also called to be (and are) a distinct new people of God.

H. Richard Niebuhr (1894-1962), a professor at Yale University,
offered some answers to those questions in *Christ and Culture,* a book
published in 1951. In it Niebuhr identified the options as "Christ
against culture," "the Christ of culture," "Christ above culture,"
"Christ and culture in paradox" and "Christ the transformer of culture."[1] Niebuhr's study leads to a more complex treatment than I
need to introduce here, but it points in a helpful direction. Therefore, I want to follow Niebuhr's lead by discussing four possibilities
that have bearing on the relationship of Christianity and culture
today. I call them: Christ over culture, Christ apart from culture,
Christ the servant of culture, and Christ and the two cities.

Christ over Culture

The first answer to this question was that of the medieval Roman Church and possibly the Roman Church in our time. It is also, as we will see, the viewpoint of many evangelical Christians. This view starts with an entirely correct idea, namely that Jesus Christ is King of all kings and Lord of all lords. But then it makes the erroneous jump that because Jesus is sovereign over this world's rulers and cultures, therefore the church or at least the highest representatives of the church should be sovereign over the world's rulers and cultures too.

In the Middle Ages this meant that the pope was the highest authority on earth, with the right to crown or depose kings and receive their homage. It also meant that the pope had the right to wage war against non-Christian princes. This period of history witnessed the emergence of warrior popes like Alexander VI (ruled 1492-1503), Julius II (1503-1513) and Leo X (1513-1521), who actually led troops into battle like a secular king. Earlier, the same ideas had led to the Crusades (1095-1291) in which the knights of Christendom, carrying the banner of Christ, attempted to drive the "infidel" out of the Holy Land. In practice, of course, the crusaders also attacked Christian strongholds, the most notorious being the siege and sack of Constantinople, a Christian city, in A.D. 1204.

The church's claim to dominance did not go uncontested, of course, and in some ways the history of the Middle Ages is the history of the struggle between the pope and the kings. From the church's side the ultimate triumph was the moment when Henry IV, the secular head of the Holy Roman Empire, knelt barefoot in the snow outside the castle of Gregory VII (Hildebrand) at Canossa on January 25, 1077, begging for forgiveness and the restoration of his kingdom.

The details of this history will seem remote to today's evangelicals, if they are aware of them at all. But they are relevant to the current clashes in the culture wars, since the claims of the medieval Roman Church under the warrior popes is the precise view of today's militant evangelicals who want to "reclaim America" by establishing godliness through legislation.

Here is a typical expression of this view. Randall Terry is the founder of Operation Rescue, the evangelical organization most prominent in the fight against abortion. In an entertaining book, *Why Does a Nice Guy like Me Keep Getting Thrown in Jail?* he writes,

> If righteousness is going to prevail, if paganism is going to be turned back, then we must move to restore this nation to being a Christian nation. Otherwise we will lose the war for America's soul, and the United States as we know it will perish.
>
> And if we are going to reform and rebuild our country, we're going to have to deliberately infiltrate the power bases of America. We'll deliberately have to raise up men like John Adams and Teddy Roosevelt to be "morally correct," not "politically correct" statesmen. May God grant it.[2]

Some of this might be dismissed as mere rhetoric, an attempt to rally the troops for battle. But the basic view is still inescapable. It is a call to recover America by *legislation*—by infiltrating the power bases, taking control, so that America once again becomes a Christian nation. But was America ever truly a Christian nation? Was any nation? And what about the doctrine of the two cities, the City of God and the city of man? Will America as a nation ever be anything other than man's city? And what about America's soul? Is there such a thing as an American soul to be redeemed—or fought over?

Before we allow ourselves to be carried away by this rhetoric we should take note of the fact that this is precisely what has alarmed our secular contemporaries. Listen to them on radio and television, and you will find that this is what they are complaining about. They are saying that they dare not allow the Religious Right—that is what they call it—to take over and impose its narrow idea of what is right and wrong on everyone else. I share their apprehension, for I too fear the ignorance, harshness and even tyranny that would result if this particular block of the electorate should "win" the culture wars and become politically dominant.

President Bill Clinton was stating the reaction of many secular people carefully but accurately when he said in a speech to the Yale

University Alumni Association, "The problem I have [with the Religious Right] is that so many of them seem to believe that their number-one obligation is to make whatever they think is wrong illegal, and then not worry about what kind of affirmative duties we have to one another."[3]

Christ Apart from Culture

The second answer to the question of Christianity and culture is that of the monastics of the early church and of the Anabaptists at the time of the Reformation. Faced with what they regarded as a hopelessly corrupt and immoral government and culture in the early Christian centuries, the monastics retreated into the desert, trying to get as far away from their corrupt world system as possible. Some lived by themselves in isolated places. Others developed communities into which the devout could escape and from which the world could be shut out. To be fair, we owe the preservation of most ancient literature to these monks, who copied and so saved it while the rest of the world was destroying itself during the long Dark Ages.

The same view was present in many of the Anabaptists at the time of the Reformation. In his fine discussion of this movement Michael Horton cites a particularly telling paragraph from the Anabaptist "Schleitheim Confession" of 1527.

> We are agreed on separation: A separation shall be made from the evil and from the wickedness which the devil planted in the world; in this manner, simply that we shall not have fellowship with them and not run with them in the multitude of their abominations. This is the way it is: since all who do not walk in the obedience of faith, and have not united themselves with God so that they wish to do his will, are a great abomination to God, it is not possible for anything to grow or issue from them except abominable things. For truly all creatures are in but two classes, good and bad, believing and unbelieving, darkness and light, the world and those who [have come] out of the world, God's temple and idols, Christ and Belial; and none can have part with the other. . . . He further admonishes us to withdraw from Babylon

and the earthly Egypt that we may not be partakers of the pain and suffering which the Lord will bring upon them.[4]

It does not take a great deal of thought to see that this approach errs in two ways. First, it overestimates the godliness of the godly. The righteous are not as free of this world's evil as they suppose. Second, it underestimates the value of this world's culture and government, since there is such a thing as common grace by which even rank unbelievers are able to create objects of beauty, launch worthwhile social projects and perform secular responsibilities with integrity and skill. Paul tells us that "the authorities that exist have been established by God" and thus have valuable, God-assigned functions to perform (Rom 13:1; see vv. 1-7).

Generally speaking, this was the choice of the majority of evangelicals in this country in the first half of our century up to the decade of the seventies, when they awoke to the current culture battles. *Newsweek* called 1976 the "year of the evangelical" because of this resurgence. But before that time evangelicals were mostly content to withdraw from the culture to form their own independent society with evangelical schools, books, movies, social groupings and scores of independent churches, answerable to no one.

Christ the Servant of Culture

The first two answers to the relationship of Christianity to secular culture are widely different—in fact, they are the two opposite poles of an answer—but they have one thing at least in common. They believe that there is something unique about Christianity and that this unique worldview or ethic is preferable to the world's worldview or ethic. The answer we come to now rejects that belief. It says that Christianity is not better than the world. Therefore, it is not the world that needs to be changed but Christianity. The church and Christian people must be secularized. We must become servants of this world's culture.

This is the view of liberal Christianity, which is not even authentic Christianity. However, the particular expression of this view that we are contending with most today is one that emerged in America in the 1960s. It is associated with the so-called death of God theologians—Thomas J. J. Altizer, William Hamilton, Gabriel Vahanian and Paul van Buren—and it has received classic treatment in a book by Harvard Divinity School theologian Harvey Cox called *The Secular City*. His book hit the religious world like a bombshell in 1965, and the views he expressed there commanded the allegiance and efforts of many leaders in the mainline denominations for the next several decades. Although Cox later retreated from some of his ideas, *The Secular City* argued strongly that secularism is a good thing, something to be affirmed and applauded rather than denied, and that the Judeo-Christian tradition itself leads to and endorses the secularization.

Cox found his biblical basis in three areas. First, he argued that the Genesis account of creation teaches the "disenchantment" of nature. No longer were trees, rocks, glens and groves to be seen as the abode of gods or spirits. Nature was neutral. Cox called this disenchantment the necessary precondition for the development of the natural sciences and the creation of our present technological world. He wrote that in this sense the Bible's account of creation is really a form of "atheistic propaganda."[5]

A second area in which the biblical tradition led to secularization, according to Cox, is politics. He traced this to the exodus from Egypt in which God sanctioned, as it were, an act of civil disobedience. From this time on no one was to believe in the "divine right" of rulers but only in the rights of the people or the democratic process.

The third area of biblical desacralization is the Sinai covenant, which Cox called the "deconsecration of values." Contrary to any traditional understanding of Sinai, according to which God laid down certain absolute moral and governmental laws, Cox affirmed that what happened on Sinai was the relativizing of moral values. How could that possibly be? It was due to the law's opposition to idolatry, Cox answers, referring to Exodus 20:3 ("You shall have no other gods before me"). Because the Jews believed in Jehovah rather than in the heathen gods, they experienced liberation from all arbitrary religious moral systems and had their values relativized. They learned that no values were ever absolute.

On this fanciful biblical basis Cox taught that modern man living with his technology, urbanity and pragmatism is the product of biblical faith and divinely directed historical forces. This secular human lives in the secular city from which for all practical purposes God is banished. He enjoys a freedom made possible by technology and undergirded by almost total privacy. Values are private, as each is left free to live as he or she desires. And this is good! Cox called on Christians to support this outlook. He wrote,

> Clearly, those whose present orientation to reality is shaped by the biblical faith can hardly in good faith enter the lists as adversaries of secularization. Our task should be to nourish the secularization process, to prevent it from hardening into a rigid world view, and to clarify as often as necessary its roots in the Bible. Furthermore, we should be constantly on the lookout for movements which attempt to thwart and reverse the liberating irritant of secularization.[6]

How can we explain the tremendous attention that Cox's book received in the late 1960s? The answer is that the secularization of the church that Cox described was already well under way. In fact, it was already entrenched in many church bureaucracies. When *The Secular City* appeared these bureaucrats naturally hailed it as a theoretical justification of a policy and lifestyle that they were already following.

Their presence is what I have long called the secular church.[7] We can gain a better understanding of it by the following four categories.

The World's Wisdom

One element in the secularization of the mainline churches, which clearly preceded Cox, was their exchange of the ancient wisdom of the church, embodied in the Scriptures, for the world's wisdom. In earlier ages Christian people stood before the Bible and confessed their ignorance of spiritual things. They even confessed their inability to understand what was written in the Bible except for the grace of God through the ministry of the Holy Spirit to unfold the Bible's secrets to us. This ancient wisdom, which was the strength of the church, was set aside, and the reforming voice of God through the Scriptures was forgotten.

What has happened as a result of this abandonment of the church's ancient wisdom? Several things. First, it has produced a pitiful state of uncertainty and insecurity in church leaders. This is often covered up, of course. But at times it is honestly stated, as in these words from an address by Robin Scroggs when he was installed as professor of New Testament at Chicago Theological Seminary.

> We are thus in no secure place. We have found no single author-
> itative standard from the past of what to say or how to live. Neither
> have we a secure self-understanding erected on the basis of our
> immediate experience. We in fact find ourselves in the abyss of
> a continual uncertainty, but we are kept from falling into chaos
> by the very tension between past and present. . . . We have no
> assurance that where we happen to be is the best or final place
> to stand.[8]

That is a pitiful confession, but it is accurate. For it describes much in the life of the contemporary liberal church and explains why so many people are deserting the mainline churches. People are not attracted to a church that does not know what it believes.

The second result of the church abandoning the wisdom of the Bible for the world's wisdom is that it embraces the moral values of the world. Nothing makes it distinct. To be sure, evangelical churches have also embraced the world's values, as we will see. But this has been for the same reason. Evangelicals have also forgotten their theology, even though they usually give extravagant lip service to the Bible's authority.

Third, the church that has forsaken the God-given wisdom of the Bible finds that its values, goals, objectives and decisions do not depend on a word from God, but on the 51 percent vote. So it does business by consensus or, failing that, by power politics. If Christians throw out a transcendent authority, an earthly authority will always take the Bible's proper place.

A final consequence of the church's abandonment of God's wisdom is that the church becomes increasingly irrelevant to nearly everything (as even Cox's *The Secular City* must seem to most people today). This irrelevance has been noted widely, and not just by perceptive evangelicals. Speaking in the early 1970s at a meeting of the Consultation on Church Union in Denver, Colorado, Peter Berger of Rutgers University pointed to a lack of authority and thus the resulting irrelevance of the old denominations.

> If there is going to be a renaissance of religion, its bearers will not be people who have been falling all over each other to be "relevant to modern men." . . . Strong eruptions of religious faith have always been marked by the appearance of people with firm, unapologetic, often uncompromising convictions—that is, by types that are the very opposite from those presently engaged in the various "relevance" operations. Put simply: Ages of faith are not marked by "dialogue" but by proclamation. . . . I would affirm that the concern for the institutional structures of the Church will be vain unless there is also a new conviction and a new authority in the Christian community.[9]

The World's Theology

The older denominations have also been secularized by adopting the world's theology. The world's theology is easy to define. It is the view that human beings are basically good, that no one is really lost and that belief in Jesus Christ is not necessary for anyone's salvation, though it may be a helpful spiritual crutch for some people.

In this approach many of the old biblical terms are retained, but they are given different meanings. Thus, *sin* does not mean rebellion against God and his righteous law, for which we are held accountable; it means ignorance or the oppression found in social structures. The way to overcome it is by social change, new laws or revolution. *Jesus* becomes not the incarnate God who died for our salvation, but rather a pattern for creative living. We are to look to Jesus as an example, but not as Savior. *Salvation* is defined as liberation from oppressive social structures. *Faith* is becoming aware of oppression and then beginning to do something about it. *Evangelism* does not mean carrying the gospel of Jesus Christ to a perishing world, but rather working through the world's power centers to overthrow injustice.

The World's Agenda

In the mainline churches the phrase "the world's agenda" is quite popular. It means that in order of priority the church's concerns should be the concerns of the world, even to the exclusion of the gospel. If the world's first priority is the alleviation of world hunger, well, that should be the church's priority too. If the problem is poverty in undeveloped Third World countries, that should be the church's problem also. Racism. Ecology. Aging. Whatever it is, it should be uppermost in the concerns of Christian people.

I do not want to suggest here that there are areas of life about which God, and therefore the church, is unconcerned. That would be a retreat to the "Christianity apart from culture" idea that I have already discussed or a surrender to a dualism that would deny the sovereignty of God over all life. These problems ought to trouble Christians. Moreover, to the extent that they have skills or opportunities to help they should do what they can to solve the problems. I am going to explore some of what might be done in the next chapter. The point I am making here is that none of these problems should be allowed to eclipse the gospel or the unique truths of Christian theology, which are far more important. If they do, Christians will have nothing of any unique value to offer to the world. Indeed, without the gospel the church will no longer even be the church, and its members will have lost the framework from which alone they can actually be useful.

The World's Methods

The final capitulation of the secular church to the world is in the area of methods. God's methods for the church are prayer and persuasion. But today in large segments of the church those methods are laughed at as being hopelessly inadequate, and what is offered up instead are power politics and money. A cartoon that appeared

in *The New Yorker* magazine years ago got it exactly right. Two Pilgrims were coming over on the *Mayflower* and one was saying, "Religious freedom is my immediate goal, but my long-range plan is to
go into real estate."

Not only are money and political power used to work at what
liberal churchmen consider to be the church's new task. In actuality,
raising money and acquiring power are equated with God's work
itself.

Here is an example. Some years ago the program agency of one
large denomination published a brochure entitled "God's Work in
God's World." Looking at the title one might think that it would be
a report on what was being done in evangelism, social services, the
mission field, the building of new churches or such things. Opening
it, one found in bold type the words "The Good News." At that point
a reader might imagine the report to have something to do with the
gospel. Yet what was this "good news"? It was that the results of a
special emergency appeal had "provided the first increase" in general mission receipts in several years. In other words, the "gospel" was
that the church had received more money recently. The brochure
then went on to show what could be done with the money. It said
that these new dollars "provided the capacity to increase the over-
seas missionary force by twenty-four persons." That sounded good.
But if one read carefully, it did not say that the missionary force *was*
increased by twenty-four persons, only that there was now enough
money to do it if those in charge would like to. But they did not. That
year the total missionary force declined, just as it had the year before
and has done since. At the time the brochure was published the
missionary force was only 17 percent of what it had been some years
earlier.

What about evangelicals? As I have discussed the various options
to the Christianity and culture question I have tried to show how in
each case some evangelicals have bought into that approach. They
have embraced the goal of "Christ over culture" by trying to impose
their vision of the just society on others by legislation. They have
embraced the "Christ apart from culture" option by trying to escape

their own secular environment. Can it be that evangelicals, who have always opposed liberalism and its methods, have bought into the "Christ the servant of culture" option too? Yes, they have, in the sense that they have fixed their eyes on a worldly kingdom and have made power and money their weapons of choice for winning it.

How else are we to explain the emphasis so many evangelical churches and organizations place on money? Or that evangelicals support a National Association of Evangelicals lobby in Washington, D.C.? Or that they have created social action groups to advance specific evangelical legislation? Or that many pastors tone down the hard edges of biblical truth in order to attract greater numbers of people to their services?

Christ and the Two Cities

It is time to talk about the fourth option. But here we have to leave the "Christ . . . culture" way of speaking and speak instead about "Christ *and* the two cities," because that is what is involved, after all. "Christ and . . ." means that God is sovereign over the city of man as well as the church and that Christians belong to both spheres— but as Christians. They can have worldly occupations and involve themselves with worldly concerns, but they should never do this uncritically or forget what it should mean to be a Christian man or woman in those areas.

Where do we see this answer to the Christianity and culture question? We see it as a fruit of the Reformation. Michael Scott Horton, in *Beyond Culture Wars,* highlights this important Reformation insight.

> The reformers avoided [two] tendencies: on the one hand, to confuse the two kingdoms (Rome) and, on the other, to divorce the two kingdoms and reject any Christian involvement in the kingdom of culture (Anabaptists). Instead, they insisted that Christians should be involved in the world. They should neither seek to escape it, like the monks, whose lives were often more "worldly" than the world, nor seek to rule it, like the popes, whose own houses were not quite in order. Every believer is a "priest" before

God, and each person (believer *and* unbeliever) has been given a vocation or calling, by virtue of creation, to participate in some way in culture. We are social beings, created to enjoy each other's company, whether Christian or non-Christian. Redemption does not change our participation in culture; rather, it changes *us* and, therefore, the character of our involvement. Separation from the world is not physical, according to the reformers; rather, it is a matter of divorcing our dependence on the things of this world: its vanity and rejection or perversion of things heavenly. Luther and Calvin said that the calling of the magistrate or public official was "one of the noblest" (Calvin), inasmuch as it serves the society so well.[10]

Because of this outlook Protestants were able to encourage each other and their children to pursue secular vocations, if that was their calling from God, not as a second-rate vocation—inferior to a church vocation—but as a work in which they could fully serve God and others. But carefully! It was by doing this, not by identifying Christ with culture or by trying to escape the culture, that they effected the profound social changes that we rightly associate with the Protestant Reformation.

It is important to see that the Reformers' assessment of culture and a believer's proper involvement in it was based on theological understandings. There were three key doctrinal ingredients, as Horton points out.

The first ingredient was the doctrine of creation, which affirms the essential goodness of the world. When God created the physical universe he declared at each stage of creation, "It is good." God established families by giving the first woman to the first man and encouraging the couple to "be fruitful and multiply." He endorsed secular vocations by placing Adam and Eve in a beautiful garden with meaningful work to do. They were given management responsibilities, because they were to take care of the garden, and they had what we would call scientific tasks, because they were to classify and name the animals, which was not an easy thing to do.

Even after the Fall God called people to be kings and other government officials. He gave laws for the division of the land among the families of Israel so that the people could settle down and raise crops. When the tabernacle was constructed God gave skills to design and create beautiful things to Bezalel and Oholiab, who were Israel's leading artisans (Ex 35:30—36:1). God endorsed the work of the Hebrew midwives (Ex 1:20-21), a valid secular occupation. This did not only involve God's people. He raised up secular rulers such as Cyrus, who released the people of Israel to return home following their Babylonian exile.

The second ingredient was the doctrine of the Fall, which explains why, even though creation and secular life have been created by God and retain great value so that virtue, truth and beauty can be advanced even by unbelievers, the secular world is not to be embraced uncritically. It is still a fallen world, and because it is fallen there will never be any possibility of creating a perfect society or utopia—even when Christians are attempting it. The great example and warning here is earthly Jerusalem, which, although it was the city of God's Old Testament people, was nevertheless a corrupt earthly city that was judged in time just as the other cities and nations have been and are being judged.

With appropriate humility the Reformers acknowledged that God's people also participate in the Fall in that they themselves have a corrupt, sinful and deceptive nature. So even when they participate in secular affairs with a view to doing good, they must acknowledge that they do not have all the answers, that secular people also have important insights and skills to offer, perhaps better than their own, and that Christians sometimes wrongly advance their own selfish concerns to the hurt of other people and need to be reproved and corrected for such errors.

Third, the Reformers drew from the Bible's teaching about redemption to form their understanding of the Christ-and-culture question. This meant not only personal redemption from sin's penalty and power, which evangelicals rightly insist on today, but also a restoration of society at the end of time when a new heaven and a new earth, including a new Holy City, the new Jerusalem, will be created (Rev 21—22). The Reformers did not see this as something to be realized in history now, as if the efforts of God's people will culminate in their creating the new Jerusalem on earth. But a vision of the heavenly city gave them ideals for what might be done now and, at any rate, encouraged them to keep working optimistically, knowing that God guarantees that the end result will be good and not evil.

The result of the Reformation answer to the Christ-and-culture question was thus both responsibility and realism. It was responsibility to be in the world and work responsibly for its improvement. But at the same time it was also a realistic understanding that the world will remain sinful and corrupt until God's final restoration of all things.

Citizens of Two Kingdoms

The bottom line of what I have been arguing in this chapter is that Christians are citizens of two kingdoms, the kingdom of this world and the kingdom of our Lord Jesus Christ, and they have responsibilities in each. Those responsibilities are not on an equal plane. Christians are citizens of God's kingdom first, which means that they will enter the secular world as Christians and work for its good as Christians both should and can, but they should not enter the Christian world as unbelievers, attempting to modify the church to accommodate the world's concerns. Nevertheless, they will be part of the world in which God has placed them.

But what are they to do practically? Christians have some idea of what government, life and culture might look like from a Christian point of view. How do they go about moving toward this better world if the solution is not merely trying to impose their vision of the just society on others by power legislation? As a starting point, I suggest the following three priorities.

Participation

In the first place, Christians need to participate in secular life rather than merely shoot from the sidelines at secular people and at what secular people are doing. In other words, we must participate in man's city—but in the right way.

One of the arguments Michael Horton makes in *Beyond Culture Wars* is that at this moment in history evangelicals have little to offer in the cultural battles, first, because they have not participated in culture enough for their views about it to be taken seriously and, second, because they do not know the Bible or their own theology well enough to be able to give a distinctly Christian contribution if they did. All they can do is be negative. They are not making their own positive contributions.

It was not always this way. We need to remember that in the past America's great academic centers, such as Harvard, Yale, Dartmouth, Brown, Princeton and other schools, were established by orthodox Christians. Many, though not all, of America's founding fathers had Christian commitments and contributed to the formation of the American democratic experiment out of a biblical world and life view. Thinking back to Europe, we remember that the Reformation faith gave content and motivation to such cultural giants as Johann Sebastian Bach, George Frederick Handel, Rembrandt, John Donne, John Milton, Sir Isaac Newton and others. Evangelicals are just not producing people of their caliber today.

Until we produce our own quality art, our hysterical denunciations of what is admittedly "artistic trash" will fall on deaf ears. Until we show how Christians in government can and should function, being concerned not just for our rights and privileges but for the good of all and with justice for all, we will rightly be ignored. As Horton says, "If we have not paid our dues by years of making positive contributions to culture, we simply do not have the cultural clout to pontificate about cultural crises."[11] Only by participating in such cultural endeavors and thus by modeling what we believe can and should be done will we gain a hearing and actually begin to be effective.

Persuasion

The second thing evangelicals need to learn if they are to be effective in moving the world in a more righteous direction is the art of persuasion. There are two parts to this. First, evangelicals must learn to think about the issues, really think about them. Second, they must learn the art of persuasion itself.

Evangelicals are not great thinkers. To be sure, the current age is not a thinking age even for non-Christians. In fact, I have argued in *Mind Renewal in a Mindless Age*[12] that these are exceedingly mindless times and that this is due primarily to television. Television does not operate by rational thought but by images, which means that not only does it not encourage thought in those who watch it but that it actually helps to destroy rational processes. As a result, most people become susceptible to mere manipulation not only in buying commercial products (which they usually do not need) but also in trying to fulfill such serious duties as voting in national elections. Politics at the highest level has become not a politics of positions and arguments but mere attempts to present the candidate as a nicer guy than his or her opponent.

All of this is true. Nevertheless, there are those at the top of our society who are manipulators rather than the manipulated, thinkers rather than the mindless hordes, and these are the leaders that Christian thinkers must engage. It is here the battle must be won, if it is to be won, and it must be won by arguments.

Moreover, our arguments must be formed by genuinely *Christian* thinking. A few years ago the board and staff of the Bible Study Hour, the radio and conference ministry in which I am engaged, met to work out a focus for the ministry. We knew what programs we were conducting. But we met to ask what it was that we were really hoping to accomplish and what we might want to do differently to achieve those goals and not some other ends. At the end of a day and a half of careful self-examination we expressed our goal as "teaching people to think and act biblically." Those words said that although we are concerned with right action, we recognize that right thinking comes before right action. Furthermore, because we are Christians we also recognize that right thinking must be biblical, that is, informed by biblical truths and controlled by biblical categories.

In Romans 12:1-2, at the start of the application section of Paul's great letter to the Romans, there is an important reference to renewal. The verses say, "Therefore, I urge you, brothers, in view of God's mercy, to offer your bodies as living sacrifices, holy and pleasing to God—this is your spiritual act of worship. Do not conform any longer to the pattern of this world, but be transformed by the *renewing of your mind*. Then you will be able to test and approve what God's will is—his good, pleasing and perfect will." In this important passage renewal is the key. But it begins with the renewal of our minds, and this means that it begins with the individual believer first of all. The Christian must become a person who thinks as God thinks because he or she has a deep and perceptive knowledge of the Bible in which the mind of God is disclosed.

The apostle had a renewed mind himself. So he described his battle with the world in these terms: "Though we live in the world, we do not wage war as the world does. The weapons we fight with are not the weapons of the world. On the contrary, they have divine power to demolish strongholds. We demolish arguments and every pretension that sets itself up against the knowledge of God, and we take captive every thought to make it obedient to Christ" (2 Cor 10:3-5). The battle in which the apostle Paul saw himself engaged was not a battle for political power by which he hoped to gain his objectives, but a battle of arguments. It was a battle of ideas that he knew would in time change the world. Paul thought in a Christian way, and he wanted to persuade others to think along Christian lines too.

Here is an example from the Reformation period. In 1524, seven years after Martin Luther had nailed his Ninety-Five Theses to the door of the Castle Church at Wittenberg, the farmers of Germany rebelled against their feudal lords in what became known as the Peasants' War (1524-1526). It began near Schaffhausen, where Hans Müller, acting on a suggestion from Thomas Münzer, formed the peasants into an "Evangelical Brotherhood" pledged to emancipate the farmers. By the end of that year some thirty thousand farmers were in arms in southern Germany, refusing to pay state taxes, church tithes or feudal dues. In March 1525 they drafted and circulated widely a document called the "Twelve Articles," in which they claimed the right to choose their own pastors, pay only just tithes, be considered as free men rather than serfs, enjoy fair rents, and other such reasonable demands. They were also favorable to the Reformation and opposed to the Roman Catholic Church.

The peasants sent a copy of the articles to Luther, fully expecting his support. And, indeed, Luther's first response was sympathetic. Luther acknowledged the injustices about which the farmers were in arms and blamed the rulers of both state and church for their responsibility. "We have no one on earth to thank for this mischievous rebellion except you, princes and lords, and especially you blind bishops. . . . You do nothing but flay and rob your subjects, in order that you may lead a life of splendor and pride, until the poor common people can bear it no longer."[13]

But Luther did not endorse the rebellion, even though the majority of its goals coincided with those of the Reformation. And later, when hundreds of monasteries were sacked and many cities overrun, Luther denounced the violence in characteristically fierce and uncompromising terms.

Why did he react this way, when nearly everyone, the peasants above all, expected him to side with them? Luther's justified fear of anarchy was one strong reason. Another was his belief that God had established the authority of princes. To rebel against the powers that exist is to rebel against God, he said. But Luther also knew that the power of the sword has not been given either to the church or to the individual Christian, and he was aware that our weapons are not the weapons of this world and that our arguments alone have power "to demolish strongholds" (2 Cor 10:4).

According to Luther, the Reformation would proceed *non vi, sed verbo*—not by force, but by the power of God's Word. And so it did! The Peasants' War was a tragic episode in the Reformation period. More lives were lost in that war in Germany than in any tumult prior to the Thirty Years' War. Some 130,000 farmers died in battle or afterward as a result of retaliatory punishments. Germany was impoverished. The Reformation itself almost perished. But it did not, because it was moving forward by the power of the Word of God and persuasion, as God blessed the teaching and influence of the Reformers.

Prayer

Yet when all is said, it is not enough for evangelicals merely to participate in the world's affairs and attempt to persuade non-Christians of a right and better way. We must also be people of prayer since we know that apart from God's intervention the world will neither understand nor heed what we are saying.

We are not competing on a level playing field, to use a modern idiom. We are fighting for spiritual realities, and the world is blind to these truths. Moreover, the world is hostile to God, and as a result it is also hostile to those who represent him in this world. Jesus said, "If you belonged to the world, it would love you as its own. As it is, you do not belong to the world, but I have chosen you out of the world. That is why the world hates you. Remember the words I spoke to you: 'No servant is greater than his master.' If they persecuted me, they will persecute you also" (Jn 15:19-20). In that day the religious power of Israel and the secular power of Rome combined to have Jesus executed, and all he had done was to speak the truth among them.

Gene Edward Veith, dean of the School of Arts and Sciences at Concordia University, Wisconsin, thinks that in the days ahead Christians are going to experience more and more hardship and even persecution. In the postmodern world into which we are moving

> Christians must not . . . expect to fare particularly well. . . . Christians will be excoriated for "thinking they have the only truth." They will be condemned for their intolerance, for "trying to force their beliefs on everybody else." Christians can expect to be excluded from postmodernists' invocations of tolerance and pluralism. As the culture becomes more and more lawless and brutal, Christians may even taste persecution. The church may or may not grow in such a climate.

This sounds discouraging, but Veith remains optimistic because, as he says, "the church of Jesus Christ cannot be overcome by the gates of hell, much less by a culture (Matt. 16:18)."[14]

When Jesus was about to be taken from the world he prayed for all who should believe on him, that they would stand for the truth, as he did, and live as he did in the world. That is the most important thing, after all, that we should be like Jesus Christ. If we are, there will be persecutions. We will lose battles. But we will win some too, and when that happens the world will look on and occasionally confess that we were right.

8
How We Might
Move Forward

AT THE END OF THE LAST CHAPTER I suggested three important principles for Christians who would like to make a significant difference for God in this world: participation, persuasion and prayer. First, Christians must begin by a real side-by-side participation with non-Christians who are working in the same area, not merely shooting at secular people from the sidelines as evangelicals tend to do. They must actually be doing the job and doing it rightly. They must be models of what they recommend. Second, while they have rolled up their sleeves and become engaged in the work with secular people, they must use the only two weapons believers have been given, namely, persuasion and prayer. Christians must try to win people to a right course of action and away from wrong action by arguments, not by legislation, and they must pray for God's blessing on their efforts, knowing that even the best arguments will be successful only as God opens the minds and hearts of other people to receive them.

But where do we go from here? In this chapter I want to offer some suggestions about how we might proceed in several key areas. These are not exhaustive, and the suggestions are only a beginning. I am not a legislator or a specialist in any of these areas. But the suggestions flow from what I have been saying and indicate how Christians might be used for good as citizens of both Christian and secular worlds.

Some Necessary Guidelines

But we need some guidelines even here because it is possible to do the things I have mentioned—participate, attempt to persuade and pray—and still proceed wrongly and thus ineffectively in social areas. So here are four guidelines to go with the initial three principles.

First, we must stand for what is right rather than contend only for our personal advantage. We live in an age when it is difficult to argue for what is right as opposed to what is wrong, because in an age of relativism no one believes in absolutes, and principles, which have to do with what is right, are absolutes. At one time politics was the forum in which leaders contended for the right by argument. But what has happened today is that it has become an arena in which each block of the electorate is fighting for its "rights," which is a very different matter from fighting for what is *right*. Every contemporary issue is pictured as some group's rights. Thus, in a practical sense, personal rights become the only absolutes.

There are certain basic human rights, of course. At least in terms of the American Constitution we recognize the rights to "life, liberty and the pursuit of happiness," among others. But suppose the nineteenth-century struggle for the abolition of slavery were fought on the basis of rights alone, as some did try to fight it. It would not have been won, because the slave owners would have insisted on their rights to private property, that is, the slaves. They had the right to manage their plantations as they saw fit, with no interference from the government. They had the rights of citizens; the slaves had no citizen rights. It was only because the abolitionists insisted on the principle that human beings are all made in the image of God and therefore are and ought to remain free that they succeeded.

A similar situation exists in the battle against abortion today. This is an important battle. But if it is to be won, it will have to be on the basis of the broad principles that the fetus is a genuine human being and that aborting it is murder, and is wrong. If the arguments are not along these lines, opposition to abortion will seem to be only the pet prejudice of a few narrowly religious people who want to impose their ideas on others and take away their "rights."

Second, we must be guided by truth rather than by mere pragmatism. Argument from pragmatism is nearly universal today, as it must be once absolutes are thrown out. "If it works, it must be right" is the attitude. Or sometimes, which is even worse: "If it can be done, we should do it."

Here Christians must be guided by truth rather than by pragmatism, and this means that we must do careful homework on the issues so that we have a sober understanding of what the truth is. It also means that we will have to work largely behind the scenes in arguing for and devising public policy, not in the visible popular arena of the media, particularly television. Communication on television does not work by a careful discussion of ideas but by images and the emotional response they generate. There may be places for this tool at a late stage in a particular cultural battle, but it must be preceded by thoughtfully working out a right position on the issues. This is something that in our time the great majority of evangelicals have been too emotional, too impatient or perhaps even too inept to accomplish.

Third, we must work for the well-being of all people and not just those of our own group. During the nineteenth century those who opposed slavery had little to gain personally, so it was evident that they were working for the good of others and not merely for their own advantages. Evangelicals have not done as well in this area recently, or at least we have not been perceived to be doing so. We are seen as trying to impose our own moral code on everyone else, criminalizing any behavior with which we disagree. We are perceived as people wanting to make America a nice place only for ourselves. This is a sure formula for the defeat of what we stand for.

On the other hand, if we can work for the good of all people, even if they are radically different from ourselves and do not think as we do, and actually be seen as doing it, then there is a chance for us to advance our now greatly improved agenda. Don E. Eberly, a former congressional and White House staff person, has written a helpful book entitled *Restoring the Good Society*, in which he argues this point.

If the Christian faith becomes just another organized interest group—determined to take over political parties and drive through its own narrowly defined legislative agenda—neither its political power nor its spiritual influence in the culture will grow. If, however, religious conservatives are committed to a holistic social and moral vision for America—one that offers real solutions to the lack of honesty and integrity in politics, seeks to serve the common good of all humankind by offering sound ideas across a spectrum of concerns, and promotes practical ideas for strengthening homes, rebuilding schools, and restoring neighborhoods—then it could offer the leadership a society needs and wants.[1]

One way to move forward in this area and avoid merely seeking the advantage of our own group is to be concerned with justice, since justice by its very definition must be justice for all. Eberly says rightly, "When public action is committed to a pursuit of justice, it is guided by a higher commitment than simply winning a victory for one's own side. . . . Using justice as a frame of reference in public debate can safeguard activists from views and appeals that appear narrow and self-seeking."[2] If Christians will fight for what they regard as right, they will be fighting at least as much for the rights of others as for themselves.

It would do a great deal for the cause of Christian conservatives if some of them would do battle on behalf of those with whom they disagree. Homosexuals, for instance. Or abortion doctors. They could condemn harassment of both groups and fight discrimination against homosexuals in jobs and housing, just for starters.

Fourth, we must be humble in our struggles because others may actually be right and we may be wrong. One of the great dangers to which we Christians are vulnerable is pride. We easily assume that only our consciences have been enlightened and that we alone have the right answers. We do not. Nor, although we have the Word of God to guide us, do we always listen to it and do what it says. We need forgiveness for having used the Bible only to advance our own cause. And we need to listen to others, particularly well-informed non-Christians, to learn what they may know.

Do you want to start a crusade? Fine! We need a few. But if you do, be sure that the position you take is biblical and that you are not just serving yourself or trying to enhance your own crusading reputation.

Abortion: The Right to Life

For evangelicals the greatest moral issue of our day is abortion. This may or may not actually be the greatest issue. Yet it is certainly a real issue because it deals with life and death and the rights, if they are rights, of the smallest and most vulnerable members of the human race, and because it has captured the attention of Christians across a broad spectrum of America's religious life. Thus, evangelical Christians, Roman Catholics and others have joined hands to fight abortion.

Most evangelicals are dismayed that the current administration in Washington favors the right of abortion on demand and is even willing to pay for it out of taxes contributed to a new national health service. But the issue must not be obscured by whether or not taxes are being used to pay for abortions. How the government uses my money may be an emotional issue that can be exploited to raise my indignation and perhaps get me to give money to an antiabortion campaign. But it is not the issue. Taxes are used to pay for all sorts of things, and rightly. The issue is whether abortion itself is right. Evangelicals believe that abortion is wrong, because the fetus is not "tissue," as the proabortion forces want people to think of it, but is actually a tiny human being. We believe abortion is wrong because it is murder and because we believe that God will not hold America guiltless for the murder of more than a million and a half babies every year by this means.

What are we to do about it? We must protest, of course, explaining our position and arguing our case. Arguments pointing to brain waves in the unborn even in the earliest months of pregnancy are useful, as are pictures of what the fetus actually looks like in these early months and even weeks—a true baby with hands and fingers, arms and toes.

It is also helpful to argue from history, showing perhaps from the horrors of the Nazi period what can happen when any one group of society is considered to be "nonhuman" or as somehow coming short of what we begin to call "rightful" or "normal" human life. If Jews can be considered nonhuman, that is, undeserving of the rights accorded to all others, then it is only a step from killing Jews to killing off the old, the disabled, mentally retarded persons or any others that it is too much trouble and expense to care for. The late Francis Schaeffer and former surgeon general of the United States C. Everett Koop argued this case forcefully in the book and movie series *Whatever Happened to the Human Race?*[3]

And that leads to a historical observation. Prior to that film series and the resulting discussion very little about abortion appeared in the media except from the point of view of the so-called rights of the woman who was pregnant. But as a thoughtful case against abortion began to be made, by Catholics as well as evangelicals, I noticed that the way abortion was referred to began to change. Now instead of hearing only of the rights of the mother, we began to hear of "pro-life" as well as "prochoice" arguments. I thought at that time that Christians working together were actually beginning to turn the tide and had a chance of reversing America's moral slide in this area. Yet that is not the case today. At the present moment in American life the pendulum has swung back in the other direction, and the pro-life position is increasingly presented as only the narrow prejudice of the Religious Right.

What has happened? Part of the problem, a large part, may be that the world prefers its own convenience to what is right. The secular world is a hotbed of self-serving injustice, after all. But there may be more to the change in climate than this. The tactics of evangelicals may actually be the chief reason for the failure of their cause.

What is the chief tactic being employed by evangelicals in the fight against abortion today? A lot may be going on behind the scenes that we do not easily see. I personally believe that there is. But so far as what is seen is concerned, the chief tactic is obviously the blockading of abortion clinics and other forms of confrontation that have at times degenerated into violation of others' civil rights.

The problem here is that the zeal of the antiabortionists has led them to use the world's methodology—sit-ins and pressure tactics— rather than the arts of persuasion and prayer, which have been given to us by God, as I wrote earlier. Crusaders will argue that there is no time for thoughtful persuasion and prayer. Babies are being killed. Something must be done. But what the crusaders fail to see is that if we use the methods of the world rather than those given to us by God, the world will use them against us since it is far better at using its own methods than we are.

What happens when Christians decide to picket an abortion clinic? As long as the protest is peaceful and there is no injunction against the demonstration, very little happens. Neither the newspapers nor television report on peaceful attempts to persuade women about to enter the clinic that what they are actually about to do is to murder their baby and that other options are available from a caring community. But as soon as an injunction is obtained, when police arrive and the protesters who will not peaceably disperse are loaded into police vans to be taken away for arraignment, the cameras roll and pictures of stubborn, sometimes yelling and abusive demonstrators appear on the six o'clock news. Instead of appearing as reasonable, caring people who have a legitimate position to argue, we appear instead as religious fanatics who want to take away other people's rights. It is unfair, but that is nevertheless what happens. And the advantage in the battle shifts to the other side.

If we care about abortion, as we should, we need to explain that the only view of humankind that protects us from exploitation by tyrannical rulers or others who do not care about us and are interested only in themselves is that we are made in the image of God and are therefore valuable to God. Even the unborn are valuable. We must show that disenfranchising the unborn child is no different from the once-popular defense of slavery by calling blacks less than human, or the murder of Jews by calling them a threat to society. We must say that we are all made in the image of God, even people we don't like and with whom we disagree, and that no one should be destroyed for anyone's convenience, even that of an unborn child's mother.

The Cities: Who Would Want to Live There?

I do not need to prove the accelerating urbanization of the world in this century. At the time of Jesus Christ there were only about 250 million people in the world, about equal to the current population of the United States. It took fifteen hundred years for that to double to one-half billion at the time of the Protestant Reformation. It doubled again by the end of the eighteenth century, to one billion in three hundred years. By the start of the twentieth century, one hundred years later, it was two billion. Today there are four and a half billion people. By the end of this century, that is, in slightly more than one additional decade, the population of the world is expected to reach six billion. The vast majority of these new people will live in the world's cities.

Two hundred years ago only 2.5 percent of the world's population lived in cities. The figure was 40 percent by 1970. Today it is almost half, and it is projected to reach a startling 90 percent by the year 2000.

Think of the cities. How many of the world's cities do you suppose have more than a million inhabitants? The answer to that question is 175. Twenty-nine of these are in the United States, but the United States does not have the largest number of these megacities. China and Russia have more cities with over a million persons than all other countries. The fastest-growing cities in the world are in Latin America. Mexico City, now the largest city in the world, has twenty million residents. By the year 2000, India will have twenty cities with twenty million residents. In America 70 percent of our citizens now live in urban areas.

What does that say about the proper focus for Christian witness today? What does it suggest for our mission priorities? And what about the social needs of the cities? What about drugs, runaway crime, urban blight, the demise of city families and the plight of the poor?

I suggest that the starting point here is the "participation" I put forward earlier as one of the principles that should guide Christians in their concern for today's world. For too long evangelicals in particular have been guilty of what has been called "white flight." We have moved from the action, where we have been needed, to where it is nice! Because of our suburban/rural orientation, we have carried the same pattern over into our approach to world missions. We have focused on the remotest areas, while the people in those areas have been leaving them and streaming into the metropolitan environments. I would argue that the greatest challenge to a serious Christian witness today is to establish an evangelical presence in the world's cities.

Ronald J. Sider, an associate professor of theology at Eastern Baptist Theological Seminary in Philadelphia, says that it should happen in our own country first. He puts it in stark terms: "Evangelicals must reverse the continuing evangelical flight from the cities. . . . Tens of thousands of evangelicals ought to move back into the city. . . . If one percent of evangelicals living outside the inner city had the faith and courage to move in town, evangelicals would fundamentally alter the history of urban America."[4]

So here is an outline of a plan.

We Must Live in the Cities

The first and most obvious step for dealing with the problem of our cities is to get Christians to stay in or move back to them, as I have indicated. Not every Christian needs to live in our cities, but far more should live in them than do now. They should live in them as their mission field of choice.

How many should there be? It is difficult to say. In Nehemiah's day, when Israel's economy was largely agricultural, the proposed figure for repopulating Jerusalem was one in ten. These were the city dwellers, plus others who lived in the cities round about (Neh 11:1). In America in our day, where the economy is industrial and service-based rather than agricultural, 50 percent of the general population lives in cities. That suggests that at least 50 percent of the Christian population should also. But since this percentage is going up—estimates of 90 percent by the year 2000—and since we want to be ahead of the times rather than lagging behind them, we should probably lead the way with an even higher percentage of Christians relocating to the urban areas. Many thousands should move there.

Sadly, in places where evangelicals have in some measure developed a concern for the cities they have tended only to import programs from the suburbs, staffing them with people who do not live in the city or understand city problems. And when the job is done, perhaps only on a part-time basis, these admittedly well-meaning people escape back to the suburbs where they suppose themselves to be safe and where life is comfortable.

That is not good enough. As a city dweller myself, I can say that I appreciate what people who do not live in the city might offer—money, for example, or, better yet, partnerships between wealthy suburban churches and struggling inner-city parishes. But that is only help around the edges. It does not go to the heart of what is needed.

Let me give one illustration of what needs to happen on a large scale. One of my associates, the missions pastor of Tenth Presbyterian Church in Philadelphia, located his family on a narrow inner-city street about four blocks from the church. It was a terrible place to live. The houses were falling apart. The street and sidewalks were torn up. Garbage was thrown about. There was a vacant lot where one small row house used to stand that had become a dumping place for whatever the people who lived there didn't want—old refrigerators, tires, parts of cars and other refuse. To top it off, a few doors from the end of the street there was a drug dealer who sold to people who would drive down the street just long enough to load up on their stimulant of choice.

My associate and his wife began by renovating their own home, starting from the wall studs outward and doing most of the work themselves. To put that much effort into a house in the neighborhood attracted the attention of their neighbors and was favorably received. This family, particularly the wife of my associate, began to get to know the neighbors and within a short time had organized a block community. They began to clean up the street and to investigate what help they might have from the city. At their request the city repaved the street and repoured the sidewalks. Next they got the local community hospital, which was anxious for good community relations, to swing by twice a week to collect their garbage—a better and more frequent collection than I receive in a better part of the city just several blocks away. They cleaned up the vacant lot, turning it into a playground for their children, and they brought pressure on the drug dealer to stop selling drugs or at least to move his retail business elsewhere.

The last I heard the drug dealer was driving around the neighborhood in a car sporting a bumper sticker that said: "Just say no!" For a while, as long as it was possible, Tenth Presbyterian Church expected all of its staff to live within the city's bounds.

We Must Be Organized as Christians in the Cities

This example of city living leads to a second step in my plan: the organization of people, particularly Christians, to be a genuine city presence and do good. Organization is the key word here. For it is not enough merely to have Christians living in the city, as many undoubtedly do already. They must also know each other, meet together often in formal and informal ways, talk about the cities' problems and what might be done, and actually work together to help others.

In my judgment the most effective way of doing this is by small Bible study fellowship groups encouraged by city churches but allowed to develop their own individual concerns and outreach. Tenth Presbyterian Church has between eighty and a hundred of these groups at any given time. One reasonable goal might be the development of an organized Christian presence in each block of each major city in America. Here is an example.

E. V. Hill is the pastor of the Mount Zion Missionary Baptist Church in Los Angeles and one of the great urban leaders of our time. Before he entered the ministry he lived in Texas, where he was a ward leader for the Democratic party. His assignment was to get out the vote for Democratic candidates, and his chief strategy for doing this was to have a block captain for each block of his ward. On election days the block captains were to contact each resident of their blocks to make sure they voted. When Hill came to Los Angeles he asked himself why he should not do the same for the kingdom of God, if he had done it for the Democrats. Why not have a Christian block captain for every block of Los Angeles? Does that sound crazy? Impossible?

It is not as absurd as you might think. The city of Los Angeles has about 9,000 blocks. In E. V. Hill's area of the city, south central Los Angeles, the number is 3,100. That is what Dr. Hill's church tackled. When I first heard him tell about this goal they had already established a Christian presence in 1,900 blocks of their area.

How many blocks are in the immediate area of Tenth Presbyterian Church in Philadelphia? The number is not even that overwhelming. In fact, it is not overwhelming at all. Our immediate neighborhood is bounded by Market Street on the north and South Street on the south. Starting at Broad Street, which divides Center City in two, and going westward toward the Schuylkill River, the area in which we are located, there are just 74 blocks. If the area is extended eastward toward the Delaware River, that is, taking in the entire Center City residential area east to west, there are only 87 more. Only 161 blocks in Center City! It should not be too difficult to have a Christian presence in every block of that small area.

Can it be done? Of course. Can it be done in other U.S. cities? Yes, in them too. Would the effort be felt? I am sure it would.

Hill tells of what happened in Los Angeles on one occasion. One man had been so put off by the captain of the block in which he lived—she was always inviting him to church and other religious meetings—that he decided to move. He decided to move the whole way across Los Angeles. The truck came. He loaded up his possessions. His block captain came out to say goodby. The truck started off. But as soon as he was gone, the block captain went back into the house, got out the directory of the Mount Zion block captains in Los Angeles, found the person in charge of the block to which her offended neighbor was moving, and when he got to his new area there was the new block community captain standing on the street in front of his new home to welcome him and invite him to church.

His comment was a classic. He said, "My God, they're everywhere." That should be our goal—to be a visible presence everywhere in the cities.

We Must Be a Community in the Cities

It is not enough just to be in the cities and organized, of course. The world can do that. The third requirement is that we must be a Christian community. It is only as a community that we can model what we want. It must be Christian, because we want to model the unique qualities of life that being a Christian brings. The great twentieth-century poet T. S. Eliot asked:

> When the Stranger says, "What is the meaning of this city? Do you huddle close together because you love each other?" What will you answer? "We all dwell together to make money from each other"? or "This is a community"? (Chorus from "The Rock")

Anthony T. Evans is a successful black pastor in Dallas, Texas. He is an excellent Bible expositor, and his goal is to have the great population centers of America experience spiritual renewal. Evans publishes a monthly newsletter called *The Urban Alternative* in which there appeared an article entitled "10 Steps to Urban Renewal." It mentioned sound Bible teaching, rejection of government dependence, use of spiritual gifts, the discipling of converts and other such things. One important requirement, according to Evans, is to become a community. He wrote, "The church is first and foremost a spiritual family, a community. That's why the Bible refers to the church as a 'household of faith,' 'family of God' and 'brothers and sisters.' It's meant to function as a family, model family life, and care for the families it encompasses."[5]

The church can do that as no other organization can—not businesses, not schools, not the centers of entertainment or social life, not government or city agencies. Only the church! Besides, churches have an extraordinary opportunity to model community at a time when other forms of community are breaking down. There is no better place than the fellowship of Christians for embracing those suffering from ruptured marriages, fractured homes and other broken relationships.

What makes a community? A community holds together only by some higher allegiance or priority, and the only adequate base for real brotherhood or community among people is devotion to God. Without this people soon become little more than competing or warring factions. Cyril J. Barber put it well in a book on Nehemiah and the reforms he brought to the city of Jerusalem six centuries before Christ.

> A strong religious commitment is essential if a democratic form of administration is to succeed. Without adequate spiritual values it is hard, if not impossible, to retain the idea of obligation and responsibility. Individualism cannot long be held in check by the concept of a calling embodying good works and self-restraint. When this control is weakened, legislation takes the place of spiritual convictions and becomes the foundation of the community. And with the increase in legislation there is a corresponding increase in bureaucracy with a minimizing of efficiency and a diminution of personal worth.[6]

If Christians have a commitment that goes beyond mere individualism—and they should—they can model Christian communities in a church setting. Moreover, if they can do it there, they can begin to model it in other environments, as Christians in business show what it is to have a Christ-centered business, Christians in education show what it is to educate in a Christian way, politicians act as Christian politicians, and so on in all the professions.

We Must Have a Vision for the Cities

This leads to the fourth necessary ingredient for an effective Christian impact on the city. We must have a vision for what a city can and should be. Sadly, up to this point evangelicals have not provided our culture with much of a vision for anything. Colonel V. Doner, in a book entitled *The Samaritan Strategy: A New Agenda for Christian Activism,* claims that this was the specific failure of the Christian Right in the 1980s. It was able to marshal effective support for a few select causes, such as the fights against abortion and pornography. But it had no vision for the kind of society we should want to see established. Thus, the Christian Right came to be seen as a movement only for Christian interests as well as a threat to people who had even slightly different goals. Doner wrote,

> To many, it appeared that all the Christian Right had to offer was a negative reactionary collage of "don'ts" rather than a comprehensive and constructive agenda of "do's." Worse yet, most Christians could not understand how all the issues connected to each other. . . . Without a clear Christian worldview, Christians were unable to act in unison behind a comprehensive and clearly understood agenda.[7]

That carefully thought out and well-articulated Christian worldview has not yet emerged overall, and it has certainly not emerged as a vision for our nation's cities. Developing such a vision should be a primary objective for thinking evangelical Christians in our time.

And while we are working on it we should not think that the world is utterly opposed to us. Society is often less hostile than we think. Not long ago the Gallup Poll organization conducted a survey of residents of cities with populations that exceed fifty thousand, asking what organizations they perceived as trying hardest to improve city life. There were all kinds of suggestions: the mayor, city council, local newspapers, local businesses, neighborhood groups, the chamber of commerce, banks, service clubs, builders, almost anything you can think of. Do you know what group led the list? The local churches! They received 48 percent of the vote, ahead even of the mayor, who came second with only 39 percent. So let us not be negative. The world may yet be waiting to see what Christians can do.

Pornography: The Trash Avalanche
This country has a strong and valuable tradition of the right of free speech and free expression, something we do not want to lose. We

do not want to take away people's right to express their opinions in print or by graphic media. But no freedom is utterly without limits. So when we deal with pornography we need to say that freedom to print sexually obscene material stops at the point at which it harms others.

And it does! Defenders of the pornography industry deny this, of course, just as makers of cigarettes deny that cigarettes cause lung cancer, emphysema and other lung-related illnesses. But in this case, it is our job to show that pornography really is harmful. In other words, we need to document our case. We need to remind people that Ted Bundy, who in 1989 was executed for multiple serial murders of young women in Florida and elsewhere, said on death row that the chief contributing influence to his violent murderous course was pornography. We need to highlight the Federal Bureau of Investigation report that convincingly links pornography to sex-related murders, and the Michigan State Police study that linked pornography to 40 percent of its assault cases.[8]

What can one person do? Or even a group of persons? Donald E. Wildmon has been making this case through the American Family Association, which he has directed since 1977. Another man who has done something is Jack Eckerd. When he became a Christian in 1983 he decided that selling *Playboy* and *Penthouse* magazines in his extensive drugstore chain was displeasing to God. He called his company's president and told him that he wanted the pornographic magazines removed from all 1,700 of the Eckerd drugstores. The president protested, because the sales brought in millions of dollars for the firm. Eckerd persisted and won. He owned the stores.

Moreover, his action caused something of a chain reaction. One by one Revco, Peoples, RiteAid, Dart Drug, Grey Drug and High's Dairy Stores followed Eckerd's lead. The last holdout was 7-Eleven, which in 1986 finally removed pornography from all 4,500 of its stores and recommended that its 3,600 franchises do the same.[9]

All this happened without a single law being passed. Why? It is no great mystery. It was because one man did what he thought was right to do because he had become a Christian. Not many Christians are

in such an influential position, of course. But all have areas of influence, whether great or small, and we are far from seeing what
might be accomplished if each believer would follow his or her
conscience in such areas.

Education: The Opening of America's Mind

What about education? What about the public schools? I do not want
to argue here that prayers and Bible readings ought to be reinstated.
Many Christians doubt that is a good idea, and this would be an
insignificant victory anyway, even if it could be attained. My concern
is with education itself, for that is what schools are for after all. The
problem is that in many school systems today education is just not
happening. Or where it is happening, it happens in an environment
that is destructive of character and even of sound citizenship. People
who have values should not be forced to submit to this destructive
system. They should be free to create other options and not be
penalized even financially by having to pay for their own schools
while at the same being required to support the disasters that pass
for public schools in some communities.

Our task here should be to expose the serious educational failures
of our time, encourage quality alternatives, even secular ones, and
begin to create first-class educational models ourselves. We should
probably support voucher systems or something of that nature. We
should certainly back all forms of quality education and not just our
own. Above all, we should model what we believe should be done.

We can do it in two ways.

We Can Pursue Further Education Ourselves

The first challenge is to show that we value education ourselves.
How? We can do it by turning off the television and by reading some
worthwhile books or magazines (secular as well as Christian). We
can do it by taking a few stimulating college courses. There are many
valuable continuing education programs being offered today. We
can do it by attending seminars. Anything to get our minds working,
especially about the important issues of our day. There is a strong

anti-intellectual strain in evangelical religion, but it was not always this way. Don E. Eberly reminds us of the intellectual life and achievements of the American Puritans.

> Unlike much of today's evangelicalism, the Puritans achieved towering accomplishments in many fields and left few aspects of life unexamined. They probably wrote more scholarly books than any similar group of their size in history. Producing great poetry, literature, or scholarship was not inconsistent with their spiritual mission; it was, in fact, a conscious expression of it.[10]

As often noted, the American Puritans were the founders of most of our first great universities—Harvard, Yale, Dartmouth and others. Instead of looking down on intellectual matters, evangelicals should lead the way in intellect, thinking through and then proposing strong reasonable answers to the problems that confront today's society.

We Can Develop Alternative Christian Schools

The other way that we can model what we think might be done in education is by developing alternative Christian schools. This is already underway in most areas of this country by means of home schooling, Christian grammar and high schools and centers of higher education. Many of the institutions have been with us for a long time, but there are also new ones. The move to home schooling is new. The challenge here is to provide quality education in all fields and not just private forums for evangelism or indoctrinating students in a Christian way of life.

Let me give a personal illustration. In 1984 my wife and I began a Christian high school in Philadelphia known as City Center Academy. Until then we had placed each of our three daughters in the city's schools. Two were in the best of the city's public schools. But over the years we saw the level of education in these schools deteriorate. At the lowest levels, in grade school, it was possible for a conscientious student to get by, particularly if he or she had strong parental support. But as the students reached seventh or eighth grade, it seemed to us that education virtually stopped—whether because of too large classes, the unruly nature of today's young people or simply disinterest or incompetence on the part of the teachers or faculty. Our daughters had stopped learning. The only alternatives were the Catholic parochial schools or private secular schools, which were very expensive. Even if we might have been able to afford the expensive private schools, what were other city families to do, especially the Christian families?

Out of that dilemma we created City Center Academy. The school is a Christian school. The teachers are Christians, and we do have assemblies with Christian teaching as well as classes in Bible and apologetics. But City Center Academy is above all a place to receive quality precollege education at low cost. From the beginning we conceived it not as an elite school for the children of well-to-do families, but as a school for nearly any child whose parents wanted it. We have four years of instruction in literature, with two-hour writing labs each week. There are four years of history, covering the development of civilization in the Western world. We teach Latin in the ninth and tenth grades. We also have complete high-school-level offerings of math, science and foreign language courses. We teach computers and have art classes and even a simple athletic program.

Over the years City Center Academy has graduated scores of students who would have had no future at all if our school had not existed. They would have dropped out of high school and ended up working in a convenience store or, worse, selling drugs. Instead nearly all go on to some form of higher education. As I write, the last two graduations have seen every student go on to college, some to the very best schools both secular and Christian. We need to see similar efforts everywhere with the goal of having the highest possible quality teaching and student achievement.

A Biblical Summary

What do we need to do? The answer is no mystery. It is stated clearly in 2 Chronicles 7:14: "If my people, who are called by my name, will humble themselves and pray and seek my face and turn from their wicked ways, then will I hear from heaven and will forgive their sin and will heal their land." These are the steps to God's blessing.

First, we must humble ourselves. By nature we are not humble. We are proud and feel a need for nothing. Only when we come before God are we genuinely humbled, for only then do we see ourselves as the sinful and rebellious creatures we truly are.

Second, we must pray. We do not naturally pray either. Why? Because we feel self-sufficient. This is why God often has to bring us very low. It is often only in the depths of life, when everything is crumbling around us, that we are willing to turn from ourselves and ask God for the help we need.

Third, we must seek God's face. To seek God's face means to seek his favor, rather than the favor of the world around us, and to seek his will rather than our own. To seek God's face means a radical change in the use of our time, talents and resources, our lifestyle.

Finally, we must turn from our wicked ways. If we do not think we have wicked ways, we will not turn from them—and we are fooling ourselves. But when God brings the reality of our sin home to us, we will find ourselves distressed by sin and unwilling to rest until we confess it to God, find his forgiveness and turn from everything that displeases him. Everything! Not just the "great" sins. Not just the sins that have obviously gotten us into trouble or that offend others. All sins. God does not ask for 50 percent of what we are or look only for 60 percent (or 70 percent) righteousness. He wants all of us, and he insists on genuine holiness. We cannot serve God and sin too.

Is it hard to repent? It certainly is! Nothing is harder or goes more against the grain of our sinful natures. But it is necessary for personal happiness and God's blessing. But the promise is that, if we will repent of our sins, then God will hear from heaven (he never turns a deaf ear to the repentant), forgive our sin (how much we need it) and heal our land.

9

God &
Caesar

*I*N THE FALL OF 1561 AN IMPORTANT conversation took place in Scotland between Queen Mary and the Calvinist Protestant preacher John Knox. Mary was a Catholic. She had been educated in Catholic France, and she believed that sovereigns had absolute power over the consciences of their subjects. Knox was a Reformer. For his uncompromising preaching he had been sentenced to serve as a galley slave for nineteen months. After his release, he had studied in Geneva under John Calvin (1553-1559). Then, in the summer of 1560, he had participated in the drafting of the Scottish Confession of Faith, which stated that Jesus Christ "is the only Head of His Kirk" (sections 11 and 18). Knox had returned to Scotland just two years before his celebrated conversation with Queen Mary.

In the interview Mary accused Knox of having wrongly taught the people to receive another religion than their princes allowed. "And how can that doctrine be of God, seeing that God commands subjects to obey their princes?" she asked. She was referring to Romans 13:1 and other texts.

Knox answered, "Madam, as right religion took neither [its] origin nor authority from worldly princes, but from the Eternal God alone, so are not subjects bound to frame their religion according to the appetites of their princes." He admonished Mary, "God commands queens to be nurses unto his people."

"Yes, but you are not the church that I will nourish," she retorted.

Knox replied, "Your will, Madam, is no reason."[1]

In this way the issues of church and state and the proper role and function of the state were framed in Scotland in the sixteenth century. Scotland saw no relief until Mary's forced abdication in 1567.

What is the role of the state in human affairs? How is the state to relate to the church of Jesus Christ? And conversely, how are Christians to relate to the government's authority?

The Starting Point: God Is Sovereign

My starting point for this chapter will be Paul's discussion of the role of the state in the first seven verses of Romans 13, specifically, Paul's reason for his categorical opening statement that "everyone," not only Christians, "must submit himself to the governing authorities" (v. 1).

Why must we do so? The answer is not that you will get into trouble if you do not, or even that obedience is necessary for maintaining social order. Those are excellent pragmatic reasons that Paul understands and will bring into the discussion later, but they are not his starting point. What he says in verse 1 is that we must obey the authorities because "there is no authority except that which God has established" and "the authorities that exist have been established by God." In other words, the starting point is the sovereignty of God in regard to human rulers. Those who exercise authority do so because God has established them in their positions.

We need to think about this carefully because, although it is easy for us to accept God being sovereign when we are given Christian rulers or when people of high moral character are elevated to positions of responsibility, it is much more difficult when our leaders are evil or act badly. What about Nero, the corrupt emperor who was reigning in Rome at the very time Paul was writing this letter? What about rulers who persecuted the church? Or, for that matter, what about leaders from our own time who have done evil? What about dictators such as Adolf Hitler, Joseph Stalin or Idi Amin? Or even elected officials like Richard Nixon who betrayed his trust and disappointed us? Or others today?

Romans 13:1 tells us that even these authorities have been established by God, and that we have a legitimate (though not unlimited) responsibility to obey even them.

One example of an evil but nevertheless God-established ruler is Pharaoh. Pharaoh was the oppressor of the Jews. He worked them as slaves and arrogantly resisted Moses' demand that he let God's people go. God judged his arrogance. But evil as this man was, he had nevertheless been put into his position by God, which Paul clearly states in Romans 9:17. He quotes God as telling Pharaoh, "*I raised you up* for this very purpose, that I might display my power in you and that my name might be proclaimed in all the earth" (quoting Ex 9:16). God raised Pharaoh up so that he might display his wrath in judging him. It was not a desirable appointment, but still it was God who had raised him up simply because God is sovereign in all things.

A second example is Nebuchadnezzar, whom we looked at in an earlier chapter. Nebuchadnezzar was another arrogant ruler. He thought he was superior to Jehovah, because he had been able to conquer Jerusalem, raze the temple and carry off to Babylon the gold and silver objects that had been used by the Jewish priests in their worship. The first four chapters of Daniel are a record of the struggle that took place as Nebuchadnezzar contended for sovereignty and God worked to humble him and show him that God alone, not Nebuchadnezzar, is the Most High God and ruler of all (see Dan 4:17, 25, 32).

In the end, Nebuchadnezzar seems to have gotten the message, for he confessed, "I, Nebuchadnezzar, raised my eyes toward heaven, and my sanity was restored. Then I praised the Most High; I honored and glorified him who lives forever.

His dominion is an eternal dominion;
    his kingdom endures from generation to generation.
All the peoples of the earth
    are regarded as nothing.

He does as he pleases
> with the powers of heaven
> and the peoples of the earth.

No one can hold back his hand
> or say to him: "What have you done?" . . .

Everything he does is right and all his ways are just. And those who walk in pride he is able to humble" (Dan 4:34-35, 37).

A third example is Cyrus the Persian, who is also mentioned in Daniel (1:21; 6:28; 10:1). He was an unusually humane ruler, whom God used to bring the Jews back to Jerusalem from Babylon. In Isaiah 45:1 this pagan king is even called the Lord's "anointed," which means "messiah," the very title given to Jesus as the Messiah of God.

These rulers—Nero, Pharaoh, Nebuchadnezzar, Cyrus and all others—have been set in their places by God, simply because God is sovereign and, as the Westminster Confession of Faith says, "God from all eternity did, by the most wise and holy counsel of his own will, freely and unchangeably ordain whatsoever comes to pass" (3.1).

Of course, the problem for us is not so much that God has established whatever rulers there may be. We can believe that abstractly and either like and approve of our rulers, or not like them and disapprove of them—perhaps even reject them! The problem is that we are told that it is the duty of Christians to obey those who exercise such authority, and that includes *all* authorities, not just kings and presidents but also policemen, judges, schoolteachers, bosses in our companies and other such "governing authorities." We do not want to do that.

There are many obvious problems at this point, and I will be dealing with some of them as we go along. One problem is that Paul does not answer a lot of questions that we would like him to have answered. For example, When is a government a legitimate government, and when isn't it? When is it right to rebel against an unjust or tyrannical government? Or is it not permitted at all? What about our own American war of independence? If we had been living then,

on which side should we have been? With England or with the
colonists? What are we to do when there are rival claimants to the
throne? Which one should we obey? Again, at what point does an
unjust ruler become legitimate?

Or what about limits? We are to obey the governing authorities.
That is what Paul says. But does this mean that we are to obey
everything they command? What about unjust acts commanded by
an evil government? Killing civilians? Lying? Clandestine operations
even for such an important branch of government as the CIA? Are
there no limits to what must be obeyed? I am going to explore the
limits to the obedience Christians can give a civil government next.
But the point I am making here, the first point, is that obedience to
those in authority cannot be taken lightly, as we are inclined to do.
So far as Romans 13:1 is concerned, it would be difficult, probably
impossible, for anyone to write a more all-encompassing, absolute
or utterly unqualified statement than the one Paul has given: "Everyone must submit himself to the governing authorities."

Power or Authority?

There *are* limits, of course, and we need to discuss them. But even here
the place to begin is not with the limits themselves, but by trying to
understand the nature of the authority that has been given to civil rulers. The key word is *authority*. It occurs six times in Romans 13:1-7.

In the Greek language the two words used of political power are
closely connected but need to be distinguished. The first is *kratos*.
Kratos refers to what we might call "the naked power of rule." It can
be legitimate or illegitimate, as in the case of the devil, who, we are
told, has "the power of death" (Heb 2:14) but who will lose it when
Jesus returns. His power will be taken away, and he will be cast into
the lake of fire. This word has proved useful in describing some
types of government. We speak of democracy, for example. *Dēmos*
means "people," "crowd" or "public assembly." *Kratos* means "rule."
So democracy means "rule by the people (or by many people)."
Plutocracy is a system in which the rich (or aristocrats) rule, because
ploutos means "wealth."

So when we speak of "power" *(kratos)* we recognize that there can be both legitimate and illegitimate power. And, of course, Christians are under no obligation to obey a power that is illegitimate. Just because a man with a gun orders us to do something does not mean that we should do it necessarily. The man has power, but it is an illegitimate power. What we need is a legitimate power, a policeman, to subdue him.

The other word that is used of political as well as other kinds of power is *exousia,* which is the word Paul actually uses in Romans 13. *Exousia* is a delegated power. That is, it is power that is given to a person or group of persons by another. Paul uses it in Romans 13 because he wants to make explicit that the authority of the governing powers is from God, and because it is from God these powers are responsible to God for how they exercise it. They are responsible to God precisely because God has given them the power. So here in one word is both the legitimacy and the necessary accountability of human government.

The all-important example of this is the conduct of Jesus in his trial before Pontius Pilate. Jesus was tried for treason because, as his accusers put it, he "claim[ed] to be a king" (Jn 19:12). It did not take Pilate long to discover that the kind of kingdom Jesus was talking about was no direct threat to Rome, because it was a kingdom of truth. Jesus told him, "I am a king. In fact, for this reason I was born, and for this I came into the world, to testify to the truth. Everyone on the side of truth listens to me" (Jn 18:37). After he had heard that, Pilate knew that this was a religious matter and was of no concern to him. Yet the leaders of the people were still clamoring for Jesus' death, and it became clear that Pilate was soon going to bow to their wishes. He wanted to help Jesus, but Jesus was not speaking to him.

"Do you refuse to speak to me?" Pilate said. "Don't you realize I have power either to free you or to crucify you?" (Jn 19:10).

At this point Jesus replied with one of two classic texts for helping us understand the God-given role of government and the right relationship of the church to the state.[2] Jesus answered, "You would have no power over me if it were not given to you from above. Therefore the one who handed me over to you is guilty of a greater sin" (Jn 19:11).

The word that is translated "power" in this verse is the same word that Paul uses in Romans 13, and it is used in exactly the same way. The power that was given to Pilate was a delegated authority, because it had been given to him by God. It was a true authority. Pilate had the right to try Jesus and render judgment as he thought right. But he was responsible to God for what he did and for how he did it. That is why Jesus was able to remind him, "Therefore the one who handed me over to you is guilty of *a greater sin.*" The sin of the Jewish leaders was greater than the sin of Pilate, because they were sinning against the Scriptures and their conscience, which even Pilate recognized ("It was out of envy that they had handed Jesus over to him," Mt 27:18). Nevertheless, Pilate was also sinning. He was sinning by condemning an innocent man, and he would have to answer to God for it.

Pilate had authority in Christ's trial. He could decide as he wished. He decided wrongly as we know, but he had authority to make the decision even if it was wrong. This is because his authority was from God, and Jesus did not suggest that it be wrested from him even because he had made so great an error as condemning the Son of God.

Having been told that we must obey the authorities, the next two verses give us reasons why we should. First, if we disobey the state we will be disobeying God, and God will punish us (Rom 13:2). Second, the government will also punish us (v. 3). Verse 2 says, "Consequently, he who rebels against the authority is rebelling against what God has instituted, and those who do so will bring judgment on themselves."

But this raises some immediate questions. For example, are there no conditions under which rebellion against the existing authority is justified? Or demanded? Suppose the state is tyrannical? Suppose it is violating human rights? And what about obedience itself? Must obedience be absolute? Or are there limits? Can we obey in some areas and not in others? Must Caesar *always* be obeyed?

These questions bring us to the second classic text for understanding the God-given role of government and our rightful relationship to it. The setting is this. Jesus' enemies had come to him with a trick question: "Is it right to pay taxes to Caesar or not?" (Mt 22:17). They thought that if he said it was right to pay taxes, they could discredit him with the people who hated Rome and for whom taxes were a greatly resented burden. He would be dismissed as a collaborator. On the other hand, if Jesus said that they should resist Rome by refusing to pay their taxes, then his enemies could denounce him to the Romans as an insurrectionist.

Jesus asked for a coin. When they produced it, he asked whose portrait was on it and whose inscription, probably holding it out to them so they could see it. "Caesar's," they replied.

"Give to Caesar what is Caesar's," Jesus said, thus laying the basis for the exact teaching Paul gives in Romans 13:7 when he says, "Give everyone what you owe him: If you owe taxes, pay taxes." However, at this point I think Jesus must have flipped the coin over, exposing the back on which there would have been a portrait of one of the Roman gods or goddesses. And he continued, making the contrast, "and to God what is God's" (Mt 22:21).

The first part of Jesus' answer reinforced Caesar's authority, even in such an unpopular matter as taxes. His second part drew limits. Although the state has a God-given and therefore legitimate authority, the authority of God is greater. Therefore, those who know God must worship and obey him, even if it means disobeying Caesar.

Four Logical Options

Jesus' words in response to the question about taxes suggest four options that I have found useful in dealing with this matter of the state's authority and the rightful limits of a Christian's compliance with it. These are: God alone as an authority with the authority of Caesar denied; Caesar alone as an authority with the authority of God denied; the authority of both God and Caesar but with Caesar in the dominant position; and the authority of God and Caesar but with God in the dominant position.

God Alone as an Authority

The first option is one some Christians have embraced at some periods of history, especially when the state has become excessively oppressive or corrupt. In the early church persons called anchorites went off into the desert, thus separating themselves from all social contacts and living, as they believed, solely for the service of God. This was the birth of the monastic movement, and for that reason I call this option that of monasticism.

However, we must not think that this has been practiced only by members of some monastic orders. It is also the essential approach of those evangelical Christians who so separate themselves from the secular world that they withdraw from the surrounding culture, refuse to participate in elections, have only Christian friends or work only for a Christian company.

Caesar Alone as an Authority

The second option is that of most secularists and sometimes even of so-called Christians: the choice of Caesar alone. It was the way chosen by the Jewish leaders at the time of Christ's trial, when they told Caesar (incredibly, in view of their past history and their knowledge of the Old Testament), "We have no king but Caesar" (Jn 19:15).

This is the most dangerous of the four options, because if God is left out of the equation, Caesar is left with no ultimate accountability. He has nothing to restrain his whims or cruelty.

In America we recognize the need for checks on governmental power. In fact, each of our three main branches of government—the executive branch, the legislative branch and the judicial branch—has a check on the others. The president appoints Supreme Court justices; but if the president gets out of line, the Senate (part of the legislative branch) can impeach him. The president initiates programs, but Congress must fund them. As for Congress, it can make laws, but the president can refuse to sign them (the power of the veto), or the judicial branch can declare them unconstitutional. The Supreme Court is carefully protected out of respect for our laws. We claim to be a nation governed by laws, not by people. But the court cannot initiate legislation; it can only pass on it, and the president has the power to appoint the justices.

We have created this system of checks and balances because we recognize that persons in positions of power are untrustworthy. But if that is true on the merely human level, how much truer it is on the cosmic level. Human rulers regularly conspire against God and his Anointed. "Let us break their chains . . . and throw off their fetters," they say (Ps 2:3). If we forsake God, we are at the mercy of our governors.

The Authority of God and Caesar, but with Caesar in the Dominant Position

The third option is one many persons would prefer, but it is the position of cowards. If God's authority is recognized at all, it must be supreme simply because God is supreme by definition. That is what it means to be God. So if anyone claims to obey the state before God or rather than God, while nevertheless still believing in God, it can only be because he is afraid of what Caesar might do to him.

This was the case with Pilate. He knew Jesus was innocent of the charges brought against him. He declared him to be innocent, but in the end he gave in and had Jesus crucified. Why? Because he was afraid of Caesar. Toward the end of the trial, when he was holding out against their wishes, the Jewish authorities played their trump card, crying out, "If you let this man go, you are no friend of Caesar" (Jn 19:12). Pilate, who feared Caesar and wanted to be a friend of Caesar more than anything else in the entire world, gave in and thus condemned the sinless Son of God. The irony is that Pilate failed to secure Caesar's friendship even so, because a few years later he was removed from office and banished to France, where he died.

**The Authority of God and Caesar, but with God
in the Dominant Position**

The last option is the only valid one: God and Caesar, but with God
in the dominant position. It was the position Jesus articulated when
he said, "Give to Caesar what is Caesar's, and to God what is God's."

Because Christians recognize the authority of the state, they
should be the very best of citizens, and that in two ways. First, they
should obey the state in all areas of its legitimate authority. We
should obey the speed limits, pay our taxes honestly, support worthy
civic endeavors, speak well of our rulers, and support and pray for
them. John Calvin expressed this well when he wrote, "We are not
only subject to the authority of princes who perform their office
toward us uprightly and faithfully as they ought, but also to the
authority of all who, by whatever means, have got control of affairs,
even though they perform not a whit of the princes' office."[3] Jesus
exemplified this when he did not show disrespect to Pilate. He did
not warn him that if he failed to rule justly, Jesus' followers would
rise up and do their best to unseat him and the Roman government.
Jesus knew what the governor would do, and he accepted it as from
God, which it surely was.

But Jesus was not silent either. He spoke of truth, reminding Pilate
that Pilate was sinning and would therefore one day himself have
to answer for it. That is our role. We speak often today of the separation of church and state, and we should be thankful for that
separation. It is a dearly won liberty to have a church free from
government interference or control and to have a state free from
clerical domination.[4] But the separation of church and state does not
mean the separation of God and state. So although we do not rule
the state, nor should we, it is still our duty as Christians to speak out
against the civil ruler's sins and remind the governing authorities
that they are accountable to him from whom their authority comes.

This means that we are accountable too! We are accountable to
speak up. We do not have the power of the sword. That is reserved
for the civil authorities, as Paul will show (Rom 13:4). Our weapon
is truth, for we are a kingdom of the truth. The truth is stronger than

the sword. But woe to us if we do not wield the sword of truth powerfully.

Some Important Limitations

But now we have to go a step further and ask if there are areas that demand more than mere words from Christians. Not the sword; we have eliminated that option. But something beyond words, such as noncompliance. Although Christians are to be the best of all citizens, obeying the government if at all possible, there are nevertheless times when they must refuse to obey the state and resist its decrees. When is this necessary? We need to look at several of these areas carefully.

Evangelism

The first area in which Christians cannot recognize the authority of the government and must therefore disobey it is whenever the state forbids the preaching of the gospel or evangelism. Christians have a God-given duty to evangelize. We call it the Great Commission. Jesus said, "Go into all the world and preach the good news to all creation" (Mk 16:15). He told the eleven, "Go and make disciples of all nations" (Mt 28:19). He said, "You will be my witnesses in Jerusalem, and in all Judea and Samaria, and to the ends of the earth" (Acts 1:8).

What must happen when the authorities demand differently is illustrated in Acts 4 and 5. The disciples had been preaching in Jerusalem, but they had created such a stir that the leaders of the people called them in and, meeting in solemn assembly, commanded that the apostles keep silent. Peter and John replied, "Judge for yourselves whether it is right in God's sight to obey you rather than God. For we cannot help speaking about what we have seen and heard" (4:19-20).

The apostles were threatened and released. But they went right back to their preaching. They were arrested again. "We gave you strict orders not to teach in this name. . . . Yet you have filled Jerusalem with your teaching and are determined to make us guilty of this man's blood" (5:28).

The apostles replied, "We must obey God rather than men" (v. 29).

The incident makes it clear that Christians are to give preference to the preaching of the gospel and are not to cease from it even though commanded to do so by the civil authorities. They may suffer for it. Many of the early preachers were arrested and beaten. Some were killed. But they evangelized anyway. We need to remember this in our age, which is becoming increasingly intolerant of any public articulation of Christian faith and truth.

Moral Behavior

A second biblical limit on obedience to human authorities is in moral areas affecting Christian conduct. No government has the right to command Christians to perform immoral or non-Christian acts. During the Nazi era Christians in Germany were faced with a devilish state and its openly anti-Christian and even antihuman practices. German citizens were commanded to have no dealings with the Jews. They were not to trade with them, have friendships with them or even acknowledge them. This was an unjustified demand on Christians to behave immorally, and those who disobeyed these laws were right to do so.

Corrie ten Boom and her family were right to hide Jews and thus try to save their lives.

Dietrich Bonhoeffer was right to speak out against Hitler, organize an underground church and strengthen its opposition and witness.

Martin Niemoeller was right to go on preaching the truth even to the point of being imprisoned for it. We are told that another minister visited him in jail and argued that he would be set free if only he would agree to keep silent about certain subjects. "So why are you in jail?" he concluded.

"Why aren't you in jail?" Niemoeller replied.

In our country Christians must also speak out against racism, government and corporate corruption, sex and age discrimination, and other evils. At the present moment in America it is unlikely that you will be imprisoned for speaking the truth, though that may come in time. But you might lose your job for refusing to be dishonest or for calling to account those who are not honest. You might lose your chance for promotion. You might be cut out of the leadership circle. No matter. You must still speak up, and you must act justly even if you are pressured to comply.

Civil Disobedience

A third area in which Christians may consider disobeying the state is when the state flagrantly ignores righteousness or justice and those who are sensitive to these wrongs feel the need to do more than merely speak out. It differs from the previous area in that the former limitation concerned times in which Christians are pressured to act immorally themselves and must refuse, while this refers to government injustice toward other people and the need Christians feel to do something to change it. We usually speak of this as civil disobedience, and there are excellent examples of its having being done rightly and with success. The civil rights movement of the 1960s is a good example.

But here is the problem. As soon as we move away from the area of words only (that is, speaking the truth and calling the rulers to account) and into the area of direct action, it is fatally easy to cross over the line into a wrong method of responding and thus become guilty too, not merely of breaking an unjust law, but of breaking just and even moral laws. Let me give two examples, one from the past and one from the present.

Dietrich Bonhoeffer is my example from the past. I have commended him for his stand against the evils of the Nazi state, and he is also to be commended for courageously returning to Germany from America, where he was living at the time, to help the struggling church and give it leadership. But Bonhoeffer was not executed for speaking out against Nazism. He was executed for being involved in a plot to assassinate Adolf Hitler. We can understand how he might have felt that assassination was the only course left to him to stop the growing evil. But desperation does not make murder right, and at this point he went beyond any possible biblical sanction.

We can contrast his conduct with that of David in his struggle against King Saul. God had already removed his blessing from Saul, and Saul was seeking David's life. David did not have to wait in Jerusalem to be killed. He had every right to flee. This was a form of disobedience. But David did not cross over the line and try to kill Saul. On the contrary, he spared his life on at least two occasions while he waited for God to remove him, which God did in the end (see 1 Sam 24; 26).

My second, current example is the attempt of Christians to stem the terrible destruction of human life through abortions, which are legal by today's laws. This effort is best known as Operation Rescue, though that is not the only effort or the sole organization involved.

When I am talking about the abortion problem, as I often do, I usually challenge the blockading of abortion clinics on the basis of the methodology being used. I say that we live in a television age and that television turns our tactics against us to the point of our losing the battle against this great evil in the popular mind. I say that television will never record a serious discussion about the true nature of abortion or the value of a life made in the image of God conducted between an antiabortionist and a woman who is considering an abortion. It is not good television. But as soon as a restraining order is issued and the police arrive to begin arresting the demonstrators and placing them in paddy wagons, then the cameras roll. For this makes good television, and we who oppose abortion appear on television as people who are violent and who want to take away other people's rights. This is the argument I made in the last chapter.

But that is not the issue here. There is nothing wrong with being arrested in itself. The problem is the carryover from mere protest and the attempt to persuade people by speaking the truth to breaking otherwise perfectly valid laws, like rights of private property, freedom of movement and such things.

We can applaud the courage of those who demonstrate. We should endorse the issue they represent. We must love them as Christian brothers and sisters. But we must still say that it is not right to trespass on others' property. It is not right to make it difficult for people to enter abortion clinics, if they choose to do so. It is not right to invade the clinics, destroy records and equipment, or do things that are even worse. The problem in this area can be seen in the Florida case in which one, probably deranged, demonstrator shot and killed a doctor who had been performing abortions. Or in the case of the man who shot several abortion clinic personnel in New England. These acts were not courageous or godly. They were murder.

I want to make every allowance for the right exercise of the consciences of other people in these areas. Many believe that they must do something to attract attention to evil rather than merely sit on the sidelines doing nothing. But as Charles Colson observes, "In our day, breaking laws to make a dramatic point is the ultimate logic of terrorism, not civil disobedience."[5] And what is also true, "Civil disobedience, like law itself, is habit-forming, and the habit it forms is destructive of law."[6] Rightly practiced, civil disobedience has its place. But we have to be very careful how we use it and what we may be unleashing if we do.

There is no moment in all of life in which we must be more diligent to hear and obey the Word of God in Scripture as when we are calling on another person or group to do the same. We tend to be self-righteous at the best of times. But we are especially self-righteous when we embark on a crusade, since crusades encourage passion and passion often blinds us to our personal faults. At times we must disobey. Caesar is not God. Though we must give Caesar what is Caesar's, we must be careful to give God what is God's. But we need to look carefully to God to know the difference.

The Power of the Sword

As we saw when we studied Romans 13:2, the first reason that Christians should obey governments is that God has established them; therefore, if we resist those who have been raised up to govern us, we are resisting God and God will judge us accordingly. The second reason we should obey is that the state will judge us too. That is, we will get in trouble, and the reason we will is that the state has the power to enforce its decrees and laws.

Paul expressed this idea by writing, "For rulers hold no terror for those who do right, but for those who do wrong. Do you want to be free from fear of the one in authority? Then do what is right and he will commend you. For he is God's servant to do you good. But if you do wrong, be afraid, for he does not bear the sword for nothing. He is God's servant, an agent of wrath to bring punishment on the wrongdoer" (Rom 13:3-4).

What does this power of the sword mean? It means only one thing, and that is force. This is what the state has been given by God, and it is the very basis for how the state conducts its affairs.

We do not like to think about this too much, because force or forcing someone to do something is not supposed to be good in our "free" society. Think of raising children, for example. Most people today think it is bad to force children to do anything. So instead of saying, "Make your bed" or "Eat your dinner or else," we give them options, presenting the good as "being in their best interests," or offering them "rewards" instead of punishments. We say, "Would you rather eat your dinner now or for breakfast?" or "Would you rather eat your potatoes or your spinach first?" And so far as we are concerned, we bristle as soon as someone says that we *have* to do something.

Because of this mindset, whenever we think of government, especially if it is one we favor, we refuse to think of it existing by force or operating through force. Instead we think of it giving moral guidance and appealing to the best in its people while providing an environment for self-fulfillment or expression. We will admit that totalitarian systems like the former communist states of eastern Europe operated by force. That is what was wrong with them, we think. We suppose that our government must be different. Or at least we hope it is different.

But it is not! "Kinder and gentler" perhaps, its cast-iron fist hidden by a velvet glove. But it too is based on force, for the simple reason that every government is based on force. That is the nature of governments. There is no other way in which they can operate.

Here is an example. We have a system of so-called voluntary self-assessment of income tax in this country. When you fill out your form each April you can read on the front of the tax booklet that we are a country unique in the world in that each year millions of Americans "voluntarily" assess their own tax and "voluntarily" pay those billions of dollars that keep the government running. How wonderful, "voluntary self-assessment." But it is not true, of course. Income tax is not voluntary. If you do not believe it, try refusing to pay your tax some year. Or refuse to pay just a part of it. Tell the government, "Since our tax system is voluntary, I think I will just keep my money this year." You know what will happen. You will be billed for the deficient amount, plus interest. And if you refuse to pay, you will be arrested and your assets seized to pay the delinquent taxes.

Paying taxes is not voluntary at all. It is mandatory, and the proof that it is mandatory is the government's final use of force to accomplish its objectives.

We need to explore the areas in which this power, given to the state by God, is to operate. But we need to note, as a parenthesis, that the right to enforce laws by force is a right given to the state and not to the church. When Jesus was tried by Pilate he acknowledged Pilate's authority over him, which included the right even to put him to death. But Jesus did not claim that power for himself or his followers. When questioned about his kingdom, he replied that his kingdom was a kingdom of truth (Jn 18:37).

The church has always gotten into trouble when it has tried to take the state's power—that is, force—into its own hands. The church tried to do this in the Middle Ages, after Christianity had been embraced by Constantine as the religion of the empire. But the result was disastrous for the church. The leaders of the church became power hungry, true religion diminished and corruption increased. Religious leaders make bad rulers, because secular power seems to corrupt them even more than it corrupts secular rulers. Therefore, the power of the sword has been given to Caesar, not to the church, and it must not be used to advance the cause of Christ. Caesar alone has the right to cut off heads.

However, when we say that the power of the sword has been given to the state, we do not mean either of two wrong things. First, we do not mean that this power can be exercised in any way whatsoever. There is an illegitimate as well as a legitimate exercise of power. And second, we do not mean that the state can do by the exercise of power what the church alone is able to do by its proclamation of the gospel and the truth.

A Wrong Use of Power

I do not mean that the state's power, however legitimate it may be when used in the areas for which God has given it, can be exercised in any way whatsoever. The state has no God-given right to massacre its citizens, for instance. It has no right to use its power to advance evil. Paul makes this clear in Romans 13:3-4, when he speaks repeatedly of those who do good and those who do evil, and of the state's exercise of its power to reward those who do the one and punish those who do the other.

How, then, is the power of the sword to be used? There are two main areas. First, the state is given power to defend its citizens. It does this in two ways. It defends its citizens from enemies outside the state, that is, from other nations. It has power to wage war, including all necessary powers that go with it: power to conscript its people into the armed forces, power to tax for the war effort, power to redirect the nation's economy to a wartime footing. These are legitimate powers, but they are justified only by the need for the common defense. The power to regulate the economy in order to wage war does not necessarily carry over into peacetime, for example.

The state also has power to defend its citizens from evildoers within. That is, it has been given responsibility to provide and maintain social order. The biblical writers seem to have been particularly concerned about this, probably because they were more aware than most of us of how terrible anarchy can be. Nobody is safe in such times. Therefore, even a bad government is to be preferred to chaos. That is one reason why we are told to pray even for evil rulers. Paul told Timothy, "I urge, then, first of all, that requests, prayers, intercession and thanksgiving be made for everyone—for kings and all those in authority, that we may live peaceful and quiet lives in all godliness and holiness" (1 Tim 2:1-2). Social order is good by itself, but it is particularly good for Christians because it gives us an opportunity to advance the gospel.

The second area in which government has been given power by God is in establishing, exercising and maintaining justice, that is, in rewarding good behavior and punishing bad behavior. This is what Paul chiefly has in mind in Romans 13:3-4 when he says, "For rulers hold no terror for those who do right, but for those who do wrong. Do you want to be free from fear of the one in authority? Then do what is right and he will commend you. For he is God's servant to do you good. But if you do wrong, be afraid, for he does not bear the sword for nothing. He is God's servant, an agent of wrath to bring punishment on the wrongdoer." In order for the state to properly fulfill this role, there must be a conviction that there is such a thing as good and, by contrast, that there is such a thing as evil.

Here is where the church can contribute. Christians, and particularly their spokespeople, must articulate this moral standard.

A Useless Use of Power

The second wrong idea is that the state can reform evildoers by power. It cannot. The power of the sword has been given to the state only to defend its citizens and to punish wrongdoing. Or, to put it in other words, the state has a God-given responsibility to punish bad or evil behavior. But it has no authority, still less does it have power, actually to change or reform the evildoer. Government cannot develop morality in its citizens.

The important word is *develop*, of course. For I am not suggesting that government is not to be concerned with morality. On the contrary, morality is precisely what it is to be concerned with, for morality is the only true basis for law. If the government passes a law against stealing and enforces it with the power of the sword, the only valid basis for the law and the penalty affixed for breaking it is that stealing is wrong. Or to put it the other way, there is a God-given right to private property. If stealing is not wrong, then the act of government to oppose it and punish it is tyranny—an unjustifiable restriction of freedom. If stealing is wrong, then the government is acting properly. In the same way, the only valid base for capital punishment is Genesis 9:6, which says that the murderer may be killed because he has killed one made "in the image of God." It is the same with all laws. The only valid basis for any law is a previously existing morality.

Government must be concerned with moral issues, then. But this is not the same thing as saying that the government can develop morality in its citizens, for it cannot. It can proscribe penalties. It can enforce them and thus perhaps also restrain evil somewhat. But it cannot change the people involved. The only thing that ever changes people at a fundamental level is the power of God working through the gospel.

Where Are God's People?

If government cannot develop morality in its citizens, then morality must come in another way and from another source. What is that source? Where can morality come from? There is only one answer. It comes from revealed religion, and it must work its way into national life through those citizens who know God through Jesus Christ and who sincerely desire to please him.

Religious people are the best thing a country can have and the only citizens who will actually advance the nation in the direction of justice and true righteousness. Today the need is not for more laws. If we do not have a moral citizenry, even the laws can be used immorally. They can be used to get out of paying one's debts, escape a prison sentence, cheat the innocent, oppress the poor and many such things. What we need are people who know and are willing to live by the moral laws of God.

Remember 2 Chronicles 7:14. That great Old Testament text does not offer healing for a nation through the election of a better president or the ouster of an old one. It does not even recommend passing better laws. It calls for renewal through the repentance of God's people. It says, "If my people, who are called by my name, will humble themselves and pray and seek my face and turn from their wicked ways, then will I hear from heaven and will forgive their sin and will heal their land."[7]

10

Nehemiah: Rebuilding the Walls

*P*EOPLE ARE DESPERATE FOR LEADERS today—in politics, business and the church—since many of those we thought were leaders have let us down. This provides a splendid opportunity for Christians since they, in theory at least, should be people of integrity who will use their skills for the common good and not merely for their personal enrichment. But leadership, like everything else, must be learned. How can we learn to be leaders? There are many books on the subject, such as Dale Carnegie's successful classic *How to Win Friends and Influence People* or Peter Drucker's studies: *The Practice of Management, Managing for Results* and *The Effective Executive.* And there are many other books, some good, some less commendable.

In this chapter I want to look at the first book on leadership ever written and study it for what it can teach evangelicals who are trying to exercise leadership today. It is in the form of the memoirs of a man named Nehemiah, who served as governor of Jerusalem from 445 to 432 B.C.

Meet the Governor
Nehemiah was born in exile after the fall of Jerusalem to Babylon in 586 B.C. This meant that he lived in a bad age so far as the destiny of his people was concerned. Yet like other Jews before him—Daniel and his three friends, Shadrach, Meshach and Abednego, as well as

Mordecai and his young ward Esther, who became the queen of Persia—Nehemiah rose to a position of influence, in this case in the court of Artaxerxes. He was cupbearer to the king, as he tells us in Nehemiah 1:11 and 2:1.

The office of cupbearer sounds rather menial today, but this was not the situation. This office arose in ancient societies because of the danger that an emperor or king might be poisoned by some rival. The cupbearer was a trusted person appointed to care for and taste the wine to make sure it was safe before it was served to the king. Such a person was obviously highly esteemed and trusted to begin with. And because of his constant and regular access to the ruler he usually acquired influence beyond all but a handful of military leaders and nobles. In such a position many people might have been content to rest on their achievement or even retire to the good life. But Nehemiah showed his greatness precisely at this point. Although he was a man of the greatest possible influence in the Persian court, he left this enviable position to lead an effort to rebuild the walls of the city of Jerusalem, the city of his fathers, which now lay in ruins, and to restore its influence.

The problem was presented to Nehemiah at the beginning of his book (vv. 1-4). His brother Hanani and some other men came to the capital city of Susa, where Nehemiah was attending the king, and reported that the walls of Jerusalem were broken down and its gates burned with fire. This probably took place at a time of unrest described in Ezra 4. Others had been trying to rebuild the walls and thus restore Jerusalem's influence for nearly one hundred years. Nehemiah accomplished this Herculean task in only fifty-two days. Then he led a series of reforms that were to have the greatest possible influence on the Jewish nation up to the time of Jesus Christ.

First Things First
Where did Nehemiah begin? Peter Drucker has a chapter in one of his books on leadership entitled "First Things First." It concerns priorities, as one might suspect from the title, and it introduces what Drucker rightly calls one great "secret" of effectiveness: "Effective

executives do first things first and they do one thing at a time."[1] This is an important principle. In fact, it is two principles: establishing priorities and managing time effectively. But it raises the follow-up question: What should a leader's priorities be? What things really are "first things"?

Some managers would put relationships with people first. Others would stress personal thought time, time for planning.

It is significant that when the problem of Jerusalem's broken walls was presented to Nehemiah, the first priority of this great and (later) very successful leader was *prayer*. The first thing he did was unburden his heart to God, the gist of which is given at the close of his first chapter. Why did he start here? There may have been several reasons. For one thing, he was a man who prayed frequently about everything. Prayer was a habit for him. But I suspect also that, in this case at least, Nehemiah prayed for the simple reason that no one but God could accomplish what needed to be accomplished if the walls of the city were to rise again.

Prayer is what made Abraham Lincoln the man he was, and for the same reason. He said on one occasion, "I have been driven many times to my knees by the overwhelming conviction that I had nowhere else to go. My own wisdom and that of those about me seemed insufficient for the day."[2] Is this what makes a leader? The world may not think so, but the Bible teaches that this is the first and greatest priority. Chuck Swindoll has it right, I think, when he refers to Nehemiah as "A Leader—From the Knees Up!"[3]

Nehemiah was an important man even before his success in rebuilding the walls of Jerusalem, and many important people are arrogant—arrogant with others and, I suppose, arrogant before God. Nehemiah does not show this spirit. He was a man of courage and bold action, as we will see later on in the story. But here he humbles himself before God even to the point of tears and fasting. He is not presumptuous, but he knows that God can do what he asks him to do. Therefore he comes submissively and seriously. We see his submission in his tears and mourning. We see his seriousness in his fasting.

The most important part of Nehemiah's prayer is his confession of sin: "I confess the sins we Israelites, including myself and my father's house, have committed against you. We have acted very wickedly toward you. We have not obeyed the commands, decrees and laws you gave your servant Moses" (vv. 6-7).

Nehemiah knew that the sin of the Israelites had caused the judgment of God that resulted in the destruction of Jerusalem. So if Jerusalem was to be restored, it would need to be restored on the basis of a confession of the sins that had caused its destruction. Nehemiah is specific about them: "We have not obeyed the commands, decrees and laws you gave your servant Moses." What is most striking about this confession is that he includes himself in acknowledging these sins: "the sins we Israelites, including myself and my father's house, have committed against you."

There are two important principles here. First, Nehemiah recognizes that he was one with the people so that his sins were their sins and theirs were his. He did not try to distance himself from them. Second, he knew that he was himself a sinner. There was no sin of the people that led to the fall of Jerusalem of which he was not guilty or of which he would not have been capable of committing under the same circumstances.

So here is a secret of true leadership. A good leader is not aware so much of the talents he has that others do not have as of the fact that he is as capable of sin as anyone. When leaders forget their sinfulness they fall into sin and lose their authority. This is true of many of today's evangelicals. They do not think that they are sinners. Therefore they project a superior, self-righteous attitude and forfeit God's blessing.

Having acknowledged God's greatness, confessed his sin and reviewed God's promises, Nehemiah then laid his petitions before God, saying: "O Lord, let your ear be attentive to the prayer of this your servant and to the prayer of your servants who delight in revering your name. Give your servant success today by granting him favor in the presence of this man" (v. 11). "This man" was King Artaxerxes, whom Nehemiah introduces in the next verse, the first of chapter 2. The king was key to the plan he was already making, but God was the key to changing this powerful king's heart.

Harry S. Truman, the thirty-second president of the United States, referred to leaders as "people who can get other people to do what they do not want to do—and make them like doing it." But that is not easy. How do you get people to change their minds? Generally you cannot. But God can, even in the case of kings. Hudson Taylor, the founder of the China Inland Mission, knew this secret. He said, "It is possible to move men through God by prayer alone."

Problems of Middle Management

The first dynamic of effective leadership illustrated by Nehemiah might be called the relationship between the leader and God, Nehemiah's ultimate superior. But a Christian must relate not only to a heavenly superior but also to earthly ones. For this reason the second dynamic for any true leader involves what we generally refer to as the role of middle management. Most leaders are in middle management positions. At the beginning of this story Nehemiah was in just this position, and the superior he reported to was Artaxerxes.

Middle management is difficult. If a manager is alert, visionary and innovative, he is frequently a threat to his boss—or his boss perceives him to be so. On the other hand, if he is merely an echo of his boss, he is of little value either to him or to the organization.

But think of Nehemiah. The Persian kings were impossible at best, and often cruel. They were almost always in danger of sudden assassination or revolt, and they were therefore usually suspicious of any wrong moves or lack of loyalty by their subordinates. We see a trace of this in Nehemiah 2:2, where the king notices that Nehemiah is sad and asks about it ("Why does your face look so sad when you are not ill? This can be nothing but sadness of heart"). Nehemiah tells us he "was very much afraid." He had a right to be. Persian rulers did not like their subordinates to be gloomy.

Nehemiah's difficulties did not stop there either. What he wanted was to go to Jerusalem and rebuild its walls, and it was precisely this king who earlier had been petitioned against the rebuilding of the walls and had stopped the work as a result of that petition (see Ezra 4). Nehemiah's plan meant asking Artaxerxes to reverse his own former policy. Yet he succeeded. Chapter 2 reveals five secrets to Nehemiah's triumph.

Loyalty

When the king asked why Nehemiah's face looked sad and Nehemiah replied with the expected court greeting, "May the king live forever!" we do not think of this as hypocrisy or even mere formality. Nehemiah seems to have had the king's interests genuinely at heart. Many persons in middle management err at just this point. Sometimes they err obviously and openly by trying to outshine their boss or make him look bad. Or they try to change their boss, expecting to correct his weaknesses rather than to build on his strengths. Peter Drucker says that the right sort of loyalty is to the advantage of the middle manager as well as the boss.

> Contrary to popular legend, subordinates do not, as a rule, rise to position and prominence over the prostrate bodies of incompetent bosses. If their boss is not promoted, they will tend to be bottled up behind him. And if their boss is relieved for incompetence or failure, the successor is rarely the bright, young man next in line. He usually is brought in from the outside and brings with him his own bright, young men. Conversely, there is nothing quite as conducive to success, as a successful and rapidly promoted superior.[4]

Tact

The second secret of dealing successfully with a superior is tact. Christians are notorious for their lack of tact. They think that it is more needful for them to "express their frustrations," "speak their mind," or "let it all hang out." Notice how tactfully Nehemiah dealt with Artaxerxes.

First, when the king asked why he was sad, Nehemiah answered with a disarming question, not defensively. Many of us would have said, "I'll tell you why I'm sad. Thirteen years ago, in the seventh year of your reign, a delegation of Jews went to Jerusalem with the Jewish scribe Ezra. They tried to carry out the decree of your predecessor Cyrus to rebuild the temple and walls. But as soon as the governors of Trans-Euphrates heard about it and appealed to you to have the work stopped, you stopped it, and you didn't even wait to hear the other side of the story. You couldn't see that these governors were simply jealous of us and were afraid a revitalized Jerusalem would be detrimental to their own selfish interests."

Many of us would have replied like that. But although our reply might have made us feel better, we would have experienced the failure such an arrogant attitude deserves. The king would have become defensive, and our cause would have been lost.

Instead of this, Nehemiah asked, "Why should my face not look sad when the city where my fathers are buried lies in ruins, and its gates have been destroyed by fire?" (v. 3). This question, instead of making Artaxerxes defensive, actually won him to Nehemiah's side. The king had ancestors of his own. So he understood that Nehemiah had cause to be sad and wanted to help him.

Second, Nehemiah presented his desire as a personal matter and not as a political one. He knew that what he wanted would require the reversal of Artaxerxes' former public policy (Ezra 4:7-23), and he understood that any request to fortify a city was suspicious. So he did not treat this as a political issue at all. In fact, he did not even mention Jerusalem by name. He treated it as a matter for personal grief, which the king, who was proud of his own city, could understand.

Honesty

To be tactful does not mean that one is to be insincere, however. On the contrary, a Christian leader must always be straightforward or honest. When the king asked what he wanted, Nehemiah did not pretend that he wanted to take a vacation to Jerusalem or merely look the city over. He told the king that he wanted to rebuild it.

This is very important. A good leader is willing to have those who work under him develop their own programs. He wants this if he really is a good leader. But he does not want to be surprised by the plans of subordinates, and understandably so. Subordinates quite properly want their personal plans to succeed. But the boss is responsible not merely for the subordinate's plan but for the success of the entire operation. He needs to know what is going on and be able to approve, disapprove or redirect those plans according to the larger picture.

So here is an important principle to remember: If you want to succeed with your boss, don't surprise him. Be creative, but be sure he is with you as you plow along.

Prayer

The fourth secret of middle management success is prayer. We have already looked at Nehemiah's model prayer in chapter 1, noting especially his confession of sin. Here we see something else that is important, something the New Testament calls being "instant in prayer" (Rom 12:12 KJV). It means being ready at any moment to bring a new situation before God for his assistance. Nehemiah is talking to the king. The king asks what he wants. He realizes that after months of prayer the decisive moment has arrived. He is ready to speak. But before he speaks he utters a quick additional prayer "to the God of heaven" (v. 4). He is afraid to say even a word without God's blessing.

Planning

The most striking secret of middle management success revealed in Nehemiah's encounter with king Artaxerxes is careful planning. To put it in simple language: Nehemiah had a single fixed goal (he wanted to rebuild Jerusalem), and he had worked out how he would achieve it.

First, Nehemiah had a goal. Earlier I quoted Peter Drucker's statement that "effective executives do first things first and they do one thing at a time." I was speaking about prayer there, but the same principle applies to goal setting. We need to put first things first here also. How can we put first things first unless we work our goals out carefully? It cannot be done. Unless we have a clear understanding of what we are trying to do and why it is important, other important but lesser matters will crowd out the proper goals.

By way of illustration, there is a story involving Yogi Berra, the well-known catcher for the New York Yankees, and Hank Aaron, who was then the chief power hitter for the Milwaukee Braves. The teams were playing in the World Series, and as usual Yogi was keeping up his ceaseless chatter, intended to pep up his teammates on the one hand and distract the Milwaukee batters on the other. As Aaron came to the plate, Yogi tried to distract him, saying, "Henry, you're holding the bat wrong. You're supposed to hold it so you can read the trademark." Aaron didn't say anything. But he hit the next pitch into the left-field bleachers. After rounding the bases and tagging up at home plate, Aaron looked at Yogi and said, "I didn't come up here to read." He knew his goal, and he did not allow Yogi to distract him.

The second part of planning involves ways to achieve the chosen goal. For four or five months Nehemiah had been praying for direction on how he might rebuild Jerusalem, but he had not been inactive during those months. He gathered information. As his requests to Artaxerxes unfold we are impressed by his knowledge of the area to which he is going. He even knew the name of Asaph, the keeper of the king's forest. He had worked out what he would need to get the walls built. He was specific: he knew how long it would take; he needed letters of safe-conduct for the governors of the Trans-Euphrates region; and he asked requisitions for the supplies that would be needed.

It is surprising how often careful planning is overlooked by persons in leadership, whether in the church or in business or in government. Christians sometimes have a false spirituality that goes like this.

"God has told me to do so and so."

"Yes? And how are you going to do it?"

"I don't know. I guess I'm just going to start out and see how the Lord leads."

People who start like this usually return with the job unfinished. From the beginning Nehemiah had planned where he wanted to go, and he got there.

Taking Command

When Nehemiah arrived in Jerusalem he faced an overwhelming task. Commentators differ over the size of the city at this time and therefore over the length of wall that Nehemiah was to build. But even by the most modest estimates the circumference of the city was one-and-a-half to two-and-one-half miles. Moreover, the destruction of the walls had been great and the stones that had to be reassembled were massive. These great blocks had been tumbled down into the valleys below and now had to be exposed and then hauled back up to the site of the wall and reassembled. This required an army of workers, diverse skills and even, we may suppose, a certain amount of lifting and moving machinery.

Besides, the task had been attempted before in the second year of King Cyrus in 538 B.C., more than ninety years earlier, and had been given up then, which meant that Nehemiah was bucking a previous history of defeat. If he had approached the matter without careful preparation, the people would have said, "We cannot do it. We have tried several times already and we have failed each time. We cannot change the situation."

Overwhelming? Yes. But overwhelming tasks are opportunities for great people, and Nehemiah was a great man. In chapter 2 we see how he went about changing the situation so that within fifty-two days (less than two months) the work was accomplished. The story reveals several secrets to his success.

He Worked Out a Plan

Nehemiah was a great planner—a pray-er *and* a planner. Before he spoke to Artaxerxes about wanting to go to Jerusalem he had formulated a plan for how he could accomplish his goal. Here, in the second chapter, we find him doing exactly the same thing. Only now he is on the site, and the plan needed to be more specific.

One of the best-known incidents in Nehemiah's account is the one in which he rode out by night to inspect the wall of the sleeping city. We might have expected Nehemiah to do several things when he arrived in Jerusalem—perhaps make a great show of arriving and assuming power, perhaps hold private interviews with the chief men of the city, perhaps even try to set up alliances with the leaders of the cities round about. But he did none of these things. For the first three days he did nothing. Then, on the third night he took a few trusted men and set out on a careful examination of the walls. He is so detailed in his account that even today this is the best extant record of the extent of the city in the postexilic period.

Arnold Toynbee, the great English historian, said, "Apathy can only be overcome by enthusiasm, and enthusiasm can only be aroused by two things: first, an ideal which takes the imagination by storm, and second, a definite intelligible plan for carrying that ideal into practice."[5] Nehemiah was confronted with great apathy, and his first step was to formulate a plan to carry his vision into practice.

He Timed His Announcement Carefully

If Nehemiah had acted too quickly, without gathering the necessary facts, his ideas would have been dismissed as the uninformed and impractical daydreams of a novice. On the other hand, if he had delayed longer, he would have lost the initiative that his prestige as the newly appointed governor gave him. By the end of the three days his presence had aroused considerable curiosity. It was the moment to tell why he had left Susa for the 1,500-mile trip to Jerusalem.

He Threw Out a Challenge

Verse 17 records what Nehemiah said "to them." Since the immediate antecedent to the pronoun must be "the Jews . . . priests . . . nobles . . . officials or any others who would be doing the work" (v. 16), Nehemiah must have addressed them all, which he could only have done by calling a large meeting. The advantage of this was that he could speak to each directly. Each one could make up his or her own mind about the challenge. No one had a chance to misinterpret

Nehemiah's words to the others.

Dale Carnegie tells of a mill manager whose men were not producing. The owner, whose name was Charles Schwab, asked why. The manager had no idea. "I've coaxed the men; I've pushed them; I've sworn and cussed; I've threatened them with damnation and being fired. But nothing works. They just won't produce."

"How many heats did your shift make today?" Schwab asked.

"Six."

Without saying another word, Schwab picked up a piece of chalk and wrote a big figure 6 on the floor. Then he walked away.

When the night shift came in they saw the 6 and asked what it meant. "The big boss was here today," someone said. "He asked how many heats the day shift made, and we told him six. He chalked it on the floor."

The next morning Schwab walked through the mill again. The night shift had rubbed out the 6 and replaced it with an even bigger 7. When the day shift reported in they saw the 7. So the night shift thought it was better than the day shift, did it? They'd show them. They pitched in furiously, and before they had left that evening they had rubbed out the 7 and replaced it with a 10. It was a 66 percent increase in just twenty-four hours, and all because of Schwab's challenge.[6] Nehemiah knew that secret and threw out a challenge as well.

He Identified with the People in the Task

Even though we have only a brief record of what Nehemiah said to the people, his identification with them in the effort is striking. Notice the personal pronouns *we* and *us*. "You see the trouble *we* are in: Jerusalem lies in ruins, and its gates have been burned with fire. Come, let *us* rebuild the wall of Jerusalem, and *we* will no longer be in disgrace" (v. 17). If he had said, "You see what trouble *you* are in; *you* need to rebuild the wall," he would have gotten nowhere. It is amazing what the equal participation of a leader can do to build morale. It is this "we together" and not "what you should do" that inspires confidence.

He Took the People into His Confidence

Nehemiah kept the people informed both here at the beginning and later when the work got underway. At this stage it was the progress already attained. It had two parts. First, there had been a victory at the highest level: the king had altered his policy to permit the rebuilding. Second, God was behind the great project. Nehemiah reports, "I also told them about the gracious hand of my God upon me and what the king had said to me" (v. 18). If you are trying to lead others, don't forget this element. It is said of Martin Luther that one reason for his success in leading the Reformation was that he kept the German people informed of what was happening and what he was doing at each stage.

How the Work Was Done

The third chapter of Nehemiah is a detailed account of how the gates and walls were rebuilt, focusing on the names of those who were involved in the construction. Can anything be more uninteresting than a list of names, particularly names most of us can hardly pronounce? Actually chapter 3 is an important section, one of the most important sections of the book.

The most striking thing about chapter 3 is that Nehemiah divided the work into manageable sections. If the rebuilding of the walls had been tackled as a task whole in itself and if one person or even one group of people had been assigned to it, the work would have seemed impossible, and rightly so. Who could rebuild an entire mile-and-a-half or two-and-a-half-mile wall? Nobody could do it. But when the project was divided into forty or forty-one separate segments, as the chapter shows it was, then the two-and-a-half-mile project became possible. Nehemiah succeeded by engaging all the people and dividing them into units with manageable assignments.

Most managers know how to subdivide projects, of course. So this is perhaps a superfluous point for them. But lots of people do not know how to manage projects. When faced with a large assignment most people make one or more mistakes. They underestimate the task. They let the work go until the end of the available time, when it is too late to get all that is necessary done. They waste time on easier, more interesting tasks, rather than tackle the basic and more demanding tasks first. Or they try to do too many things at once.

Church workers especially need to learn this strategy. Ephesians 4:11-13 explains what the pattern is to be. It says that Jesus

gave some to be apostles, some to be prophets, some to be evangelists, and some to be pastors and teachers, to prepare God's people for works of service, so that the body of Christ may be built up until we all reach unity in the faith and in the knowledge of the Son of God and become mature, attaining to the whole measure of the fullness of Christ.

This is the basis of what we today call "an every member ministry," that ministers are to prepare the people to do God's work. Unfortunately, many churches have it completely turned around. They resemble a football game in which there are eighty thousand spectators in the stands who badly need some exercise and twenty-two men on the field who badly need a rest.

Dealing with Opposition

The distribution of material in Nehemiah 1—6 is interesting. Chapter 1 is given to Nehemiah's response to the challenge to build Jerusalem's walls; chapter 2 to his audience with Artaxerxes, his trip to Jerusalem and his nighttime inspection of the ruins; chapter 3 to the way the walls were actually built. But then three whole chapters (4—6) discuss the opposition Nehemiah encountered while building the wall and how he dealt with it. This distribution shows the importance of a leader's approach to opposition. To succeed at a task when there is no opposition requires only a technocrat, a task specialist or "bean-counter." It takes a genuine leader to triumph over determined opposition.

In the fourth, fifth and sixth chapters of Nehemiah we see how Nehemiah dealt successfully with six forms of opposition.

Opposition by Ridicule

The easiest way to oppose something you do not like is to ridicule it, and this is the first thing that Sanballat and Tobiah, Nehemiah's most determined enemies, did. The text tells how Sanballat got Tobiah, his associates and the army of Samaria together and made fun of the Jews in what must have been a great public forum, saying, "What are those feeble Jews doing? Will they restore their wall? Will they offer sacrifices? Will they finish in a day? Can they bring the stones back to life from those heaps of rubble—burned as they are?" (4:2).

The reason that people ridicule those they oppose, aside from it being so easy, is that it is demoralizing and frequently effective. It is effective because it strikes at the hidden insecurities almost everybody has. Each of Sanballat's five rhetorical questions and Tobiah's taunt struck at a legitimate sense of weakness that Nehemiah and the others must have had.

How did Nehemiah deal with this attack? First, he did not retaliate. Second, he prayed. He is always praying. Third, he went on with the work. Since he had left the taunts of his enemies with God, he no longer needed to be concerned about them and could get on with the task that God had given him. What he says is nice: "So we rebuilt the wall till all of it reached half its height, for the people worked with all their heart" (v. 6).

The Threat of Violence

The larger second half of Nehemiah 4 contains a second form of opposition to the governor's work, the threat of physical violence. Nehemiah introduces the problem in verses 7 and 8 and describes how he met it in verses 9-23. The introductory verses say, "But when Sanballat, Tobiah, the Arabs, the Ammonites and the men of Ashdod heard that the repairs to Jerusalem's walls had gone ahead and that the gaps were being closed, they were very angry. They all plotted together to come and fight against Jerusalem and stir up trouble against it."

Nehemiah must have known that it was unlikely that his enemies would attack the city in full force since he had the imposing authority of the king of Persia behind him. If the coalition of the governors

of Trans-Euphrates attacked him, they would be opposing Artaxerxes, the very thing they were accusing the Jews of doing. On the
other hand, Nehemiah must have known that what we might call
guerrilla warfare was likely. It would not take much of an effort for
his enemies to sneak up on the city, surprise the builders and kill
some—and deny that they had anything to do with it. This would so
demoralize the people that the work would stop and would never get
going again. What Nehemiah did was extremely wise. He dealt with
the real threat, not the imagined one, while lifting the people's low
self-esteem and raising their confidence. He turned Jerusalem into
an armed camp.

When the threat became known he responded by posting a guard
day and night (v. 9). When the rumors of violence continued and
began to have a demoralizing effect on morale he went further: he
stopped the work (see vv. 13, 15), armed the people (v. 13) and
rearranged them in family groups at the most exposed places along
the wall (v. 13). He knew that they would fight most fiercely where
the lives of their own family members were at stake.

Throughout this period Nehemiah continued to boost morale by
reminding the people that God would fight for them. "Don't be
afraid of them," he said. "Remember the Lord, who is great and
awesome, and fight for your brothers, your sons and your daughters,
your wives and your homes" (v. 14). "Our God will fight for us" (v.
20). Nehemiah had many good traits, but what made him really great
here was his faith that the God who had given him the task of
rebuilding the wall would stand by him and the others until the job
was done. Has God given you a task? You should know that he will
enable you to carry your work to its completion too.

Opposition from Within

Suddenly, to judge from the tone of chapter 5, a new form of opposition erupted—and from an unexpected source. The first two forms
of opposition had been from without, from Israel's enemies. This
new form was from within. It arose because of wrong conduct by
some of the Jewish people themselves.

Isn't that the way it always is? You are engaged in some important work. You have been opposed by people who are not Christians and do not share the vision. You have overcome that form of opposition and are pressing on, when suddenly there is a problem within the Christian community itself, and this threat is more of a problem than the external threat. It had been true of Israel before this. During the days of the monarchy the Jewish states had been opposed by their pagan neighbors. There had been many wars. But when God sent prophets to call the people to righteousness, it was not the pagans who killed God's messengers but the Jews themselves. An examination of church history will show that the most successful attacks on the church have come not from unbelievers, but from people who have professed to know Jesus Christ. Who is responsible for most opposition to Christian work today? Isn't it true that the greatest opposition is from apparent believers, from those who profess a form of godliness but reject true Christianity?

The problem that erupted at this point is described in verses 1-5.

Now the men and their wives raised a great outcry against their Jewish brothers. Some were saying, "We and our sons and daughters are numerous; in order for us to eat and stay alive, we must get grain."

Others were saying, "We are mortgaging our fields, our vineyards and our homes to get grain during the famine."

Still others were saying, "We have had to borrow money to pay the king's tax on our fields and vineyards. Although we are of the same flesh and blood as our countrymen and though our sons are as good as theirs, yet we have to subject our sons and daughters to slavery. Some of our daughters have already been enslaved, but we are powerless, because our fields and our vineyards belong to others."

These verses describe a classic example of the gap between rich and poor and the way in which the rich usually try to control things so that they get richer while the poor get poorer. It was a case of exploitation, and what made it worse was that it occurred within the Jewish community, among those who should have been helping one another.

Nehemiah "pondered" this problem rather than acting precipitously and eventually decided to confront the offenders privately. He reports this briefly: "I told them, 'You are exacting usury from your own countrymen' " (v. 7). What Nehemiah was doing in this private confrontation with the wealthy was following the first principle for dealing with sin among brothers, which Jesus spelled out in Matthew 18. "If your brother sins against you, go and show him his fault, just between the two of you. If he listens to you, you have won your brother over" (v. 15). We do not know whether Nehemiah had witnesses along for this first one-on-one meeting with the offending nobles and officials, but he was following this procedure. He was trying to resolve the problem privately.

Did Nehemiah succeed in this first effort? He did not seem to. There was no response from the nobles. They seem merely to have dug in their heels and said nothing, as people in the wrong often do. Nehemiah moved to a public confrontation.

I am indebted to Frank R. Tillapaugh for some important thoughts at this point, based on the fact that in order to have a public meeting Nehemiah must have pulled his workers off the wall. In normal circumstances this would not have been remarkable, but the situation was not normal. Nehemiah's goal was to build the wall, and to build it quickly before the effort could be stopped by Israel's enemies. He had everyone working, from dawn's first light until the stars came out. In fact, from the moment three days after he had arrived in Jerusalem, when he had begun the building, until now, there had been only one small interval in which the work had been stopped, and that was when a hostile armed attack had seemed imminent (4:13-14). As soon as the threat passed, Nehemiah had the people back on the walls again.

Yet now Nehemiah stops the work and holds a public meeting. Why was this? Tillapaugh says that it was because the situation had changed. There was a problem within now, and it was of such overriding importance that it was necessary to deal with it immediately. "What good was it to build the wall," asked Tillapaugh, "if inside the wall there were people who were exploiting one another?"[7]

We must ask that question again today, and we must ask it of ourselves. What good is it to build great evangelical institutions, constructing walls against the "evil" of our opposing, secular world, if within the walls the so-called people of God are indistinguishable from those without? What good is it to preserve a separate "Christian" identity if Christians behave like unbelievers? To put it in sharp terms, we need to stop calling the world to repent until we repent ourselves.

The astonishing thing about this chapter is that Nehemiah succeeded. We know that he was against stiff opposition because the nobles did not respond when he had approached them earlier. Nevertheless, after Nehemiah had exposed the wrong being done and had challenged the offenders to return the pledged fields, vineyards, olive groves and houses, refund the interest and stop the usury, the nobles agreed to give everything back (v. 12).

Opposition by Intimidation

Suddenly, just when the work seemed about to be finished, a final phase of his enemies' opposition unfolded. It was opposition by intrigue, innuendo and intimidation. Each attack was subtle, seeming to be something other than it was. So part of the challenge to Nehemiah was to see the real situation clearly.

The *intrigue* took the form of an invitation to Nehemiah to meet with his enemies on the plain of Ono (6:1-2). The reason that this was subtle and therefore dangerous is that on the surface it sounded quite plausible. What is more, it was attractive. The wall was rebuilt; only the gates remained to be set in place. It was time for a conference. Ah, but the job was not quite done. True, the walls were completed to their full height. But so long as the gates were unfinished the entire project was in jeopardy. Nehemiah knew this. So he declined the invitation.

What magnificent, single-minded concentration! And what a classic reply! "I am carrying on a great project and cannot go down. Why should the work stop while I leave it and go down to you?" Nehemiah says that his enemies sent him the message four times. Each time he gave the same answer.

After the fourth invitation and refusal Sanballat must have sensed that his anxiety was showing, so he resorted to *innuendo*. This took the form of an unconfirmed "rumor." Sanballat sent his aide to Nehemiah, holding an unsealed letter in which was written:

It is reported among the nations—and Geshem says it is true— that you and the Jews are plotting to revolt, and therefore you are building the wall. Moreover, according to these reports you are about to become their king and have even appointed prophets to make this proclamation about you in Jerusalem: "There is a king in Judah!" Now this report will get back to the king; so come, let us confer together. (vv. 6-7)

We have words for this. We call it political "hardball." It is something from the experienced campaigner's bag of "dirty tricks."

It was not new in substance, of course, but was a revival of the charge made earlier (2:19). What made it new (and "dirty") was the fact that it was an *open* letter. An open letter would have been a read letter. In other words, as in the case of all gossip, the damage was already done. Moreover, the letter was a threat to hurt Nehemiah more. For when Sanballat said, "This report will get back to the king; so come, let us confer together" (v. 7), he was not offering to help, as his words seemed to indicate; he was actually threatening to report Nehemiah to Artaxerxes if Nehemiah refused to cooperate.

What is a leader to do in such circumstances? If ever a leader needs inner strength, it is in such cases. His heart must be pure. If Nehemiah had actually been planning to become king and lead a revolt, he would have been weak-kneed with indecision.

As soon as Nehemiah heard the report, he replied with an immediate denial: "Nothing like what you are saying is happening; you are just making it up out of your head" (v. 8). And he did something else too. He prayed—because, although he denied Sanballat's false rumor as directly and emphatically as possible, he did not know whether his denial would be believed or whether he would survive the assault. Artaxerxes might have believed Sanballat. Nehemiah might have been recalled and beheaded.

The *intimidation* took the most subtle form. A man thought to be a prophet sent for Nehemiah. His name was Shemaiah, and he had an invitation: "Let us meet in the house of God, inside the temple, and let us close the temple doors, because men are coming to kill you—by night they are coming to kill you" (v. 10). This was a temptation for Nehemiah to do two wrong things: to put his own safety ahead of the work and to break God's law in order to save his life.

The second of those points deserves explanation. When Shemaiah suggested that he and Nehemiah flee to the temple to save themselves, the term he used means "the Holy Place" and not just the temple enclosure. For anyone but priests to enter the Holy Place was contrary to Old Testament teaching. Nehemiah was a layman, and laymen were not allowed into the inner portions of the temple (Num 18:7). Uzziah had violated that prohibition and had been fortunate to escape with no more than leprosy (2 Chron 26:16-21). If Nehemiah had succumbed to Shemaiah's artful suggestion he would have been seriously compromised and may even have lost his life. Because Shemaiah was suggesting something contrary to the law of God, Nehemiah knew that "God had not sent" Shemaiah (v. 12).

God does not speak out of both sides of his mouth. His yes is yes, and his no is no. He is at all times utterly consistent. If we would learn that, it would save us much trouble. Normally, instead of obeying God, we disobey him and assume that God will therefore change his mind and alter his requirement. But he does not, and we do not triumph in the situation as Nehemiah did. Cyril Barber writes that Nehemiah triumphed "not by breaking God's law to escape assassination, but by keeping it!"[8]

So the work went on, and in less than two months the "impossible" task had been completed.[9]

11
Nehemiah:
A Postscript

*I*N THE LAST CHAPTER WE SAW HOW Nehemiah organized the people of Israel to rebuild the walls of Jerusalem in just fifty-two days. It is probably the best example in the Bible of how godly leadership can operate in a secular environment on a secular task. But the story of Nehemiah's rebuilding of the walls is not the whole of the book that bears his name. It occupies the first seven chapters. But after that there is an account of his restoration of the civil and religious life of the nation, and at the end there is a chapter dealing with Nehemiah's final reforms, about thirteen years after he had first arrived in Jerusalem.

This final chapter deserves notice as a postscript because it is a study of an additional essential element in effective leadership: perseverance. Keeping on with the task. Refusing to give up. This is a lesson today's evangelicals need to learn if we are to be effective in our efforts to make a difference in our world.

The Same Old Problems
To begin with, Nehemiah 13 concerns a time somewhat removed from the first chapters. This is indicated in verse 6, where Nehemiah explains that he had returned to Babylon in the thirty-second year of Artaxerxes and that what he is recounting now was "some time later." It appears from this that Nehemiah had two governorships of

Judah. The first, which he has described in 5:14, extended from the twentieth to the thirty-second year of Artaxerxes. That is, it lasted for twelve years, from 445 B.C. to 433 B.C. Some commentators consider it unlikely that Nehemiah spent all twelve of those years in Judah, judging that he must have returned to Babylon shortly after the victories of his first great year and perhaps only returned intermittently during the twelve-year period. But Nehemiah does not say this. On the contrary, the gap in which the problems of chapter 13 developed seems to have been between the end of his first twelve-year term and the second assignment years later.

There is no way of knowing how many years this was, since Nehemiah is vague. Presumably a considerable period of time elapsed, since the problems of the final chapter are major ones that would not have developed overnight. Guesses for the year of Nehemiah's return to Jerusalem run from 425 B.C.[1] to 420 B.C.,[2] dates near the end of the reign of King Artaxerxes.

The significant thing is that Nehemiah was now considerably older. He must have been at least forty when he left Susa for Jerusalem the first time. The end of his first governorship would have brought him to the age of fifty-two, and if we are now in the years 425 to 420 B.C., Nehemiah must have been near sixty-five. This is the age most people today retire. But Nehemiah did not retire. In this chapter we see him returning to Jerusalem and achieving some of his most important victories.

But it is not just the fact that Nehemiah had to continue his struggles into old age that is significant. It is also that he had to deal with exactly the same problems he had dealt with earlier.

The end of chapter 12 deals with the provisions made for the temple service (vv. 44-47), and the beginning of chapter 13 deals with the purification of the people by excluding from their official number all who were of foreign descent (vv. 1-3). Some commentators have called these sections parenthetical. But that is not how Nehemiah viewed them. He links these sections to the dedication by using the words "at that time" and "on that day," though what they describe was probably spread out over a period of weeks or months.

It is his way of saying that the purity of the people was the very heart of what he was trying to accomplish. These were exactly the problems he faced when he returned to the city some seven or twelve years later. In other words, his second governorship did not deal with a new set of problems but with the same old problems.

And there is this too. In chapter 10 there is an account of a covenant made by the people at the time of the religious revival under Ezra. The covenant contained six items.

1. The family. The people promised not to intermarry with the people of the nations about them. This was not racial snobbery or prejudice. It was to preserve their religion and the unique quality of the spiritual life that flowed from it.

2. The Sabbath. The people promised to abstain from all commercial activity on this day, preserving it as a day to worship God and remember his blessings.

3. The temple tax. The people promised to pay the tax required of them by Exodus 30:11-16. They took it as an annual obligation.

4. Additional provisions for the temple. The people were not content merely with paying the tax for the temple but also promised to provide the temple with wood for the altar and the first-fruits of their crops and trees.

5. Dedication of the firstborn. This was a matter of priorities. It was a way of acknowledging that all we are and have is a gift from God and is owed to him.

6. The tithe. The final thing the people promised was to be faithful in paying tithes to God. The tithe was paid to the Levites, and the Levites paid a tithe of all they received to the priests. This was the way the people provided for the temple service.

But it was exactly these matters that Nehemiah found to have been neglected when he returned for his second period as governor in 425 or 420 B.C. In fact, of the six items solemnly covenanted in chapter 10, the only one that does not recur in chapter 13 is the obligation to dedicate the firstborn to God, and that is probably because it is subsumed under the greater problem of the family and intermarriages with foreign peoples dealt with extensively in verses

22-28. How pious the people were in promising these things in the revival! How solemnly they declared: "We will not neglect the house of our God" (10:39). But they did neglect it. They broke their promises.

A Worm in the Big Apple

These problems were dramatically illustrated by what Nehemiah found to be going on at the temple. Eliashib, the high priest (13:4-7) with whom he had worked closely during his earlier governorship and whom he had placed in charge of the temple storerooms, had affiliated himself with Tobiah the Ammonite, Nehemiah's old enemy (vv. 4-5). Later we learn that Eliashib had also given a daughter in marriage to Nehemiah's other archenemy, Sanballat the Horonite of Samaria (v. 28). We are told that he had provided Tobiah with rooms in the temple, putting him in a suite of rooms where the temple articles, tithes and offerings had formerly been stored.

Why had Eliashib done this? Probably because, as he would have said, "We are living in a new day. Nehemiah has returned to Babylon. His old style of aggressive leadership was good in the old days, but it is not the right style for this time. Today we need compromise, building bridges, a hand out to old friends."

We can be sure that Tobiah had been working his side of the alliance too. He would have been maneuvering for entree into the highest leadership positions in the city. Tobiah had a Jewish name, and when Nehemiah had first come to Jerusalem he discovered (and reports) that Tobiah had married the daughter of Shecaniah son of Arah, one of the leaders of the city, and that his daughter had married Meshullam son of Berekiah, another leader (Neh 6:18; cf. 3:4; 7:10; 10:7; 12:3, 14, 33). Tobiah would have done anything to get even a toehold in the city. He must have been delighted with the splendid arrangements Eliashib made for him. From the temple precincts he had a base from which to foment intrigue and increase his bad influence.

When Nehemiah got back to Jerusalem and discovered what had been done, he did not waste a moment in either investigation or negotiation. He simply threw Tobiah and all his possessions out! He dumped his possessions outside the door onto the sidewalk, fumigated the room, and then restored the temple articles. Just like that! Charles Swindoll, who is entertaining on this point, says, "Nehemiah didn't even want the smell of Tobiah to hang around the building."[3]

Was Nehemiah angry? He was. He says he was "greatly displeased" (v. 8). Was he right to be angry? The answer is yes to that too. Christians are uneasy with anger, and rightly so. But they forget that deep-seated wrongs are seldom corrected except by people who have first become agitated and angry about them. The cool, the complacent do not change anything.

It is possible to be wrongly angry, of course. That is often the case when the wrong is only against ourselves. We can also be wrong if we do nothing more than get angry. But wrong anger is not our major problem in today's Christianity. The bigger problems are compromise and cowardice. John White says rightly,

> In Christian work our cowardice in avoiding unpleasantness is currently doing more damage than any damage from irascibility on the part of Christian leaders. And what irascibility we do give way to is usually verbal. It wounds without correcting. The church has become flabby, . . . inept, unwilling to act. Discipline should be reconciliatory and loving, *but it should take place.* And on the whole it doesn't. . . . Who are we—who condone every manner of evil in our midst—to criticize one of those rare leaders who does not hesitate to act when the integrity of God's temple is in question?[4]

Apparently Nehemiah did not fear to place his actions before God for judgment, for he says in verse 14, "Remember me in this, O my God, and do not blot out what I have so faithfully done for the house of my God and its services." We should all be so bold!

Nehemiah's Final Reforms

After dealing with the erring Eliashib and Tobiah, Nehemiah moved with determination to right the other wrongs that he discovered. These correspond to the promises made by the people in chapter

10. They concerned the family, the Sabbath, the temple tax, other provisions for the temple, dedication of the firstborn, and the tithe. Nehemiah's dealings with these constitute his final reforms.

The Tithe

Nehemiah learned that the tithes had not been paid and that the Levites and others responsible for the temple worship had therefore left Jerusalem and gone back to their own fields to earn a living. Probably there was a connection between this problem and the earlier one. If Eliashib the high priest was acting in an unprincipled manner, the people had probably begun to lose confidence in the priestly establishment, and it is understandable that the tithes would be neglected. On the other hand, the tithe obligation remained for the people regardless of the spiritual quality of the leadership; the tithe was a biblical command. It is probably true that the people were just neglecting this responsibility.

Nehemiah dealt with this problem through the proper officials, since the responsibility for collecting the tithe was theirs. He rebuked them, reinstated the Levites in their position and reestablished the system for collecting tithes.

Other Provisions for the Temple

Additional provisions for the temple had also suffered, no doubt for the same reasons as the neglect of the tithe. Nehemiah corrected this abuse too. He dismissed the old custodians, who had failed in their responsibilities and who would have been in tight with Eliashib, and installed Shelemiah, Zadok, Pedaiah and Hanan in their places because, Nehemiah says, "these men were considered trustworthy" (v. 13).

The Sabbath

The longest single section of Nehemiah 13 deals with the desecration of the Sabbath. Like a trickle through a dike, commercial activity on the Sabbath had probably begun slowly—in the countryside with the farmers harvesting grain and treading grapes. But it had grown steadily stronger. Having harvested their grain and made their wine, the farmers next brought these to the city to be sold—again on the Sabbath. And following quickly on their heels were traders from Tyre, who had fish and "all kinds of merchandise" for the markets.

Nehemiah did four things that were typical of his leadership style. First, he rebuked the nobles who were responsible for the city's life, warning them that it was for such abuses that the judgment of God had come on the people years before. It was characteristic of Nehemiah to work through those who were officially in charge.

Second, he locked the gates on the Sabbath, placing some of his own men over them. This was a practical device by an eminently practical man. If the gates could not be opened, it was certain that no merchandise would flow into the city through them.

Third, when the merchants (probably the merchants from Tyre) camped outside Jerusalem hoping for a change in the Sabbath regulations or perhaps looking for a way to get around them, Nehemiah threatened them with forceful action if they did not move on. He did not want temptation even to be hanging around the perimeter of the Jewish city.

Finally, Nehemiah put the Levites in charge of guarding the city gates. He wanted this to be their responsibility, and he knew that he and his men would not always be around to do it for them.

The Family

The final abuse was an old one, going back to the people's early days in the land: intermarriage with the nations round about, the very thing that they had promised to avoid in chapter 10. Half of the children of these marriages did not even know how to speak the Jews' language, and the problem had extended upward even into the families of the leaders of the city. As Nehemiah explains in verse 28, a grandson of Eliashib the high priest had married a daughter of Sanballat the Horonite.

In this case, Nehemiah did not act as radically as Ezra had done when he required the Jewish men to divorce their foreign wives (Ezra 9—10). Nevertheless, he gave them a thorough dressing down and publicly humiliated some of them, extracting renewed promises that the people would abstain from damaging marriages with foreign peoples (v. 25). As for the grandson of Eliashib, Nehemiah simply drove him from the city.

So ended the last of the reforms.

Keep On Keeping On

Leighton Ford, the son-in-law of Billy Graham and head of the Lausanne Committee on World Evangelization, had a son named Sandy. When he was fourteen years old Sandy developed a heart problem from which he later died, at the age of twenty-one. Nevertheless, for a time the problem seemed to be corrected and the young man returned to running track and cross country, in which he excelled. On one occasion, Sandy was in a mile race, close to the tape and moving ahead to a record-setting victory with a forty-yard lead on the second-place runner. Suddenly he developed a problem in his legs, stumbled and fell. The fall was probably brought on by his old heart problem. He picked himself up, stumbled forward a few yards more and fell again. Looking back, he saw the second-place runner closing in on him. So he got up on his hands and knees and crawled under the tape, across the finish line, and fell there, having won the race.[5]

That is perseverance. It was a major quality of Nehemiah, and it is a quality of all great leaders. Is it true of us? In our following after Jesus Christ in faithful discipleship? In our efforts to make a difference for good in this sad world? We should "keep on keeping on" until we can say with the apostle Paul, "I have fought the good fight, I have finished the race, I have kept the faith. Now there is in store for me the crown of righteousness, which the Lord, the righteous Judge, will award to me on that day—and not only to me, but to all who have longed for his appearing" (2 Tim 4:7-8).

Part 4

The Marks
of the Church

And what does the LORD require of you?
To act justly and to love mercy
and to walk humbly with your God.

MICAH 6:8

12

One Nation Under God?

T HESE ARE CRITICAL DAYS IN AMERICAN history.[1] In 1984, in the course of his last presidential campaign, President Ronald Reagan said, "Just about every place you look, things are looking up. Life is better—America is back—and people have a sense of pride they never thought they'd feel again." But not long afterward, after the upheavals of the Iran-Contra affair, the insider-trading scandals on Wall Street and the revelations of misconduct by some of the television evangelists, *Time* magazine reported perceptively, "America, which took such a back-thumping pride in its spiritual renewal, [now] finds itself wallowing in a moral morass." *Time* asked sharply, "Has the mindless materialism of the '80s left in its wake a values vacuum?"[2]

The Values Vacuum

A values vacuum is what we are dealing with, of course. But it is not something that suddenly burst on us in the 1980s. It had been with us (and growing) for a long, long time before that.

Francis Schaeffer traced our values crisis to the thought of Georg Wilhelm Friedrich Hegel, the German philosopher who invented the idea of the "historical dialectic." Hegel believed that history is always in a state of development. At any one period there may be something that a majority of the people agree on and are willing to regard as truth. Hegel called this a "thesis." But this "truth" is always countered by a contradictory idea, which Hegel called an "antithesis." And the result is a struggle between the "thesis" and the countering "antithesis" through which a new "truth" or "synthesis" develops. This new "truth" becomes the new "thesis," and the process repeats itself indefinitely. If this is the way things are, there can never be any absolute truth but only what is truth for you (but not necessarily for me) or me (but not necessarily for you). And what is truth today was not necessarily true yesterday and probably will not be true tomorrow.

The majority of our contemporaries live in this philosophical house, whether or not they realize that they are Hegelians. For them, truth is relative. And where truth is relative there can be no absolutes. There can be no valid values.

Even secular writers have begun to mourn this missing element. One who has done so brilliantly is Allan Bloom, the author of the bestselling critique of American higher education, *The Closing of the American Mind.* Bloom, a professor at the University of Chicago, does not have a Christian answer to the problem. This is an unfortunate shortcoming of his book. He calls only for a return to classical learning, at least for a small core of intellectuals. But Bloom sees the problem clearly, and he has analyzed where it has come from and where it is going. In the very first lines he states: "There is one thing a professor can be absolutely certain of: almost every student entering the university believes, or says he believes, that truth is relative."[3]

If that is so, then there is no point in pursuing truth, no point in asking what is right as opposed to what is wrong, and the result is a downward spiral that has more in common with the first chapter of the book of Romans than with the popular Western or American ideal of "human progress."

In the July 3, 1987, issue of *National Review* former Secretary of Education William J. Bennett courageously exposed the "value neutral" stance of our public schools' sex education programs as a factor in the alarming rise of teenage pregnancies in the last decade. According to Bennett, sex does involve values—absolute values—and we are harming our children by failing to say so. "We should recognize that sexual behavior is a matter of character and personality and that we cannot be value-neutral about it. Neutrality only confuses children and may lead them to conclusions we wish them to avoid." Instead of the values morass in the area of sex education, Bennett rightly says that we should teach children "sexual restraint as a standard to uphold and follow."[4]

The International Council on Biblical Inerrancy was created to fight this relativism, particularly in the church, where it has spread. It argued that Hegel is wrong and that our entire civilization is on a disastrously wrong path. We cannot survive without absolutes. But because we can never discover a basis for ultimate truth or absolutes in ourselves, we must receive these from God, who has provided them for us in the pages of the Bible. That is where we learn who we are, who we are meant to be, who God is, how we can be reconciled to God through faith in Jesus Christ, and what God requires of us as Christ's followers. Only on this basis can ours or any other culture move forward.

I liked the title one of our television networks chose for a prime-time special on a visit of Pope John Paul to the United States. It was called "God Is Not Elected." We need to say that as Christians. God is not elected. Nor are right moral values. Values cannot be determined by the freedom of personal choice or a 51 percent vote.

Politics: A Misplaced Confidence

A second reason that these are crisis days for the United States touches on the practices of evangelicals in particular. Either we have detached ourselves from the problems of our country, believing that the political system and the government that flows from it are so corrupt that no true Christian should have anything to do with them—an error more characteristic of the past—or else we have become so enamored with the political process that we have been swept up into the idolatrous notion that the kingdom of God can come by the political involvement of Christians. We need to repudiate both errors and work to articulate the correct role of

Christians as Christians in a secular state.

How should we do that? Where should we start? Here are five balanced statements to keep in mind as we begin.

> 1. Church and state must be separate from each other, in the sense that the church must not control national policy and the state must neither establish nor limit the free exercise of religion. But this does not mean that the state is independent of God or that either church or state is unanswerable to the other for how it carries out its functions.

The doctrine of the separation of church and state means that presidents are not to appoint clerics, define doctrine or establish church polity, and clerical authorities are not to appoint presidents or do the state's work. Nevertheless, church and state are both responsible to God in whose wisdom each has been established. Each is to remind the other of its God-appointed duties and recall it to upright, godly conduct if it strays. If Christians do not do their job of speaking to the civil authorities on moral issues, spiritual and moral principles will be eliminated from public debate, the state will become its own god, and the only functioning political principle will be pragmatism. This is precisely what has been happening in the United States in recent years.

> 2. Christians are free to seek elected office, and some should be encouraged to do so. But elected officials do not have to be Christians to be effective leaders, and merely being a Christian does not in itself qualify one for any office.

The Westminster Confession of Faith in its chapter on the "Civil Magistrate" states rightly that "it is lawful for Christians to accept and execute the office of a magistrate." This means that it is as proper for Christians to engage in secular pursuits such as politics as it is to become missionaries and ministers. But while missionaries and ministers must be born again to perform their function, civil leaders do not have to be. A Christian does not have to vote for the "Christian" candidate if a choice is offered. Moreover, since none of us is able to see into another person's heart, if we think that we have to vote only for Christian candidates, we subject ourselves to base manipulation by whatever candidate is willing to use the proper evangelical terms when speaking to us.

3. The Bible gives Christians guidelines for approaching national and social problems, and Christians will seek to be consistently biblical in all their thoughts and actions. But the Bible does not necessarily give specific answers to problems, and reasoning from a biblical principle to a specific public policy must be done carefully.

It is a valid complaint of seasoned politicians that many Christians leap too quickly from a valid truth of Scripture to a specific program and are overly hasty in denouncing anyone who disagrees with their program as being unbiblical or anti-God. If Christians are to gain a hearing in the rough and tumble of the political arena, they must be willing to fill in the gaps, showing how a suggested program best expresses and advances the desired principle. Moreover, Christians must argue their case with unbelievers, appealing to them on behalf of what is good for them and society and not retreating into an unassailable citadel of "revelation."

As Chuck Colson said in a positioning letter to Congress on the Bible II speakers and workshop leaders, "To be successful, this congress must equip and mobilize Christians, not to march down Pennsylvania Avenue, but effectively to bring biblical principles to bear on the mainstream issues of our culture."

4. In attempting to advance a specific proposal Christians must depend on moral persuasion, asking God through prayer to give their reasoning favor with those having different points of view. They must not retreat from this high calling to tactics of mere naked pressure or coercion.

It is tempting to resort to such pressure. The political process is slow, riddled with compromise and frustration. It is tempting to try to shortcut the hard work. Again, some people know only the tactics of public demonstration, economic boycott, media hype and back-room power politics. Since these things often work for others, the Christian activist reasons that they should also work for him. And sometimes they do, although the results are frequently unsubstantial. Christians must not forget that the only truly lasting reforms come from God and that they have usually been a product of periods of great spiritual awakening.

5. Christians must think, work and pray effectively, trying always to place their specific programs within the framework of an overall Christian world-and-life view. But they must also strive no less personally to model the reality suggested.

How Real Is Our Religion?

Can we do that? Will Christian people do it? In my opinion that question leads to the most important reason for the crisis before us and to our greatest challenge. For it is a way of saying that in the final analysis our problems are neither primarily philosophical nor programmatic but spiritual. As Aleksandr Solzhenitsyn said in London a few years ago on the occasion of his receiving the coveted Templeton Prize, "These things [he was referring to the evils he had observed in the Soviet Union and to the evils of the West as well] . . . these things have happened to us because we have forgotten God."

We like to think of America as a religious nation. But American religion is shallow, and it is increasingly difficult to believe that most of it is achieving a lasting impact on society.

Several years ago, George Gallup Jr., president of the American Institute of Public Opinion, reported on the nation's religious life in an address entitled "Is America's Faith for Real?" His studies had shown that 81 percent of Americans consider themselves religious (only Italians, with 83 percent, rate higher). Ninety-five percent of Americans believe in God. Seventy-one percent believe in life after death. Eighty-four percent believe in heaven. An astonishing 67 percent believe in hell. Large numbers believe in the Ten Commandments. Nearly every home has a Bible. Almost all pray. More than half of all Americans can usually be found in church on Sunday morning. But these statistics are misleading. For, as Gallup also reported in the same address:

1. Only one person in five says that religion is the *most* influen-

tial factor in his or her life,

2. Although most Americans want religious education of some sort for their children, religious faith ranks below many other traits parents would like to see developed, and

3. Only one person in eight says that he or she would even consider sacrificing everything for God.

Gallup's surveys showed a glaring ignorance of the Ten Commandments, even though we profess to believe in them; high levels of credulity (for example, high proportions of Americans, even churchgoers, believe in astrology); lack of basic spiritual disciplines; and a strong anti-intellectual bias where religious ideas are concerned. Americans want private emotional experiences rather than sustained, rigorous thought and the challenge of applying strong biblical values to their personal and public lives.[5]

John R. W. Stott, rector emeritus of London's All Souls Church, calls Western Christianity "skin-deep." He asks, "How can we have so many people claiming to be born again and yet have so little impact on society?"[6]

In the late 1970s columnist William Reel wrote an article for the New York *Daily News* entitled "Mean Street . . . X-Rated Streets," citing the terrible statistics at that time—400,000 alcoholics, 500,000 narcotics users, 300,000 compulsive gamblers, 658,147 felonies in the preceding year (assaults, robberies, muggings, rapes, murders)—in New York City alone. But then came his bottom line, a surprising conclusion that asked for spiritual renewal.

You gave up on New York politicians long ago. They are pathetic and embarrassing. But what is worse than the abdication of political leadership in New York is the abdication of spiritual leadership. There is no one willing to speak the truth, to call the Neros to account, to warn of the wrath of God.

When was the last time a Catholic leader said anything more forceful than "God bless you"? New York needs a John the Baptist and Catholicism gives us Caspar Milquetoasts. The Protestant leadership is effete and insipid, debating Holy Orders for lesbians at a time when grandmothers are regularly and brutally assaulted by muggers and rapists. The Jewish establishment is moribund. Jeremiah must weep when, looking down from above, he contemplates these sad sacks sitting in their studies composing Passover messages that have no more spiritual content than a press release from the Liberal Party.

New York was a great city when it put a great emphasis on spiritual values. Maybe we can get back to this. . . . Let's hope so. It can't happen a moment too soon. A beginning has got to be made immediately.[7]

A Much Needed Text

What we need to do is spelled out in Micah 6:8. "What does the LORD require of you? To act justly and to love mercy and to walk humbly with your God." That verse is sometimes cited as if it were listing requirements for secular rulers, who, of course, are to provide for justice and show mercy. But it is actually a challenge to God's people to model what they recommend to others.

The verses immediately before this (vv. 6-7) contain four questions asked by the ungodly but religious inhabitants of Jerusalem to the effect that they were willing to do anything God might require of them—if only he would make his desires known. Does he want "burnt offerings . . . calves a year old"? That can be arranged. Does he want "thousands of rams," perhaps "ten thousand rivers of oil"? The people are willing to bring those. Perhaps God wants the "first-born" children? The text suggests that the people might even be willing to offer their children to God, as their pagan neighbors had been doing. Throughout this entire prophecy God has been faulting those who profess the name of God for unrighteousness. But they come back to God with the arrogant suggestion that the fault is not theirs but God's. It is because God has not been explicit. "Tell us what we haven't done," they demand. The implication is that they are far more ready to serve God than he is to reveal his requirements.

So God answers them, and what he says is not new. He does not lay down further religious ordinances. All he asks is what he has asked from the beginning. And it is not ritual! It is not mere verbal assent! It is not even sacrificial giving to religious causes. It is to act justly, to love mercy and to walk humbly with God.

To Act Justly

This does not mean merely to talk about justice or to get other people to act justly. It means to do the just thing yourself. Moreover, it means to do it, if necessary, over a long period of time.

There are two problems here. The first is knowing what the just thing is. This is not as easy as some people think. Is the just thing simply what the laws of the land require? It must be related to law, of course. But laws can be unjust, oppressive. They can be tools of favored classes to control those less favored. How can we be sure that a given law is unjust? Are we able to make that determination by our own intellectual and moral powers? That might be possible if we were not sinful. But we are sinful. Our judgments are clouded by our own self-interest, and we ourselves become tools of what is wrong.

I have a friend who served in the Philadelphia police department for twenty years and whose experiences in law enforcement have made him cynical. We have often talked about justice. But he has known of innumerable cases in which the guilty have gone free and the innocent have been punished. His testimony is: "On earth there is no such thing as justice."

The only way we can begin to know what justice is and act on it is if God, the author of justice, directs us in the correct way through Scripture, enabling us to see not only the world but ourselves in that mirror. We must be a people of the Book.

The second problem is perseverance. It is one thing to know what justice is. That is hard enough. But even when we know what the just thing is, it is still difficult to establish justice, and those who are trying to do it often get tired in the attempt.

I was speaking to a student group at the University of Pennsylvania, stressing the kind of leadership needed in our nation's cities today, and a student approached me to object that he had been working in city politics and had found the situation so frustrating that he had quit. He thought my talk had been too optimistic, that I was naive. I asked what year of school he was in. He was a senior. I asked how old he was. He was twenty-two. I asked how long he had been involved in the political system. He replied that he had been involved for eighteen months. I said, "You are not old enough nor have you worked in the system long enough to be frustrated." I say the same thing to myself. I have been working in Philadelphia for nearly thirty years, but I have no more right to be frustrated than that student does.

One of my associates says, "We tend to overestimate what God is going to accomplish in one year and underestimate what he is going to accomplish in twenty years." I think that is right. God takes the long view. Our responsibility is to act justly and work for justice, however long it takes.

To Love Mercy

This does not mean merely that we are to love mercy in others or even to act in a merciful way here and there or from time to time. It means that we are to show mercy in concrete ways and to do so consistently. Moreover, it means that mere words are not enough. To be merciful means to be loving, kind and gracious to other people. But it also means helping them physically and financially. We cannot turn a deaf ear or turn our backs when others are in need.

This is what the apostle James wrote about in that classic passage about the relation of faith to deeds.

What good is it, my brothers, if a man claims to have faith but has no deeds? Can such faith save him? Suppose a brother or sister is without clothes and daily food. If one of you says to him, "Go, I wish you well; keep warm and well fed," but does nothing about his physical needs, what good is it? In the same way, faith by itself, if it is not accompanied by action, is dead.

But someone will say, "You have faith; I have deeds."

Show me your faith without deeds, and I will show you my faith by what I do. You believe that there is one God. Good! Even the demons believe that—and shudder. (Jas 2:14-19)

To Walk Humbly with God

This third matter is very important. Have you known Christians who are anything but humble in the way they go about their business? I am sure you have. Such people think that they have all the answers, when they do not, and they rightly bring the world's scorn on themselves. We do not have all the answers. We must begin by saying that. At best we are part of the solution, and we may even be part of the problem. Besides, if by the grace of God we are able to accomplish anything for good in the midst of the present crisis situation, it will be in precisely that way: by the grace of God. And this means that it is God's work, not ours. The City of God is God's kingdom. We are only servants of the King of that kingdom. If that is so, how can we who know we are sinners be anything but humble? How can we desire anything but to walk humbly with God?

Before the Watching World

The world is waiting for us to do that. It is waiting for Christians to be Christians. Most people do not want to hear about Christianity. They do not want to be reconciled to God. That is part of what it means to be in an unsaved condition. But they do want you to be what you profess to be as a Christian, and they expect to see good come from it. The world looks to Christians for more than we give it credit for.

Let me go back to the Gallup poll that showed how shallow the religious faith and knowledge of most Americans really is. Because the statistics seemed so contradictory—many who claimed to be religious seemed to know and care so little about true Christian faith—Gallup devised a scale to sort out those for whom religion really did seem to be important. They were the one in eight, or 12.5 percent, who really would consider sacrificing everything for their religious beliefs or God. Gallup called them "the highly spiritually committed."

What about these people? Gallup discovered that, unlike the oth-

ers, they were a "breed apart," different from the rest of the population in at least four key respects.

1. They are more satisfied with their lot in life than those who
are less spiritually committed—and far happier. Sixty-eight percent say they are "very happy" as compared with only thirty percent of those who are uncommitted.

2. Their families are stronger. The divorce rate among this
group is far lower than among the less committed.

3. They tend to be more tolerant of persons of different races
and religions than those who are less spiritually committed. That
is exactly the opposite of what the media suggest when handling
religion or religious figures.

And here is the most striking finding of all.

4. They are far more involved in charitable activities than are
their counterparts. A total of forty-six percent of the highly spiritually committed say they are presently working among the poor,
the infirm and the elderly, compared to only thirty-six percent
among the moderately committed, twenty-eight percent among
the moderately uncommitted, and twenty-two percent among the
highly uncommitted.[8]

Genuine conversion does make profound differences in a person's
life. And it is just those persons the country needs. Laws change
nothing. People do. And the only thing that ever really changes
people is God himself through the gospel of our Lord Jesus Christ.
So let us get on with our calling. Our King is Jesus. Our marching
orders are the Bible. Our weapons are participation, persuasion and
prayer. Our goals are the goals of God's kingdom.

Sometimes it takes a thousand voices to be heard as one voice. But
in other times, times like our own, one voice can ring forth as a
thousand. Today the people of the United States of America are
desperate for leadership. Let those who claim to know God act justly,
love mercy and walk humbly with God—for the good of all.

13

Christ's Prayer for God's City

*I*N THE SEVENTEENTH CHAPTER OF JOHN'S Gospel there is a wonderful prayer of Jesus Christ for his people, the church, that is a perfect note on which to end this study. The disciples, those who were present with Jesus at this time as well as those who would believe on Jesus through their witness (v. 20), were to be God's new humanity, the very thing that has been the subject of this book. Christ's prayer for them is an illuminating glimpse into what Jesus wanted the City of God to be.

What did he pray for?

It is significant to notice what he did *not* pray for. He did not pray that his disciples would become so numerous that they would dominate and then transform the world and its culture, though he recognizes that they are to be a missionary church. In fact, Jesus makes a distinction between his own and the world, declaring emphatically that his prayer is not for the world at all: "I pray for them. I am not praying for the world, but for those you have given me" (v. 9). He did not pray for the conversion of the Roman emperor or, failing that conquest, that a different, Christian emperor might be brought to the pinnacle of world power. Earlier he had rejected the temptation to worldly power himself (Mt 4:8-10). He did not pray that there might be Christian laws or that the theocratic political system of the Old Testament might be extended worldwide.

Jesus was not thinking of numbers, political structures or laws at all. Instead he was thinking of two things: the glorification of God, and the character and conduct of those by whom God would be glorified. It was a way of acknowledging that the city of man will always be man's city, hostile to God and thus filled with every vice and wickedness, but that the people of God are to glorify God as a people apart, God's new society, whether or not they are "successful" in terms of numerical growth or influence. They are to glorify God simply by being God's people.

To God Be the Glory

The word that dominates Christ's prayer in John 17 more than any other is *glory*. In the opening section Jesus prays that he might be glorified by the Father just as he has glorified God by completing his work on earth, thus revealing the Father to those whom God had given him: "Father, the time has come. *Glorify* your Son, that your Son may *glorify* you. . . . I have brought you *glory* on earth by completing the work you gave me to do. And now, Father, *glorify* me in your presence with the *glory* I had with you before the world began" (vv. 1, 4-5). In the next section Jesus claims that "*glory* has come to me through them" (v. 10), that is, by their having believed on him and by their having begun to live for him. Toward the end he says that he has "given them the *glory* that you gave me" (v. 22). Even closer to the end he adds, "Father, I want those you have given me to be with me where I am, and to see my *glory*, the *glory* you have given me because you loved me before the creation of the world" (v. 24).

This is a very important emphasis, because it means that the goal of the church is not to be numerical success (or any other kind of "success") but glorifying God by whatever means God might choose to do it.

To glorify God means to make him known in all his glorious attributes. Jesus did this for the disciples as a goal of his earthly ministry and would do it even more completely by his death on the cross for sin. We see God's sovereignty at the cross in the way the death of Jesus was planned, promised and then achieved, without the slightest deviation from the Old Testament prophecies. We see God's justice in sin actually being punished. Without the cross God might have been able to forgive sin (theoretically), but he could not have done it and remained just at the same time. A just God must punish sin. We also see God's righteousness at the cross, for only Jesus, the utterly righteous one, could pay sin's penalty. We see God's wisdom in the planning and ordering of such a great salvation. We see God's love, for it is only at the cross that we can know beyond any question that God loves us even as he loves Jesus. "For God so loved the world that he gave his one and only Son, that whoever believes in him shall not perish but have eternal life" (Jn 3:16).

Carrying that theme over to ourselves, we ask how the people of God are to glorify him. We cannot die for sin, of course. Only Jesus could do that. But we can glorify God by allowing his character to be developed and seen in us, and by obeying him in every area of our lives. In Ephesians the apostle Paul writes of one aspect of God's character, his wisdom, being demonstrated by the church even before the angels. "His intent was that now, through the church, the manifold wisdom of God should be made known to the rulers and authorities in the heavenly realms, according to his eternal purpose which he accomplished in Christ Jesus our Lord" (Eph 3:10).

With this in mind we can now turn to the latter half of Christ's prayer and study the specific marks that Jesus asked the Father to develop in his people, marks that would glorify God.

The church is founded on the Lord Jesus Christ and is called into being by the Spirit of Christ. It must therefore be like Christ, possessing at least some of his characteristics. What should those characteristics be? What should the church be like? One of the most comprehensive answers to that question is in the latter half of Christ's prayer, for in it he prayed that the church might be characterized by six things: joy (v. 13), holiness (vv. 14-16), truth (v. 17), mission (v. 18), unity (vv. 21-23) and love (v. 26). Jesus' life was marked by each of these qualities.

A Joyful People

The first of these characteristics is joy. Many of us would not think of joy as an important characteristic, let alone put it first. We would point to love or holiness or something else. But Jesus prayed that his people might "have the full measure of my joy within them" (v. 13). That most of us do not think of joy as a primary characteristic of the church probably indicates how far we have moved from the spirit of the early church, which was a joyous assembly.

We see their joy immediately when we begin to study the subject in the New Testament. In the Greek language, the verb meaning "to rejoice" or "be joyful" is *chairein;* it is found seventy-two times. The noun meaning "joy," *chara,* occurs sixty times. Joy is not a technical concept, found only in highly theological passages. Rather it most often occurs simply as a greeting, meaning "Joy be with you!" To be sure, *chairein* is not always restricted to the speech of Christians. It is used, for example, in the letter to Felix about Paul by the Roman officer Claudius Lysias, where it means "Greetings" (Acts 23:26). But in Christian hands it obviously meant much more than it did with pagans and is used more frequently.

Notice, for example, that the angel who announced the birth of Jesus to the shepherds said, "Do not be afraid. I bring you good news of great joy that will be for all the people. Today in the town of David a Savior has been born to you; he is Christ the Lord" (Lk 2:10-11). The word here obviously meant more than "Greetings!" Later Jesus said, "I have told you this so that my joy may be in you and that your joy may be complete" (Jn 15:11). The things he had spoken were great promises.

Paul's writings contain many uses of the word. In Philippians, the apostle, wishing to give a final admonition to his friends, wrote, "Rejoice in the Lord always. I will say it again: Rejoice!" (Phil 4:4). As William Barclay says in his discussion of this term, "This last greeting, 'Joy be with you!' rings triumphantly through the pages of the New Testament. . . . There is no virtue in the Christian life which is not made radiant with joy; there is no circumstance and no occasion which is not illuminated with joy. A joyless life is not a Christian life, for joy is one constant in the recipe for Christian living."[1]

Is the church today joyful? Are Christians? We need not doubt that we are all far more joyful than we would be if we were not Christians, or that there are places where joy is particularly evident. Joy is often evident in new believers, for example. But in most churches, if one were to observe them impartially week after week, I wonder if joy would be visible. We think of joy as something that should characterize that day when we are gathered around the throne of grace to sing God's glory. But here? Here we often see sour looks, griping, long faces and other manifestations of an inner misery.

The story has often been told—I am sure it is a true one—of a church in Scotland in which someone had obviously been bored by the sermon and had begun doodling. He had started drawing pictures of the preacher and then had gone on to writing verses. When the service was over the janitor found this bit of doggerel:

To dwell above with saints in love,
    Aye, that will be glory!
To dwell below with saints I know,
    Now that's a different story.

That is the difference between what we profess to be and what we frequently are. We should be a joyful people, but we are often gloomy, discouraged and negative. You say, "But my circumstances *are* discouraging. How is God glorified by that?" It is precisely in the discouragements that you can praise God by being joyful.

Fanny Crosby, the hymnwriter, became blind when she was just five years old, and she lived to be ninety-five—ninety years of blindness. Yet she did not complain. Instead, she apparently came to terms with her problem at an early age and determined to glorify God by a cheerful attitude even in her blindness. We know this because when she was just eight years old she wrote:

Oh, what a happy soul am I!
    Although I cannot see,
I am resolved that in this world
    Contented I shall be.

How many blessings I enjoy
   That other people don't!
To weep and sigh, because I'm blind?
   I cannot, and I won't.

It might mark the beginning of a revival in some places if the people of God would learn to stop thinking about themselves and what they regard as their imagined miserable circumstances and instead learn to be joyful in God. Someone once said to Hannah Whitall Smith, author of *The Christian's Secret of a Happy Life*, "You Christians are like a man with a headache. He does not want to get rid of his head, but it hurts him to keep it. You cannot expect outsiders to seek very earnestly for anything so uncomfortable."[2]

A Separated People
A second characteristic of the church is holiness, the characteristic of God most mentioned in the Bible. Holiness should therefore characterize God's church. We are taught this in many places besides John 17. For example, Peter said that we are to be a "holy" people (1 Pet 2:9). The author of Hebrews wrote that we are to "make every effort" to be holy since "without holiness no one will see the Lord" (Heb 12:14). Jesus spoke of this when he prayed that God would keep his people from the evil one. "My prayer is not that you take them out of the world but that you protect them from the evil one. They are not of the world, even as I am not of it. Sanctify them by the truth; your word is truth" (Jn 17:15-17).

What Is Holiness?
Some people have identified holiness with a culturally determined behavioral pattern and so have identified as holy those who do not gamble or smoke or drink or play cards or go to movies or do any of a large number of such things. This is a misconception. It may be that holiness in a particular Christian may result in abstinence from one or more of these things, but the essence of holiness is not found here. Consequently, to insist on such things for those in the

church is not to promote holiness but rather to encourage legalism and hypocrisy. In some extreme forms it may even promote a false Christianity according to which men and women feel that they are justified before God on the basis of some supposedly ethical behavior.

The apostle Paul found that to be true of the Israel of his day, as Jesus had also found it before him. So Paul distinguished between that kind of holiness (the term he used is *righteousness*) and true holiness, which comes from God and is always God-oriented. He said of Israel, "Since they did not know the righteousness that comes from God and sought to establish their own, they did not submit to God's righteousness" (Rom 10:3).

Israel had imagined that holiness was something that could be measured or graded. In other words, as we look around we see some whom we consider low on the scale of human goodness: criminals, perverts, habitual liars and other base characters. On a scale of one to one hundred, we might give them a score in the low teens, for although they are not very good by our standards they are nevertheless not entirely without any redeeming qualities. A little higher up are the average people of society. They score between thirty and sixty. Then there are the very good people. They may score in the seventies. Beyond that, if you push the score up to one hundred (or higher if that is possible), you get to God. His holiness is perfect holiness. According to that way of looking at holiness, God's holiness is only a perfection of the holiness that lies to a greater or lesser degree in all of us. We are to please him (some would say "earn heaven") by trying harder.

That is what Israel had done, and it is what nearly everyone naturally does. But it does not reflect the biblical idea of holiness. According to the Bible, holiness actually deals (on God's level) with transcendence and (on our level) with a fundamental response to God that we would call commitment or dedication.

The biblical idea of holiness is made somewhat clearer when we consider words that are related to it, namely, *saint* and *sanctify*. Christ used the second one in John 17. A saint is not a person who has achieved a certain level of goodness, although that is what most people think, but rather one who has been "set apart" for God. Therefore, in the Bible the word is not restricted to a special class of Christians, still less a class that is established by the official action of an ecclesiastical body. Rather it is used of all Christians (Rom 1:7; 1 Cor 1:2; 2 Cor 1:1; Eph 1:1; Phil 1:1; and so on). The saints are the "called-out ones" who make up God's church.

The same idea is present when the Bible refers to the sanctification of objects (as in Exodus 40). Moses was instructed to sanctify the altar and laver in the midst of the tabernacle. That is, he was to "make saints" of them. The chapter does not refer to any intrinsic change in the nature of the stones—they are not made righteous. It merely indicates that they were to be set apart for a special use by God.

In John 17 Jesus prayed, "For them [the disciples] I sanctify myself, that they too may be truly sanctified" (v. 19). The verse does not mean that Jesus made himself more righteous, for he already was righteous. Instead it means that he separated himself for a special task, the task of providing salvation for people by his death.

But if holiness has to do with separation or consecration and if believers are already holy by virtue of their being set apart for Christ by God, why did Christ pray for our sanctification? Why pray for what we already have? The answer is that although we have been set apart for God, we often fail to live up to that calling. To paraphrase William Wordsworth, it is "trailing clouds of old commitments, sins and loyalties that we come."

The Church That Is Not Holy

The opposite of a holy church is a secular church, one that is marked by the world's wisdom, theology, agenda and methods. I discussed this in detail earlier, in chapter seven. The true wisdom of the church is the wisdom of the Bible. Christian people stand before the Word of God and confess their ignorance of God's truth. They even confess their inability to understand what is written in the Bible except by the grace of God through the ministry of the Holy Spirit.

But today many consider themselves too wise for that old reliance on the Bible and they substitute another authority entirely. What is it? It is the *world's wisdom,* of course. But in the church it takes a special form, which is the authority of the majority. In other words, it is the wisdom of the 51 percent vote.

The secular church is also marked by the *world's theology.* It says that people are basically good, that no one is really lost, that belief in the Lord Jesus Christ is not necessary for salvation, and that all religions are really saying the same thing and are equally valid. In a climate like this the old theological terms are redefined. Sin no longer means rebellion against God's law. Salvation no longer means deliverance from sin, the world and the devil. Faith no longer means a turning from self to place one's entire trust in Jesus Christ as Savior. Instead, sin means imperfections, and salvation is something to be achieved by ourselves through hard work, social reform or positive thinking.

The secular church also adopts the *world's agenda.* It wants to deal with whatever the world is concerned about: racism, ecology, international brotherhood, secular liberation or whatever. It no longer is primarily concerned with evangelism or with living holy lives.

Finally, secularism in the church is seen in the *world's methods.* The methods given to the church by God are prayer and the power of the gospel, through which the Holy Spirit is able to turn people from their wicked ways, bring them to Christ and heal their land. But today in large sectors of the church these methods are laughed at, and the choice weapons of the hour become money, political power and entertainment.

But the church is called to be holy, separated unto God in order to imbibe his wisdom, learn his theology, pursue his agenda and utilize his methods. How can it do this? Only by a regular, disciplined, practical study of the Bible. Without this the church will always be secular. It will be like the church of the last days described by Paul in 2 Timothy. "People will be lovers of themselves, lovers of money, boastful, proud, abusive, disobedient to their parents, ungrateful, unholy, without love, unforgiving, slanderous, without self-control, brutal, not lovers of the good, treacherous, rash, conceited, lovers of pleasure rather than lovers of God—having a form of godliness but denying its power" (3:2-5). That is the secular church— "having a form of godliness but denying its power." But the true church is not to be like this. It is to be separated unto God and empowered and directed by him until Jesus comes again.

A Truth-rooted People

That brings us directly to the third mark of the church: truth. For it is by the truth of God, embodied in the Scriptures, that Christian people are to be filled with joy (the first characteristic Jesus prayed for) and live holy lives (the second characteristic). Jesus made the connection explicit in both cases. He said, "I have told you *this* so that my joy may be in you and that your joy may be complete" (Jn 15:11). That is, joy was to come from knowing his teachings recorded for us now in the Bible. He prayed, "I say *these things* while I am still in the world, so that they may have the full measure of my joy within them" (Jn 17:13). And in reference to holiness he said, "Sanctify them by the truth; *your word* is truth" (v. 17). Again the path is by the Bible.

A striking thing, which we realize more and more as we grow in the Christian life, is that nearly all that God does in the world today he does by the Holy Spirit through the instrumentality of his written revelation. So far as truth goes, the world lives by an illusion. What it thinks of as truth is a falsehood. Since we live in the world, though we are not to be of it, the world's views will always be a problem for us unless we have a sure way of countering and actually overturning its influence. Ray Stedman was thinking of this problem when he wrote,

The world lives by what it thinks is truth, by values and standards which are worthless, but which the world esteems highly. Jesus said, "What is exalted among men is an abomination in the sight of God" (Luke 16:15). . . . How can we live in that kind of world— touch it and hear it, having it pouring into ours ears and exposed to our eyes day and night, and not be conformed to its image and squeezed into its mold? The answer is, we must know the truth. We must know the world and life the way God sees it, the way it really is. We must know it so clearly and strongly that even while we're listening to these alluring lies we can brand them as lies and know that they are wrong.[3]

Stedman was saying that Christians should be great realists, because their realism is that of the truth of God. That by its very nature should lead to deep joy and greater sanctification—and lead to a more steadfast conviction as to what is our real authority in life!

Evangelicals must be men and women of "the Book." In theory we are. We say we are. We acknowledge that this is our standard. But much of the time, in practice, evangelicals operate exactly the way those in other churches do, or even worse.

We have to recover the biblical standard. This means that we cannot say, as I have heard evangelicals say on important issues, "Well, that particular matter just does not bother me." That response is not good enough. We have to get to what the Word of God says and perhaps become bothered. We have to study the Bible, do our homework and then ask: On the basis of this Word, what does God want for the church in this age?

We are going to have to do that sooner or later anyway, or else we are going to have to go the world's way entirely. History does not allow us to stand long in an ambiguous position. In Nazi Germany, the church went in one of two ways. Either it capitulated to the Nazi point of view, as most of the established church did, or it became increasingly a church of the Bible. Those who lived by the Book eventually established a communion of their own. They signed documents identifying themselves as the "confessing church." Why did they do this? They did it because, when the whole drift of the culture is contrary to biblical standards, it is impossible to appeal to any external norms. You cannot argue, "This is backed up by what they are teaching in the area of psychology or science or social relations," because it is not. The things that are being written in all those areas are contrary to biblical truth. So the church must increasingly fall back on divine revelation.

Has God spoken to his people in this Book? Does he speak? If he does, then we must be clear and say, "Let God be true and every man a liar."

A Missionary People

Up to this point Christ's prayer has been dealing with things that concern the church itself or that concern individual Christians personally: joy, holiness and truth. But while those characteristics are important and undoubtedly attainable to some degree in this life, it does not take much thinking to figure out that all three would be more quickly attained if we could only be transported to heaven.

We have joy here. But what is it compared to the abundant joy that we will have when we eventually see the source of our joy face to face? The Bible acknowledges this when it speaks of the blessedness of the redeemed saints, from whose eyes all tears shall have been wiped away (Rev 7:17; 21:4). In this life we undoubtedly know some sanctification. But someday we shall be made completely like Jesus (1 Jn 3:2). In this life we are able to assimilate some aspects of God's truth, but it is only a poor assimilation of what we will one day know fully. Paul wrote, "Now we see but a poor reflection . . . then we shall see face to face. Now I know in part; then I shall know fully, even as I am fully known" (1 Cor 13:12). If that is true, why should we not go to heaven immediately?

The answer is in a fourth mark of the church. The church is not only to look inward and find joy, Christward and find sanctification, to the Bible and find truth. It is also to look outward to the world and find there the object of its mission. What kind of a mission should this be? Jesus' prayer highlights two important matters.

We Are to Be in the World

The first thing that these verses tell us is where our mission is to be conducted. The word *mission* comes from the Latin verb meaning "to send" or "dispatch." A mission is a sending forth. But when we ask, To whom or where are we sent as Christian missionaries? the answer is "into the world." Jesus said, "As you sent me into the world, I have sent them into the world" (Jn 17:18).

That answer is probably the explanation of why the evangelical church in America is not the missionary church it claims to be. It is not that the evangelical church does not support missions. It does. The problem does not lie there. Rather it lies at the point of the evangelicals' personal withdrawal from the culture. Many seem afraid of the culture. They try to keep as far from the world as possible, lest they be contaminated by it. Some have developed their own subculture. It is possible, for example, to be born of Christian parents, grow up in a Christian family, have Christian friends, go to Christian schools and colleges, read Christian books, attend a Christian country club (known as a church), watch Christian movies, get Christian employment, be attended by a Christian doctor, and finally die and be buried by a Christian undertaker in hallowed ground.

What does it mean to be in the world as a Christian? It does not mean to be like the world; the marks of the church are to make the church different. It does not mean that we are to abandon Christian fellowship or Christian convictions. It means that we are to mingle with and get to know non-Christians, to make friends with them and enter into their lives in such a way that we begin to infect them with the gospel, rather than their infecting us with their outlook.

A young pastor in Guatemala went from seminary to a remote area known as Cabrican. Cabrican was unpopular; it was located at an altitude of about nine thousand feet and was nearly always damp and cold. The church he went to was small, having only twenty-eight members, including two elders and two deacons. These believers met together on most nights of the week, but they were not a growing congregation. There was no outreach. In one of his first messages to them the young pastor, whose name was Bernardo Calderón, said, "I know God cannot be satisfied with what we are doing." Then he challenged them to this program.

First, they abandoned the many dull meetings at the church, retaining only the Bible-school hour on Sunday. In their place home meetings were established. On Monday night they would meet in a home in one area of Cabrican, and everyone would attend. As they made their way to that home they were to invite everyone they encountered, even passersby on the streets. Since the Christians came from different areas of the city and took different paths to get there, this meant that quite a bit of the city was covered. On Tuesday the church met somewhere else. This time different paths were used as the twenty-eight members converged, and different villagers were invited. So it was on Wednesday and Thursday and the other days of the week, as the church literally left its four small walls to go out into the world with the gospel. The result? Within four years the church had eight hundred members. The next year a branch church was started, and soon there were six churches in that area of Guatemala, two of which had nearly one thousand members. They even created an agricultural cooperative in which church members bought land for their own poor and then bought and sold the produce their own people supplied. The entire area was revitalized.

Like Jesus in the World

The second thing that these verses talk about is the character of the ones who are to conduct this mission, which means the character of Christian people. We are to be *as Christ* in the world. Jesus compared the disciples to himself, both in having been sent into the world by the Father and in being sanctified or set apart to that work. He said, "As you sent me into the world, I have sent them into the world. For them I sanctify myself, that they too may be truly sanctified" (vv. 18-19). We are to be in our mission as Jesus was in his mission. We are to be like the one we are presenting.

In what ways? In all ways, of course. But since we are studying John 17, the answer here must be in terms of the marks of the church for which the Lord is praying: joy, holiness, truth, mission, unity and love. Jesus is to be our pattern in each case.

A Unified People

A fifth mark of the church is unity, and it is noteworthy that it was this that Jesus prayed for at greatest length. He said,

My prayer is not for them alone. I pray also for those who will believe in me through their message, that all of them may be one, Father, just as you are in me and I am in you. May they also be in us so that the world may believe that you have sent me. I have given them the glory that you gave me, that they may be one as we are one: I in them and you in me. May they be brought to complete unity to let the world know that you sent me and have loved them even as you have loved me. (vv. 20-23)

What kind of unity should this be?

One thing that the church does not need to be is a great *organizational unity*. Whatever advantages or disadvantages may be found in massive organizational unity, that in itself obviously does not produce the results for which Christ prayed. Nor does it solve the church's other problems. It has been tried and found wanting.

In the early days of the church there was much growth but little organizational unity. Later, as the church came into governmental favor under Constantine and his successors, the visible church increasingly centralized until during the Middle Ages there was literally one united ecclesiastical body covering all of Europe. Wherever one went—north, south, east or west—there was one united, interlacing church with the pope at its head. But was this a great age? Was there deep unity of faith? Was the church spiritually strong? Was morality high? Did men and women find themselves increasingly drawn to that faith and come to confess Jesus Christ as their own Savior and Lord? On the contrary, the world believed the opposite. Charles Haddon Spurgeon wrote, "The world was persuaded that God had nothing to do with that great crushing, tyrannous, superstitious, ignorant thing which called itself Christianity; and thinking men became infidels, and it was the hardest possible thing to find a genuine intelligent believer north, south, east or west."[4]

Certainly there is something to be said for some form of outward, visible unity in some situations. But it is equally certain that this type of unity is not what we most need, nor is it that for which the Lord prayed.

Another type of unity that we do not need is *conformity*—that is, an approach to the church that would make everyone alike. Here we probably come closest to the error of the evangelical church. If the liberal church for the most part strives for organizational unity— through the various councils of churches and denominational mergers—the evangelical church seems to strive for an identical pattern of appearance and behavior for its members. Jesus was not looking for that either. On the contrary, there should be diversity among Christians, diversity of personality, interests, lifestyle and even methods of Christian work and evangelism. Uniformity is dull. Variety is exciting. We see it in the variety of nature and the actions of God.

But if the unity for which Jesus prayed is not an organizational unity or a unity achieved by conformity, what kind of unity is it? It is a unity analogous to the unity that exists in the Godhead. Jesus spoke of it like this: "That all of them may be one, Father, just as you are in me and I am in you. . . . I in them and you in me" (vv. 21, 23). The church is to have a spiritual unity involving the basic orientation, desires and will of those participating. This is not to say that all true believers actually enter into this unity as they should. Otherwise, why would Christ have prayed for it? Like the other marks of the church, unity is something given to the church but also something for which the community of true believers should fervently strive.

We are helped at this point by several powerful images of the church used in the New Testament.

A Family
Christians belong to the family of God and are thus rightly brothers and sisters of one another. The unique characteristic of this image is that it speaks of relationships between and the commitments of one individual to another. These relationships are based on what God has done when he rescued us from spiritual death and made us living members of the new humanity, the City of God. We are made members of this spiritual family through God's choice and not our own. One important consequence of this is that we have no

choice as to who will be our spiritual brothers or sisters. The relationships simply exist, and we must be brotherly to other believers, whether we want to be or not.

A second consequence is that we must be committed to each other in tangible ways. I came across a speculation along these lines by a Christian writer. He said that he had asked himself what he would have done if he had gotten into financial difficulty a few years earlier, before he discovered what Christian community is all about and had actually gotten into a true Christian brotherhood. If he had a medical bill of several thousand dollars to pay and no extra money in the bank, to whom would he have turned? As he reflected on this he realized that he could never have turned to the Christians he knew at that time. They would have told him to go to a bank where he could get a loan, or perhaps have directed him to the welfare office. He realized that the only person he could have turned to was his blood brother.

This means that in some cases at least the human family is doing what the spiritual family ought to be doing but often is not. If we are serious about our unity, here is a place where we can demonstrate it tangibly. It is even an area in which the world, saddled as it is by its own selfishness, may take notice.

A Fellowship

A second important image used to suggest the unity of the church is a fellowship, which the New Testament normally indicates by the Greek word *koinōnia*. We have to pay attention to the Greek word because the English term is not very helpful in conveying what this means. With us a fellowship usually means only a loose collection of friends or, even worse, just a good time. The Greek word has as its base the stronger idea of sharing something or having something in common. Thus, the common Greek of the New Testament period is called Koine Greek. People who held property together or shared in a business were called *koinōnoi*, meaning "partners." Spiritually *koinōnia* refers to those who share a common experience of the gospel. Thus the New Testament speaks often of our fellowship with the Father (1 Jn 1:3), with the Son (1 Cor 1:9) and with the Holy Spirit (2 Cor 13:14).

But fellowship is not only defined by what we share *in* together. It also involves what we share *out* together. It points to a community in which Christians actually share their thoughts and lives with each other.

How is this to be done practically? Different congregations will do this in different ways depending on local situations and needs. Some churches are small and therefore will have an easier time establishing ways for sharing. Church suppers and work projects will help. Larger churches will have to break their members down into smaller groups.

At Tenth Presbyterian Church in Philadelphia, which I have served as pastor for nearly thirty years, we do this in various ways— through age-level classes and community service projects, for instance. The chief means is small parish Bible study and prayer groups. The number of these groups varies, but it has usually been between eighty and a hundred. The important thing about these groups is that they are scattered over the large geographical area of greater Philadelphia so that nearly anyone associated with the church can find a group fairly near at hand. These groups are the least structured of anything we do, but they are also the most exciting and profitable of all the church activities.

My experience in this area conforms to that of John R. W. Stott, who experimented with similar groups in his London parish. He wrote, "The value of the small group is that it can become a community of related persons; and in it the benefit of personal relatedness cannot be missed, nor its challenge evaded. . . . I do not think it is an exaggeration to say, therefore, that small groups, Christian family or fellowship groups, are indisputable for our growth into spiritual maturity."[5]

A Body

The third important image used to stress the unity of the church is the body. This image points to several important matters. For one thing, it speaks of the nature of the church's union. One part of the body simply cannot survive if it is separated from the whole. Again, it speaks of independence. It even speaks of a kind of subordination involving a diversity of function; for the hand is not the foot, nor the foot the eye, and over all is the head, which is Christ. Paul notes this in 1 Corinthians 12: "The body is a unit, though it is made up of many parts; and though all its parts are many, they form one body. So it is with Christ. For we were all baptized by one Spirit into one body—whether Jews or Greeks, slave or free—and we were all given the one Spirit to drink. Now the body is not made up of one part but many" (vv. 12-14).

A Loving People

At last we come to love, the greatest mark of all. Love is the mark that gives meaning to the others and without which the church cannot be what God intends it to be. Having written about love and having placed it in the context of faith, hope and love, Paul concluded, "But the greatest of these is love" (1 Cor 13:13).

With the same thought in mind, the Lord Jesus Christ, having spoken of joy, holiness, truth, mission and unity as essential marks of the church in his prayer in John 17, concluded with an emphasis on love. He said that he had declared the name of God to the disciples in order that "the love you have for me may be in them and that I myself may be in them" (v. 26). In this final petition Jesus is touching on the "new commandment" of John 13:34-35 once again. "A new command I give you: Love one another. As I have loved you, so you must love one another. By this all men will know that you are my disciples, if you love one another."

We understand the preeminence of love if we see it in reference to the other marks of the church. What happens when you take love away from them? Suppose you subtract love from joy. What do you have? You have hedonism, an exuberance in life and its pleasures, but without the sanctifying joy found in relationship to the Lord Jesus Christ.

Subtract love from holiness. What do you find then? You find self-righteousness, the kind of sinful self-contentment that characterized the Pharisees of Christ's day. By the standards of the day the Pharisees lived very holy lives, but they did not love others and thus were quite ready to kill Jesus when he challenged their standards.

Take love from truth and you have a bitter orthodoxy. The teaching may be right, but it does not win anyone to Christ or to godliness.

Take love from mission and you have imperialism. It is colonialism in ecclesiastical garb.

Take love from unity and you soon have tyranny. Tyranny develops in a hierarchical church where there is no compassion for people or desire to involve them in the decision-making process, only a determination to force everyone into the same denomination or get them to back the "program."

Now express love and what do you find? All the other marks of the church follow. What does love for God the Father lead to? Joy. We rejoice in God and in what he has done for us. What does love for the Lord Jesus Christ lead to? Holiness. We know that we will see him one day and will be like him. "Everyone who has this hope in him purifies himself, just as he is pure" (1 Jn 3:3). What does love for the Word of God lead to? Truth. If we love the Word, we will study it and therefore inevitably grow into a fuller appreciation of God's truth. What does love for the world lead to? Mission. We have a message to take to the world. Where does love for our Christian brothers and sisters lead? To unity. By love we discern that we are bound together in the bundle of life that God has created within the Christian community.

Like all divine things love is made known by revelation only. No Greek, no Roman, no Egyptian, no Babylonian in Christ's day or in any of the centuries before ever thought of God's nature as being characterized by love or as love being an important virtue for binding a people together, as it does the church. Read all the ancient documents, and you simply do not find this element. At best, the gods were thought to be impartial. Or if one chose to think optimistically, a god could sometimes be said to be favorable to those who did something for him. That is, there was a tit-for-tat arrangement:

"You serve me, and I will take care of you." So far as people were concerned, well, there was erotic love and a certain kind of affection within the family. But there was nothing like the great, steady, benevolent and unmerited love of God in the Bible. It was just not there.

But it is in the Bible. In the pages of the Old Testament we are told that God set his love on Israel even though nothing in the people merited it. That was a faithful, covenant love. Then, with the birth of Jesus, love actually entered history as a person. He loved and he continues to love as no other. The best and fullest revelation of love was at the cross. "For God so loved the world that he gave his one and only Son, that whoever believes in him shall not perish but have eternal life" (Jn 3:16).

There has never been, there never will be, a greater demonstration of the love of God. If you will not have the cross, if you will not see God speaking in love in Jesus Christ, you will never find a loving God anywhere. The God of the Bible is going to be a silent God for you. The universe is going to be an empty universe. History is going to be meaningless. Only at the cross do we find God in his true nature and learn how these other things have meaning.[6] Only there do we learn to love as God loves, which is the last and most important petition in Christ's prayer.

Notes

Chapter 1: The Barbarians Are Coming

[1]Augustine, *The Confessions of St. Augustine*, in *A Select Library of the Nicene and Post-Nicene Fathers of the Christian Church*, ed. Philip Schaff (Grand Rapids, Mich.: Eerdmans, 1974), 1:45.

[2]"My mistress being torn from my side as an impediment to my marriage, my heart, which clave to her, was racked, and wounded, and bleeding. And she went back to Africa, making a vow unto thee never to know another man, leaving with me my natural son by her" (ibid., p. 100).

[3]Ibid., pp. 107-8.

[4]Ibid., p. 121.

[5]Ibid., p. 124.

[6]Ibid.

[7]Ibid., pp. 127-28.

[8]Adolf Harnack in "Monasticism and the Confessions of St. Augustine," quoted by B. B. Warfield, *Calvin and Augustine* (Philadelphia: Presbyterian & Reformed, 1956), p. 306.

[9]Will Durant, *The Age of Faith: The Story of Civilization* (Norwalk, Conn.: Easton, 1992), 4:67. Original edition 1950.

[10]Augustine, *The City of God*, in *A Select Library of the Nicene and Post-Nicene Fathers of the Christian Church*, ed. Philip Schaff (Grand Rapids, Mich.: Eerdmans, 1977), 2:282-83.

[11]Durant, *Age of Faith*, 4:73.

[12]Charles Colson with Ellen Santilli Vaughn, *Against the Night: Living in the New Dark Ages* (Ann Arbor, Mich.: Servant, 1989), pp. 23-24.

[13]Ibid., p. 75.

[14]Ibid., pp. 76-77.

[15]Allan Bloom, *The Closing of the American Mind* (New York: Simon & Schuster, 1987).

[16]Ibid., p. 34.

[17]Colson and Vaughn, *Against the Night,* p. 85.

[18]Meg Greenfield, "Right and Wrong in Washington: Why Do Our Officials Need Specialists to Tell the Difference?" *Newsweek,* February 13, 1995, p. 88.

[19]Ibid.

[20]Colson and Vaughn, *Against the Night,* p. 94.

[21]Ibid., p. 98.

[22]Michael Scott Horton, ed., *Power Religion: The Selling Out of the Evangelical Church?* (Chicago: Moody Press, 1992).

Chapter 2: The Two Humanities

[1]Francis A. Schaeffer, *Genesis in Space and Time: The Flow of Biblical History* (Downers Grove, Ill.: InterVarsity Press, 1972), pp. 103-18.

[2]See my development of this theme in James Montgomery Boice, *Genesis 1:1—11:32,* vol. 1 of *Genesis: An Expositional Commentary* (Grand Rapids, Mich.: Zondervan, 1982), pp. 162-65.

[3]Schaeffer, *Genesis in Space and Time,* p. 114.

[4]Martin Luther, *Lectures on Genesis Chapters 1—5,* vol. 1 of *Luther's Works,* ed. Jaroslav Pelikan (St. Louis: Concordia, 1958), p. 327.

[5]John Calvin, *Commentaries on the First Book of Moses Called Genesis,* trans. John King (Grand Rapids, Mich.: Eerdmans, 1948), p. 224.

Chapter 3: Abraham: "He Looked for a City"

[1]Donald Grey Barnhouse, *Romans 3:21—4:25,* vol. 3 of *God's Remedy: Exposition of Bible Doctrines, Taking the Epistle to the Romans as a Point of Departure* (Grand Rapids, Mich.: Eerdmans, 1954), p. 272.

[2]*Roget's International Thesaurus* (New York: Thomas Y. Crowell, 1953), pp. 323-24.

[3]D. Martyn Lloyd-Jones, *Romans: An Exposition of Chapters 3:20—4:25, Atonement and Justification* (Grand Rapids, Mich.: Zondervan, 1970), p. 211.

[4]Ibid.

[5]Karl Barth, *The Epistle to the Romans,* trans. Edwyn C. Hoskyns (London: Oxford University Press, 1933), pp. 143-44.

[6]Watchman Nee, *Changed into His Likeness* (Fort Washington, Penn.: Christian Literature Crusade, 1967), p. 62.

[7]Over the years I have written about Abraham's walk of faith many times. Fuller accounts may be found in *Ordinary Men Called by God: Abraham, Moses and David* (Wheaton, Ill.: Victor Books, 1982), pp. 13-51; *Genesis 12:1—36:43,* vol. 2 of *Genesis: An Expositional Commentary* (Grand Rapids, Mich.: Zondervan, 1985), pp. 11-257; and *Justification by Faith: Romans 1—4,* vol. 1 of *Romans* (Grand Rapids, Mich.: Baker Book House, 1991), pp. 461-69, 477-92.

[8]Lloyd-Jones, *Romans,* p. 235.

Chapter 4: The Two Cities: Enoch & Nineveh

[1]Augustine, *The Confessions of St. Augustine,* in *A Select Library of the Nicene and Post-Nicene Fathers of the Christian Church,* ed. Philip Schaff (Grand Rapids, Mich.: Eerdmans, 1974), 1:45.

[2]Jacques Ellul, *The Meaning of the City,* trans. Dennis Pardee (Grand Rapids, Mich.: Eerdmans, 1970), p. 4.

[3]Simone Weil, *The Need for Roots: Prelude to a Declaration of Duties Towards Mankind,* trans. A. F. Wills (London: Routledge and Kegan Paul, 1952).

[4]Donald Grey Barnhouse, *The Invisible War* (Grand Rapids, Mich.: Zondervan, 1965), p. 192.

[5]Walter A. Maier, *The Book of Nahum* (1959; reprint Grand Rapids, Mich.: Baker Book House, 1980), p. 89. See also F. W. Farrar, *The Minor Prophets* (New York: Anson D. F. Randolph, n.d.), p. 145. The quotations are from David Daniel Luckenbill, *Ancient Records of Assyria and Babylonia* (Chicago: University of Chicago Press, 1926-1927), 1:222-23.

[6]Maier, *Book of Nahum,* p. 90.

[7]Ibid., pp. 90-91.

[8]Ibid., p. 291. Maier took the material from Luckenbill, *Ancient Records of Assyria and Babylonia,* 1:142ff.

[9]Maier, *Book of Nahum,* pp. 92-93.

[10]Martin Luther, *Lectures on the Minor Prophets,* vol. 18 of *Luther's Works,* ed. Hilton C. Oswald (St. Louis: Concordia, 1975), 1:288.

[11]Maier, *Book of Nahum,* p. 127. Diodorus's work is called the *Chronicles.* The material on the fall of Nineveh is taken in turn from *Persica,* a chronicle of Assyria and Persia in twenty-three books by a Greek physician named Cresias, of which only fragments survive.

[12]Maier, *Book of Nahum,* p. 128.

[13]Luther, *Lectures on the Minor Prophets,* 1:135.

Chapter 5: The Two Cities: Babylon & Jerusalem

[1]Martin Luther, *Lectures on Genesis Chapters 6—14,* vol. 2 of *Luther's Works,* ed. Jaroslav Pelikan (St. Louis: Concordia, 1958), p. 213.

[2]Robert S. Candlish, *Studies in Genesis* (1868; reprint Grand Rapids, Mich.: Kregel, 1976), p. 174.

[3]Henry M. Morris, *The Genesis Record: A Scientific and Devotional Commentary on the Book of Beginnings* (Grand Rapids, Mich.: Baker Book House, 1976), p. 270.

[4]Ibid., p. 264.

[5]This must be a description of insanity and the customary treatment of the insane in those days, because later in the story Nebuchadnezzar himself speaks of his "sanity" being restored (Dan 4:34).

[6]These verses are used of men and women in general here. Verses 4-6 also occur

in Hebrews 2 in reference to Jesus Christ, where they are used only because of his having become a man. That is, he became "a little lower than the angels" in order to be like us. In this way he became our "brother" (Heb 2:11).

Chapter 6: Daniel: God's Man in Babylon

[1]The content of this chapter is condensed with alterations from James Montgomery Boice, *Daniel: An Expositional Commentary* (Grand Rapids, Mich.: Zondervan, 1989).

[2]These and other comments are recorded in Franky Schaeffer, *A Time for Anger: The Myth of Neutrality* (Westchester, Ill.: Crossway, 1982), pp. 28-33.

Chapter 7: Christianity & Culture

[1]H. Richard Niebuhr, *Christ and Culture* (New York: Harper, 1951).

[2]Terry Randall, *Why Does a Nice Guy like Me Keep Getting Thrown in Jail?* (Lafayette, La.: Huntington House, 1993), p. 61.

[3]Cited by Michael S. Horton, *Beyond Culture Wars* (Chicago: Moody Press, 1994), p. 16, from a Focus on the Family newsletter, January 1994, p. 4.

[4]Cited by Horton, *Beyond Culture Wars*, p. 179.

[5]Harvey Cox, *The Secular City: Secularization and Urbanization in Theological Perspective* (New York: Macmillan, 1965), p. 23. The entire discussion is on pp. 21-24.

[6]Ibid., p. 36.

[7]See James Montgomery Boice, *Foundations of the Christian Faith: A Comprehensive and Readable Theology* (Downers Grove, Ill.: InterVarsity Press, 1986), pp. 669-76, from which this overview of Cox's views and the following discussion of the secular church are taken.

[8]Robin Scroggs, "Tradition, Freedom and the Abyss," *The Chicago Theological Seminary Register* 60, no. 4 (May 1970). Quoted in Donald G. Bloesch, *The Invaded Church* (Waco, Tex.: Word, 1975), p. 75.

[9]Peter L. Berger, "Needed: Authority," *The Presbyterian Journal* 20 (October 1971): 10.

[10]Horton, *Beyond Culture Wars*, p. 180.

[11]Ibid., p. 30.

[12]James Montgomery Boice, *Mind Renewal in a Mindless Age* (Grand Rapids, Mich.: Baker Book House, 1993).

[13]Martin Luther, "Admonition to Peace" (April 1525); quoted in Will Durant, *The Reformation: A History of European Civilization from Wyclif to Calvin, 1300-1564*, vol. 6 of *The Story of Civilization* (Norwalk, Conn.: Easton, 1992), p. 386.

[14]Gene Edward Veith Jr., *Postmodern Times: A Christian Guide to Contemporary Thought and Culture* (Wheaton, Ill.: Crossway, 1994), pp. 222-23.

Chapter 8: How We Might Move Forward

[1]Don E. Eberly, *Restoring the Good Society: A New Vision for Politics and Culture* (Grand Rapids, Mich.: Baker Book House, 1994), pp. 41-42.

[2]Ibid., p. 84.

[3]Francis A. Schaeffer and C. Everett Koop, *Whatever Happened to the Human Race?* (Old Tappan, N.J.: Fleming H. Revell, 1976).

[4]Ronald J. Sider, "The State of Evangelical Social Concern, 1978," *Evangelical Newsletter* 5, no. 13 (June 30, 1978).

[5]Anthony T. Evans, "Ten Steps to Urban Renewal," *The Urban Alternative* 4, no. 2 (September 1988).

[6]Cyril J. Barber, *Nehemiah and the Dynamics of Effective Leadership* (Neptune, N.J.: Loizeaux Brothers, 1976), p. 155.

[7]Colonel V. Doner, *The Samaritan Strategy: A New Agenda for Christian Activism* (Brentwood, Tenn.: Wolgemuth & Hyatt, 1988), p. 37.

[8]See Charles Colson with Ellen Santilli Vaughn, *The God of Stones and Spiders: Letters to a Church in Exile* (Wheaton, Ill.: Crossway, 1990), p. 42.

[9]See ibid., p. 40.

[10]Eberly, *Restoring the Good Society,* p. 43.

Chapter 9: God & Caesar

[1]J. Marcellus Kik, *Church and State: The Story of Two Kingdoms* (London: Thomas Nelson & Sons, 1963), pp. 92-93. Kik draws the quotations from Knox's own work *The History of the Reformation of Religion in Scotland* (London, 1905).

[2]The other classic text is Matthew 22:21: "Give to Caesar what is Caesar's, and to God what is God's." See discussion below.

[3]John Calvin, *Institutes of the Christian Religion,* 2 vols., ed. John T. McNeill, trans. Ford Lewis Battles (Philadelphia: Westminster Press, 1960), p. 1512.

[4]For a stirring account of the struggle going back to the earliest days of the church see Kik, *Church and State.*

[5]Charles Colson with Ellen Santilli Vaughn, *Kingdoms in Conflict* (Grand Rapids, Mich.: William Morrow/Zondervan, 1987), p. 250.

[6]A statement made by Harvard law professor Alexander Bickel, quoted in ibid., p. 251.

[7]The material in this chapter is borrowed with changes from a longer discussion of the same themes in James Montgomery Boice, *God and History: Romans 12:1— 16:27,* vol. 4 of *Romans* (Grand Rapids, Mich.: Baker Book House, 1995), pp. 1639-61.

Chapter 10: Nehemiah: Rebuilding the Walls

[1]Peter F. Drucker, *The Effective Executive* (New York: Harper & Row, 1986, 1987), p. 100.

[2]Cyril J. Barber, *Nehemiah and the Dynamics of Effective Leadership* (Neptune, N.J.: Loizeaux Brothers, 1976), p. 19.

[3]Charles R. Swindoll, *Hand Me Another Brick* (Nashville: Thomas Nelson, 1978), p. 30.

[4]Drucker, *Effective Executive,* p. 93.

[5]John R. Noe, *Peak Performance Principles for High Achievers* (New York: Frederick Fell,

1984), p. 134.

6Dale Carnegie, *How to Win Friends and Influence People* (New York: Simon & Schuster/Pocket Books, 1963), pp. 173-76.

7From a series of tapes by Frank R. Tillapaugh entitled "Reclaiming the Church for Ministry" (Denver: Bear Valley Ministries, 1984).

8Barber, *Nehemiah and the Dynamics of Effective Leadership,* p. 108.

9A fuller treatment of Nehemiah's leadership skills may be found in James Montgomery Boice, *Nehemiah: Learning to Lead* (Old Tappan, N.J.: Fleming H. Revell, 1990), from which the material in this and the next chapter has been taken.

Chapter 11: Nehemiah: A Postscript

1Howard F. Vos, *Bible Study Commentary: Ezra, Nehemiah, Esther* (Grand Rapids, Mich.: Zondervan, 1987), p. 134.

2Cyril J. Barber, *Nehemiah and the Dynamics of Effective Leadership* (Neptune, N.J.: Loizeaux Brothers, 1976), p. 168.

3Charles R. Swindoll, *Hand Me Another Brick* (Nashville: Thomas Nelson, 1978), p. 194.

4John White, *Excellence in Leadership: Reaching Goals with Prayer, Courage and Determination* (Downers Grove, Ill.: InterVarsity Press, 1986), pp. 123-24.

5Leighton Ford himself tells this story. I have found it in Mariano DiGangi, *Reaching the Unchurched: A Report on the Canadian Consultation on Evangelism* (Scarborough, Ont.: Reliable Printing, 1983), pp. 4-5.

Chapter 12: One Nation Under God?

1This chapter was originally presented as the keynote address at Congress on the Bible II, sponsored by the International Council on Biblical Inerrancy, on September 23, 1987, and published in James Montgomery Boice, ed., *Transforming Our World: A Call to Action* (Portland, Ore.: Multnomah Press, 1988). It is printed here with alterations to bring it up to date.

2*Time,* May 25, 1987, p. 14.

3Allan Bloom, *The Closing of the American Mind* (New York: Simon & Schuster, 1987), p. 25.

4William J. Bennett, "Why Johnny Can't Abstain," *National Review,* July 3, 1987, pp. 36-38, 56.

5George Gallup Jr., "Is America's Faith for Real?" *Alumni News* (Princeton Theological Seminary) 22, no. 4 (Summer 1982): 15-17.

6"Taking Aim Against Skin-Deep Christianity: An Interview with John Stott," *RTS* (Reformed Theological Seminary's alumni newsletter) 6, no. 2 (Summer 1987): 8.

7William Reel, "Mean Street . . . X-Rated Streets," New York *Daily News,* April 1, 1977.

8Gallup, "Is America's Faith for Real?" p. 16.

Chapter 13: Christ's Prayer for God's City

1William Barclay, *Flesh and Spirit: An Examination of Galatians 5:19-23* (Nashville:

Abingdon, 1962), pp. 77-78.

[2]Hannah Whitall Smith, *The Christian's Secret of a Happy Life* (Westwood, N.J.: Fleming H. Revell, 1952), p. 15.

[3]Ray C. Stedman, *Secrets of the Spirit* (Old Tappan, N.J.: Fleming H. Revell, 1975), pp. 147-48.

[4]Charles Haddon Spurgeon, "Unity in Christ," in *Metropolitan Tabernacle Pulpit* (Pasadena, Tex.: Pilgrim, 1970), 12:2.

[5]John R. W. Stott, *One People* (London: Falcon, 1969), pp. 70-71.

[6]This chapter is based on a shorter chapter on the same themes in James Montgomery Boice, *Foundations of the Christian Faith: A Comprehensive and Readable Theology* (Downers Grove, Ill.: InterVarsity Press, 1986), pp. 576-85. Additional material has been added from the author's *John 13:1—17:26*, vol. 4 of *The Gospel of John: An Expositional Commentary* (Grand Rapids, Mich.: Zondervan, 1978), pp. 395-445, 463-71.

Subject Index

Aaron, Hank, 208
abortion, 159, 162-65, 192
Abraham, 38, 42, 47, 77, 93; called by God, 57, 97-98; change of his name from Abram, 61-62; looked for a city, 56-71
absolutes, 159, 232
accountability, 186, 188
Adah, 46, 76-77
Adam and Eve, 35-37, 41-42, 47-49, 53, 55, 73, 94, 111, 149
Adams, John, 139
agenda, world's, 146, 251
ages of faith, 145
Ahab, 80
Akkad, 78
Aleric, 13, 20
Alexander the Great, 120
Alexander VI, 138
Altizer, Thomas J., 142
Alypius, 18-19
Ambrose, 17
America, 8
American Family Association, 173
Amin, Idi, 179
Anabaptists, 140, 148
anarchy, 155
anchorites, 186
angel, speaks to Abraham, 70
angels, fallen, 20, 36
anger, 44
animal behavior, 102-4
Aquinas, Thomas, 103
Arabs, 214
ark of the covenant, 98
Artaxerxes, 201, 203-8, 213, 215, 219, 221-22

Asaph, 208
Ashurnasirpal II, 83
Assyria, 78, 83, 89, 92
astrology, 96
atonement, 40
Augustine, 7-8, 14-21, 35, 47; conversion of, 18-19; early life of, 14-15; exposure to religion, 17-18; fame of, 16-17; quest for truth, 15-16
authority, 253; limits to state, 182; nature of the state's, 182-85
Azariah, 81
Babel, tower of, 79, 93-97
Babylon, 20, 35, 47, 78, 119-20, 180, 200, 221-22, 224; fall of mystery, 107-9; Nebuchadnezzar's city, 99-101
Bach, Johann Sebastian, 152
barbarians, 21-31; defined, 29-31; in the classroom, 22-25; in the parlor, 22-23; in the pews, 27-29; in power, 25-27
Barber, Cyril J., 171, 220
Barclay, William, 246
Barth, Karl, 65-66
beauty, cult of, 76-77
Belshazzar, 125-26
Bennett, William J., 232-33
Berger, Peter, 145
Berra, Yogi, 208
Beyond Culture Wars, 148, 152
Bezalel, 150
Bible, 28-29, 143; authority of, 253. *See also* Word of God
Bible Study Hour, 153
Biden, Joe, 25
Black Obelisk, 80

blood, shedding of, 43
Bloom, Allan, 24, 232
Bonhoeffer, Dietrich, 190-91
Boston Globe, 129
Brave New World, 93
Bundy, Ted, 173
Caesar, 128, 186-87
Cain, 48; meaning of the name, 41; way of, 45-46
Cain and Abel, 41-47, 77; offerings of, 42-44
Cain's city, 94; cruel, 75; Enoch, 72-78
Calah, 78
Calderón, Bernardo, 255
Calneh, 78
Calvin, John, 7, 21, 50, 178, 188
Carnegie, Dale, 200, 211
Carthage, 14
checks and balances, 186-87
China Inland Mission, 204
Christ and culture: apart from culture, 140-41; over culture, 138-40; servant of culture, 141-43. *See also* Christianity and culture
Christ and the two cities, 148-51
Christ Jesus, 31, 36, 39-40, 42, 55, 59, 91; being like, 256; church of, 179; following, 59-60; King of kings and Lord of lords, 109-10, 138; kingdom of, 121-22; redeemer, 43; redefined, 145; trial before Pilate, 183-84
Christian Right, 172
Christian thinking, 153-54
Christianity and culture, 137-57
Christians, joyful, 247

church, 20, 30; body of Christ, 260-61; a family, 258-59; a fellowship, 259-60; the first, 50; secular, 143-48, 250-52
church and state, 234
cities, challenge of the, 165-72; Christian vision for, 171-172; two, 72-91
citizens of two kingdoms, 151
city, godless, 75
City Center Academy, 175-76
City of God, 7, 20, 35, 47
city people, 75
civil disobedience, 142, 191-93
civil magistrate, 234
civil rights movement, 191
civilization, 72
Clinton, Bill, 25, 139
closeness without community, 74-76
Closing of the American Mind, 232
Code of Hammurabi, 80
coercion, 235
Colson, Charles, 21-23, 25, 27, 193, 235
command, taking, 209
community, 74; Christian, in the cities, 170-71
confession of sin, 203
Confessions, 14-15, 19
conformity, 257-58
Congress on the Bible II, 235
consensus, 144
Constantine, 14, 195, 257
Constantinople, sack of, 138
"Contract with America," 26
conversion, 242
cowardice, 225
cowards, 187
Cox, Harvey, 142-43
creation, doctrine of, 149-50
Crosby, Fanny, 247
cross of Christ, 263
Crusades, 138
culture: collapse, 11-31; godless, 125; wars, 8
cupbearer, 201
Cyrus, 150, 181, 209
Daily News, 237
Daniel, 100, 181, 200; God's man in Babylon, 113-33; and the lions, 127-28, 131-33; prayer life, 126-28
Darius, 120, 127-28, 130-32
David, 77; and King Saul, 192; settled in Jerusalem, 98
democracy, 182

demonism, 96
devil, 51-52. *See also* Satan
discipline, 225
divorce, 22
Donatists, 19
Doner, Colonel V., 172, 175
Donne, John, 152
Drucker, Peter, 200-201, 205, 207
drug addiction, 53
dualism, 146
Durant, Will, 19, 21
Eberly, Don E., 160-61
Eckerd, Jack, 173
Eden, 111
education, decline of, 22-24; improving, 174-76; pursuing further, 174
Effective Executive, The, 200
Egypt, 96
elected offices, 234
Eliashib, 224-25, 227-28
Eliot, T. S., 170
Ellul, Jacques, 73
emotionalism, 28
enmity, 36, 37
Enoch, 46; son of Cain, 46, 72
Enoch son of Jared, 46, 49-55; pleased God, 54-55; preacher of righteousness, 52-54; seventh from Adam, 51-52; walked with God, 54
Enochs, two, 50-55
Enosh, 48
enthusiasm, 210
Erech, 78
Esther, 201
evangelicals, 8, 147-48, 150, 152-53, 160, 162, 167, 171, 203, 218, 233, 255
evangelism: no limits on, 189-90; redefined, 145-46; worldly, 28
Evans, Anthony T., 170
every member ministry, 213
exploitation, 216
Ezra, 223, 227
faith, 56, 62-64; active, 67; based on God's Word only, 64-65; confident, 66-67; despite appearances, 65-66; growing, 70-71; in search of understanding, 68-70; in the furnace, 122-25; obedience of, 57-59; redefined, 145; and works, 240-41
Fall, doctrine of the, 150
family, 29, 223, 227-28; collapse

of, 22-23; stronger, 242
fellowship, 259-60
flood, the, 78
force, 194
Ford, Leighton, 228
free speech, 172-73
Galilee, Sea of, 40
Gallup, George, 236
Gallup Poll, 172, 236-37, 241-42
genealogies, two, 46-50
Gerstner, John, 105
glory, 244-45
God: attributes of, 245; comfort of, 86, 89; dependence on, 49-50; glory of, 244-45; love of, 263; of the impossible, 60-62; or Caesar, 128-30; proper view of, 47-48; reasons with Cain, 44-45; sovereignty of, 117, 123, 179-82; with Caesar denied, 186; wrath against Nineveh, 84-85
God and Caesar, 178-99: four options, 185-89; with Caesar dominant, 187; with God dominant, 188-89
God's city, Christ's prayer for, 243-63
God's promise, faith in, 62-64
godliness, 54
government policies, 22-23
Greenfield, Meg, 26
Gregory VII, 138
Guatemala, 255
Guinness, Os, 28
guns in school, 24
Hagar, 60-61, 64
Haman, 201
Hamilton, William, 142
Hammurabi, 80
Hananiah, Mishael and Azariah. *See* Shadrach, Meshach and Abednego
Handel, Georg Frederick, 152
Harnack, Adolf, 19
Hart, Gary, 25
Hegel, George Wilhelm Friedrich, 231-32
Henry IV, 138
Herod, King, 39
Hezekiah, 81
Hill, E. V., 168-70
Hippos Regius, 14, 19
historical dialectic, 231
history, 263
Hitler, Adolf, 179, 191
holiness, 245, 248-52; defined,

248-49; and love, 261-62
Holy Spirit, 52, 77, 252
home schooling, 176
homosexuals, 161
honesty, 24; in managers, 206-7
Horton, Michael Scott, 28, 30, 140, 148-49, 152
Hoshea, 81
How to Win Friends and Influence People, 200
humanities, two, 35-56
humility, 161, 177, 241
Huns, 22
Huxley, Aldous, 93
Huxley, Thomas, 74
hymns: "A pilgrim was I, and a-wand'ring," 58; "Are there no foes for me to face?" 38; "Glorious things of thee are spoken," 111
identifying with others, 211
image of God restored, 106-7
income tax, self-assessment of, 195
individualism, 28
innuendo, 218-19
International Council on Biblical Inerrancy, 233
InterVarsity Press, 7
intimidation, 218-20
intrigue, 218
Irad, 46, 72
Isaac, 42, 68-70, 77
Ishmael, 61
Israel, 38-39
Jabal, 46, 77
Jacob, 42, 77
Jared, 46
Jehoiakim, 100
Jehovah, 41-42, 142
Jehu, 80
Jerome, Saint, 14
Jerusalem, 47, 97-99, 150, 189, 200-204, 206, 208-11, 213-15, 219, 221-22, 224, 226-27;
Jerusalem, new, 75, 109-12, 150; walls of, 209
Jesus Christ. *See* Christ Jesus
John, 189
Jonah, 90
Joseph, 38
joy, 245-48, 254; and love, 261-62
Jubal, 46, 77
Judas, 40
Jude, 45, 52, 54
judgment, 52-53, 90, 227;

certain, 86
Julius II, 138
justice, call for, 239-40; for all, 161; God's, 245; maintaining, 197
Kenan, 46
kingdom of God, servants of, 241
kingdoms, two, 21; citizens of, 151
Knox, John, 178-79
Koine Greek, 259
Koop, C. Everett, 129, 163
Kyrios Kaisar, 128
Lamech, son of Methuselah, 46
Lamech, son of Methushael, 46, 48, 72; boast of, 77-78; wives of, 76
language, God's confusion of human, 97
leaders, 200
Leo X, 138
liberalism, 141-48
Lincoln, Abraham, 202
liturgy, 77
Lloyd-Jones, D. Martyn, 64-65, 71
love, 245, 261-63; God's, 245; greatest mark of the church, 261-63
loyalty in managers, 205
Luther, Martin, 21, 50, 65, 79, 86, 89, 95, 123, 154-55, 212
MacArthur, John, 28
Mahalalel, 46
Maier, Walter A., 84
man: frailty of, 48-49; image of God in, 164; mediating being, 103; proper view of, 48-49
Manichaeans, 15-16, 19
Marduk, 95
marks of the church, 229-63
Mary, Queen, 178-79
materialism, 28, 53
Medes and Persians, kingdom of the, 120
Meese, Edwin, 25
Mehujael, 46, 72, 77
Melchizedek, 98
Mene, mene, tekel, parsin, 126
mercy, loving, 240-41
methodology, world's, 164
methods, God's, 146; world's, 146-48, 251
Methuselah, 46, 54
Methushael, 46, 72, 77
Middle Ages, 138, 195

middle management, 204-9
Milan, 17
Milton, John, 152
Mind Renewal in a Mindless Age, 153
Miss America Pageant, 76
mission, 245, 254-56; and love, 262
monasticism, 186
monastics, 140
money, 146-48
Monica, 14, 19
Montaigne, 63
moral behavior, no limits on, 190-91
moral values of the world, 144
morality and government, 197-98
Mordecai, 201
Morris, Henry M., 95
Most Holy Place, 98
Mount Moriah, 68
Mueller, Hans, 154
Münzer, Thomas, 154
murder, 191, 193
"Mystery Babylon," 107-9
Naamah, 76
Nahum, 82-84
National Association of Evangelicals, 148
National Review, 232
Nazi era, 190
Nebuchadnezzar, 92, 99-102, 106-7, 113-23, 125-26, 180-81; attacks on Jerusalem, 100; bestial behavior, 102-4; dream of, 116-22; gold statue of, 122-23; judged with insanity, 101-2
Nehemiah, 200-228
Nero, 13
New American Standard Bible, 67
New English Bible, 67
new humanity, 243
New International Version, 51
New Yorker, 147
Newsweek, 141
Newton, John, 111, 152
Niebuhr, H. Richard, 137
Niemöller, Martin, 190
Nimrod, 79-80, 93, 95
Nimrod's city, growth of, 80-84. *See also* Nineveh
Ninety-five Theses, 154
Nineveh, 78-92, 94; fall of, 84-89; growth of, 80-84; guilt of, 85-86; repentance under

Jonah, 90; wickedness of, 85-86
Nixon, Richard, 21, 25, 180
Noah, 46-47, 49, 93-94
Non vi, sed verbo, 155
noncompliance, 189
obedience, 70; in small things, 116
occult, 53
offsprings, two, 35-40
Oholiab, 150
On Christian Doctrine, 19
On the Holy Trinity, 20
Operation Rescue, 192
opposition, 213-20; by intimidation, 218-20; by ridicule, 213-14; from within, 215-18; violence, 214-15
organization, Christian, in the cities, 168-70
Orwell, George, 93
Ovid, 63
participation, 151-52, 158, 166, 242
passion, 77-78
Peasants' War, 154-55
Pekah, 81
Pelagians, 19
perseverance, 221, 228, 239-40
persuasion, 146, 152-56, 158, 242; importance of, 235
Peter, 189
Pharaoh, 180
Philadelphia Conference on Reformed Theology, 70
Pilate, Pontius, 183-84, 187-88
pilgrim, 58
planning, importance of, 207-9; specific, 209-10
Plato, 24, 93
Platonists, 16
Pogo, 30
politics, 30, 142; disillusionment with, 25-26; misplaced confidence in, 233-36
pope, the, 138
Pope John Paul, 233
pornography, 172-74
power: illegitimate, 183; of the sword, 193-96; political, 182; politics, 146-48; pride in, 77-78; useless use of, 197-98; wrong use of, 196-97
power bases, 139
pragmatism, 143
prayer, 146, 156-58, 177, 214, 219, 236, 242; Christ's for

God's city, 243-63; instant in, 207; priority, 202-4
Pretty Baby, 106
priorities, 202; three, 151-56
Prison Fellowship, 21
private property, 159
problems, same old, 221-24
progress, doctrine of human, 121
promiscuity, 53
prostitution, 53
Protoevangelium, 36
Psalms of Ascent, 99
Psalms of Zion, 98-99
Puritans, 175
rape, 53
Reagan, Ronald, 25, 231
"reclaiming" America, 138-40
Redeemer, 49, 53
redemption, doctrine of, 150-51
Reel, William, 237
Reformation, 86, 140, 148, 151, 154, 165
Reformers, 49
reforms, Nehemiah's final, 225-28
Rehoboth Ir, 78
relativism, 28, 232
relevancy, 145
religion: how real is our, 236-38; of Babel, 94-97
Religious Right, 8, 139-40
Rembrandt, 152
repentance, 177, 218
Resen, 78
Restoring the Good Society, 160
resurrection, Abraham's belief in, 69-70
revelation, 262-63
Revelation, book of, 38
Revised Standard Version, 66
ridicule, 213-14
right and wrong, 26
right to life, 162-65
righteousness: God's, 245; two kinds, 249
"rights," personal, 159
Roman Empire, 13, 120
Rome, 20, 35, 128, 148; fall of, 13
Roosevelt, Franklin Delano, 74
Roosevelt, Teddy, 139
rootlessness, 73-74
sabbath, 223, 226-27
sacrifices, 73
saints, 249-50
salvation, redefined, 145, 251

Samaria, 81
Samaritan Strategy, The, 172
Sanballat, 214, 219, 224, 227
sanctification, 250, 254
Santayana, George, 63
Sarah, 60-62, 65
Sardannapalus, 88
Sargon, 81
Satan, 36-37, 109
Satanism, 96
Sawyer, Diane, 24
Schaeffer, Francis, 35, 46, 163, 231
"Schleitheim Confession," 140
schools, 29-30; alternative Christian, 175-76
Schwab, Charles, 211
Scriptures, wisdom of the, 143-45. *See also* Bible; Word of God
Scroggs, Robin, 144
secular church, 250-52
Secular City, The, 142-43, 145
secular environment, 114-16
secular humanism, 47
secularism, 142
self-esteem, 53
self-righteousness, 193
Sennacherib, 81-82, 84, 89
separation, of church and state, 188; unto God, 251-52
serpent, the, 35-36
Seth, 46, 48
Shadrach, Meshach and Abednego, 113, 115, 123-25, 130-31, 200
Shalmaneser III, 80
Shalmaneser V, 81
Shecaniah, 224
Shemaiah, 220
Shields, Brooke, 106
Shinar, 78; plain of, 93, 96
Siculus, Diodorus, 88
Sider, Ronald J., 166
sin: confession of, 203; punished, 245; redefined, 115, 251
Sinai covenant, 142
slavery, 159, 164
small groups, 260
Smith, Hannah Whitall, 248
social order, 196-97
societies, 72
Solzhenitsyn, Aleksandr, 236
sons, two, 40-46
Soviet empire, collapse of, 25
Sphinx, 96

spiritualism, 53
Stalin, Joseph, 179
standards, 30
state: authority of the, 179-82; defense of its citizens, 196
Stedman, Ray, 252-53
stone, not made with hands, 121
Stott, John R. W., 237, 260
Supreme Court, 187
Susa, 201, 222
Swindoll, Charles, 202, 225
sword, power of the, 193-96
tact in managers, 205-6
taxes, mandatory, 195; paying, 185
Taylor, Hudson, 204
television, 153, 160
temple, 220
temple tax, 223
temptation of Christ, 39
ten Boom, Corrie, 190
Ten Commandments, 78, 236-37
Tenth Presbyterian Church, 260
Terence, 63
Terry, Randall, 139
theology, world's, 145, 156, 251
Thoreau, Henry David, 93
Tiglath-pileser III, 80-81
Tigris River, 88
Tillapaugh, Frank R., 217
Time, 231
timing, 210

tithes, 223, 226
Tobiah, 214, 224-25
Toynbee, Arnold, 210
trial of Jesus Christ, 183-84
Truman, Harry S., 204
truth, 188-89, 245, 252-54; and love, 262; not pragmatism, 160
Tson, Joseph, 124
Tubal-Cain, 46, 77
two cities, 8, 20-21; Babylon and Jerusalem, 92-112; biblical basis for, 33-133; today, 135-228
tyranny, 262
ungodliness, 53
United States, 121, 242
unity, 245, 256-61; family, 258-59; and love, 262; organizational, 257
Urban Alternative, The, 170
urbanization, 165
Uzziah, 220
Vahanian, Gabriel, 142
values, 142, 232-33
values vacuum, 231-33
VanBuren, Paul, 142
Vandals, 19, 22
Veith, Gene Edward, 156
vengeance, God's, 85
violence, threat of, 214-15
Virgil, 63
Visigoths, 22

vocations, secular, 149
Wall Street, 231
Washington Post, 129
Watchman Nee, 68
Watts, Isaac, 38
Weil, Simone, 73-74
Wells, David F., 28
Westminster Confession of Faith, 181, 234
Whatever Happened to the Human Race? 163
White, John, 225
Whitewater, 25
Wildmon, Donald E., 173
wisdom, God's, 245; world's, 143-45, 250-51
Word of God, 161, 193; authority of, 253; knowing the, 124. *See also* Bible; Scriptures
words, reinterpreted, 115
work, dividing the, 212-13
world: agenda of the, 251; before the watching, 241-42; methods of, 251; theology of the, 145-46, 251; wisdom of the, 250-51
world and life view, 236
"year of the evangelical," 141
Zillah, 46, 76-77
zodiac, 96

Scripture Index

Genesis
1:28 *94*
2 *72*
3—5 *56*
3:5 *102*
3:15 *35-36, 39-42*
3:20 *41*
4 *48, 72*
4—5 *46, 51*
4:1 *41, 47*
4:2-3 *42*
4:12 *73*
4:14 *73*
4:16 *73*
4:17 *74*
4:20-22 *46*
4:23-24 *46, 78*
4:24-25 *78*
4:25-26 *47*
4:26 *49, 50*
5:21-23 *50*
5:21-24 *49, 54*
6—9 *93*
6:1-7 *53*
9:1 *94*
9:6 *198*
10 *78*
10—11 *93*
10:8-9 *79*
10:8-12 *93, 120*
10:10-12 *78-79*
11:1-9 *79, 93, 120*
11:3-4 *94*
11:4 *33, 93, 98*
11:8-9 *97*
12:1 *58-59*
12:1-3 *97-98*
12:1-9 *57*
12:4 *58*
12:5 *60*
12:10—14:16 *58*
14:18 *98*
15 *64-65*
15:5 *60, 62*

17 *65*
17:18 *61*
18:25 *86*
22:5, 18 *70*

Exodus
1:20-21 *150*
6:3 *42*
9:16 *180*
20:3-6 *86*
30:11-16 *223*
31:1-11 *77*
35:30—36:1 *150*
40 *250*

Leviticus
19:31 *96*

Numbers
18:7 *220*

Deuteronomy
18 *96*
32:35 *85*

Joshua
24:2 *57*

1 Samuel
24 *192*
26 *192*

2 Samuel
5:6-12 *98*
6 *98*

2 Kings
19:10-12 *82*
19:35 *82*

1 Chronicles
1:3 *50*
15—16 *98*

2 Chronicles
7:14 *176-77, 198-99*
26:16-21 *220*

Ezra
4 *201, 205*
4:7-23 *206*
9—10 *227*

Nehemiah
1—6 *213*
1:1-4 *201*
1:6-7 *203*
1:11 *201, 203*
2 *205, 209*
2:1 *201, 203-4*
2:2 *204*
2:3 *206*
2:4 *207*
2:16-17 *210*
2:17 *211*
2:18 *212*
2:19 *219*
3 *212*
3:4 *224*
4:2 *214*
4:6-23 *214*
4:9 *215*
4:13-14 *217*
4:13-15 *215*
4:20 *215*
5 *215*
5:1-5 *216*
5:7 *217*
5:12 *218*
5:14 *222*
6:3 *218*
6:5-8 *219*
6:10 *220*
6:12 *218, 220*
6:18 *224*
7:10 *224*
10 *223, 226-27*

10:7 *224*
10:39 *224*
11:1 *166*
12:3 *224*
12:14 *224*
12:32 *224*
12:44-47 *222*
13 *226-27*
13:1-3 *222*
13:4-5 *224*
13:6 *221*
13:7 *224*
13:8 *225*
13:13 *226*
13:14 *225*
13:22-28 *223*
13:25 *228*
13:28 *224, 227*

Psalms
2:3 *187*
8:3-7 *102-3*
9:9 *86*
46 *99*
48 *99*
50:15 *87*
76 *99*
84 *99*
84:1-4 *99*
84:10 *99*
87 *99*
120—134 *99*

Isaiah
45:1 *181*

Daniel
1 *117*
1:2 *100*
1:8 *116*
1:17-18 *116*
2:2 *117*
2:3-7 *118*
2:10-11 *119*

2:17-18 *131*
2:31 *119*
2:37-38 *119*
2:40-41 *120*
2:44 *121*
2:47 *122*
3:16-18 *123*
3:25 *125*
4:17 *180*
4:25 *180*
4:30 *33, 101*
4:32 *180*
4:33 *102*
4:34-35 *107, 181*
4:37 *107, 181*
5 *120*
5:6 *125*
5:18 *126*
5:20-22 *126*
5:26-28 *126*
5:27 *87-88*
6—7 *126*
6:4-5 *127*
6:10 *130*
6:11 *132*
6:16 *131*
6:20 *132*
6:21-22 *132*
6:26-27 *132-33*
6:28 *181*
10:1 *181*

Amos
3:7 *119*

Jonah
3:4 *90*
3:6-10 *90*

Micah
6:6-7 *238*
6:8 *229, 238*

Nahum
1:1-6 *85-86*
1:7-15 *86*
1:8-10 *87-88*
1:12 *87-88*
1:14 *87-88*
2:8-10 *89*
3:1-3 *82-83*

Habakkuk
1:6-7 *11*

Matthew
2:16-18 *39*
4:1-11 *39*
4:8-10 *243*
11:28 *90*
12:43-45 *44*
16:18 *157*
18:15 *217*
21:33-41 *40*
22:17 *185*
22:21 *185*
25:21 *55*
25:23 *55*
27:18 *184*
28:19 *189*

Mark
4:35-41 *40*
16:15 *189*

Luke
2:10-11 *246*
2:52 *55*
3:7 *50*
4:1-13 *39*
4:28-30 *39*
9:23 *59*
14:26 *59*
16:15 *252*

John
3:16 *64, 245, 263*

7:30 *39*
7:32 *39*
7:45-46 *39*
8:59 *39*
10:31 *39*
13:34-35 *261*
14:1-3 *111*
15:11 *246, 252*
15:19-20 *156*
17 *248, 249, 256*
17:1 *244*
17:4-5 *244*
17:9 *243*
17:10 *244*
17:13 *246, 252*
17:13-18 *245*
17:15-17 *248*
17:17 *252*
17:18 *255*
17:18-19 *256*
17:19 *250*
17:20 *243*
17:20-23 *257*
17:21 *258*
17:21-23 *245*
17:22 *244*
17:23 *258*
17:24 *244*
17:26 *245, 261*
18:37 *183, 195*
19:10 *183-84*
19:11 *183-84*
19:12 *183, 187*
19:15 *186*

Acts
1:8 *189*
4—5 *189*
5:28-29 *190*
23:26 *246*

Romans
1 *232*
1:7 *250*

1:18-32 *105*
1:23 *95*
3—4 *71*
4:13-14 *62*
4:16 *62*
4:18 *62, 65*
4:18-21 *61*
4:18-22 *60*
4:19-21 *66-67*
4:20-21 *62*
9:17 *180*
10:3 *249*
12:1-2 *153*
12:12 *207*
12:19 *85*
13 *183-84*
13:1 *178, 180, 182*
13:1-7 *141, 179, 182*
13:2 *193*
13:2-3 *184*
13:3-4 *194, 196-97*
13:4 *188*
13:7 *185*

1 Corinthians
1:2 *250*
1:9 *260*
10:13 *87*
12:12-14 *261*
13:12 *254*
13:13 *261*

2 Corinthians
1:1 *250*
10:3-5 *154*
10:4 *155*
13:14 *260*

Ephesians
1:1 *250*
3:10 *245*
4:11-13 *213*

Philippians
1:1 *250*
2:15 *21*
4:4 *246*

1 Timothy
2:1-2 *197*

2 Timothy
3:2-5 *252*
3:5 *77*
4:7-8 *228*

Hebrews
2:14 *182*
11 *46, 56, 67-68*
11:4 *45*
11:5 *50, 55*
11:7 *47*
11:8 *1, 58*
11:8-9 *57*
11:8-10 *56*
11:9 *58*
11:10 *1, 76*
11:11-12 *60*
11:11-17 *57*
11:12 *61*
11:17-19 *68*
11:33 *133*
11:35-38 *133*
12:14 *248*

James
2:14-19 *241*

1 Peter
2:9 *248*
3:4 *76*

2 Peter
2:5 *49*
3:6-7 *52*
3:9 *85*
3:10 *85*

1 John
1:3 *260*
3:2 *254*
3:3 *262*
3:12 *45*

Jude
11 *45*
14-15 *50, 52, 54*

Revelation
7:17 *254*
11:15 *122*
12:1-6 *38*
17:5 *108*
18 *108*
18:22 *109*
19:1-4 *108-9*
19:6-7 *108-9*
20:12-13 *109-10*
20:15 *109-10*
21—22 *151*
21:2-4 *92*
21:4 *254*
21:22-27 *110*
22:2 *110*
22:5 *110*